# Pragmatic Assessment and Intervention Issues in Language

*Edited by*

## TANYA M. GALLAGHER
The University of Michigan
Ann Arbor, Michigan

## CAROL A. PRUTTING
University of California
Santa Barbara, California

**College-Hill Press, Inc.**
San Diego, California

College-Hill Press, Inc.
4284 41st Street
San Diego, California 92105

**Library of Congress Cataloging in Publication Data**
Main entry under title:

Pragmatic assessment and intervention issues in language.

Includes bibliographical references and index.
1. Language disorders in children.    I. Gallagher, Tanya M.,    II. Prutting, Carol A.
RJ496.L35P73 1982   618.92'855   82-17752


**ISBN 0-933014-78-3**

Printed in the United States of America.

*This volume is dedicated
to the fond memory of
Thomas H. Shriner, Jr.*

1938 - 1980

# TABLE OF CONTENTS

# CONTRIBUTORS

JAMES D. AMERMAN, PhD
University of Missouri, Columbia
Columbia, Missouri

LAURENCE B. LEONARD, PhD
Purdue University
West Lafayette, Indiana

HOLLY K. CRAIG, PhD
The University of Michigan
Ann Arbor, Michigan

LYLE L. LLOYD, PhD
Purdue University
West Lafayette, Indiana

JOANNE KELSCH DANILOFF, MS
University of Vermont
Burlington, Vermont

PAULA MENYUK, EdD
Boston University
Boston, Massachusetts

JUDITH F. DUCHAN, PhD
State University of New York
Buffalo, New York

JOHN R. MUMA, PhD
Texas Tech University
Lubbock, Texas

MARC E. FEY, PhD
University of Western Ontario
London, Ontario, Canada

MARTHA M. PARNELL, PhD
Southwest Missouri State University
Springfield, Missouri

TANYA M. GALLAGHER, PhD
The University of Michigan
Ann Arbor, Michigan

CAROL A. PRUTTING, PhD
University of California
Santa Barbara, California

DIANE M. KIRCHNER, MA
University of Califoria
Santa Barbara, California

ELIZABETH SKARAKIS-DOYLE, PhD
University of California
Santa Barbara, California

*Consulting Editor:*
## *RAYMOND G. DANILOFF*
*University of Vermont*
*Burlington, Vermont*

# PREFACE

This book is one of three volumes dedicated to the memory of Thomas H. Shriner, Jr. This volume focuses upon language. Although Tom's interests and scientific contributions were broad, as this three volume series reflects, his primary focus was language. His research addressed questions that would increase our understanding of language development, language disorders, and the implications of that knowledge for assessment and intervention.

It is a fitting memorial to Tom that the volume addresses both assessment and intervention issues from a primarily pragmatic theoretical perspective. Tom presented the resolution of behaviorism and generative theory as our fundamental task. He thought both theories were too elegant to dismiss with the arguments so frequently quoted in the literature of the late 1960's and early 1970's. He would not allow us, as his students, to ally ourselves comfortably with either "camp." His counter-arguments and penetrating examples continually challenged our thinking and left us searching within ourselves and within the literature for a more satisfying characterization of language than either of these major theories presented. Pragmatic theory, as an integrated theory of communicative performance, seems to offer the kind of resolution he sought. Tom in this sense was the first "pragmatist" we knew and from him we were able to accept readily the paradigm as it became gradually explicated throughout the 1970's.

The chapters in this volume represent each author's analysis of the past, perceptions of the present, and projections into the future. In this sense the book as a whole could be characterized as a seminar or a discussion where each person shares his or her thoughts with the others. The book is organized in the following sequence: chapters dealing with primarily assessment issues, chapters dealing with primarily intervention issues, chapters dealing with aspects of communication that are broader than spoken language, and finally chapters dealing with theoretical implications for both assessment and intervention.

All of the contributors were influenced directly or indirectly by Tom. Tanya and Carol were Tom's students and wrote two of the dissertations he directed. Tanya's chapter, "Pre-Assessment: A Procedure for Accommodating Language Use Variability," discusses the integration of information needed to deal with individual differences. Tom was very sensitive to the inadequacies of standardization procedures for describing an individual. This and the synergy language use variability reflects were major themes throughout his work. Carol's chapter, "Scientific Inquiry and Communicative Disorders: An Emerging Paradigm Across Six Decades," is consistent with Tom's concerns regarding science. He incorporated historical and philosophical scientific papers into all of his courses and his teaching reflected his continual attempts to conceptualize the field as a whole.

Dr. Holly Craig, a former student and present colleague of Tanya, and Diane Kirchner and Dr. Elizabeth Skarakis-Doyle, students of Carol's, represent an intellectual continuity from Tom to the next generation of scholars. It is unfortunate that Tom did not know them because he would have admired their talent and dedication. Holly Craig's chapter, "Applications of Pragmatic Language Models for Intervention," highlights the relationship between theories of language and the formulation of intervention goals and procedures. Tom believed that the translation of theory into practice was the researcher's most difficult task and the ultimate goal of all of our work. Diane Kirchner and Elizabeth Skarakis-Doyle's chapter, "Developmental Language Disorders: A Theoretical Perspective," goes beyond the the normal model to account for the disordered child's need to adapt functionally to the environment. Carol and Diane Kirchner's chapter, "Applied Pragmatics," reflects the use of the speech act theory as a framework from which to appraise the pragmatic aspects of language. Again, these attempts to translate theory into practice were one of Tom's priorities.

Dr. James Amerman was a student of Tom's and Dr. Martha Parnell was Dr. Amerman's student. This again represents an intellectual continuity to the next generation. Martha Parnell and James Amerman's chapter, "Answers to Wh-Questions: Research and Application," discusses the impact that our increased knowledge of the development of Wh-question comprehension and response will have upon language assessment and intervention. It is also a translation of theory into practice.

Dr. Judith Duchan was also a student of Tom's at the University of Illinois. Her chapter, "Language Processing and Geodesic Domes," reflects a synergistic view of language. Tom's thinking was heavily influenced by Buckminister Fuller's writing on synergy. He believed that synergy was a fundamental definitional feature of language.

Dr. Paula Menyuk worked with Tom when he was a post-doctoral fellow at M.I.T. He always admired her personally and professionally for the important work she was contributing to speech and language pathology. Her chapter, "Language Development and Reading," discusses reading as a language based problem with implications for assessment and intervention. The theme is consistent with Tom's focus on synergy.

Dr. John Muma was a colleague Tom regarded very highly. Although they never worked together at one institution, they maintained an active correspondence and generously exchanged their views. John's chapter, "Speech-Language Pathology: Emerging Clinical Expertise in Language," discusses issues currently facing the practicing clinician. He does this with a concern for the individual and humanistic attitude that Tom admired.

Dr. Laurence Leonard and his former student Dr. Marc Fey were influenced by Tom through his work. Their chapter, "Pragmatic Skills of Children with Specific Language Impairment," reviews current studies and suggests that the data reflect three basic patterns. They discuss these as potential subgroups within that clinical population. Tom believed that the language impaired population was composed of subgroups, and he was continually frustrated by our inability to define them adequately. This chapter is an important step in that direction.

Dr. Lyle Lloyd was a fellow student of Tom's at the University of Iowa. He and his former student Joanne Kelsch-Daniloff co-authored the chapter, "Issues in Using Amer-Ind Code with Retarded Persons." Their chapter addresses communication issues beyond those typically discussed regarding spoken language development and makes concrete suggestions relative to the use of Amer-Ind Code with retarded persons. Tom was particularly concerned about the treatment of retarded persons,and his continual emphasis upon practical accommodations to their needs is consistent with the focus of their chapter.

This memorial series was conceived in early January, 1981, when several of us struggled to think of a memorial that would be appropriate for this great and dear man. We felt that this type of memorial was the most appropriate for Tom because he was first of all a scholar and a teacher. It has been gratifying to work with these contributors who gave their time and energies so generously to the project. Several shared personal memories of Tom and how he had affected their lives and work. We hope that this series will be testimony to that fact.

# A Personal Note

Several things came together at one time at the University of Illinois in the late 1960's and early 1970's that created an intense intellectual atmosphere. Tom was at the center of this activity with his exuberance, honesty, creativity, and boundless energy. Tom educated us both during our most challenging and impressionable time, our years as Ph.D. students. His teaching took a very personal form. Anywhere we were with Tom became our classroom. He had the ability to share his insights and creativity but what was perhaps even more difficult, he helped us formulate a structure for our thoughts and translate that structure into action. His commitment to and reverence for research was all consuming. Tom talked about good work with adjectives like "fantastic" and "simply beautiful."

Tom coupled this with a kindness and sensitivity toward students. He communicated his belief in us and took every opportunity to encourage us regarding what he saw as our potential. He worked with each of us side by side as though any amount of time we needed was freely available. He was a most loyal advisor before and after graduation, whose fondest goal for us was that we would become contributors to our field. It was difficult to thank Tom. He would always interrupt, saying very bruskly "I know, I know." We sincerely hope this was true, because we never thanked him eloquently enough.

We continue to embrace Tom in our inquiries as researchers and through the education of and affiliation with our own students. We dedicate this book to Thomas Shriner, Jr., our teacher, mentor, colleague and friend — a man who lived his own private agony and died sorely missed.

Tanya M. Gallagher
Carol A. Prutting

# FOREWORD

*T*homas H. Shriner, Jr. was born on February 12, 1938 in Fallowfield Township, Pennsylvania. On December 22, 1980, less than two months prior to his 43rd birthday, death cut short his career as a productive scholar and researcher and inspiring teacher.

Tom Shriner's academic history includes a Bachelor of Science in Education degree with a major in Speech and Hearing awarded by State College, California, Pennsylvania in 1962, a Master of Arts degree in Speech Pathology and Audiology in 1964 and a Ph.D. degree in Speech Pathology and Audiology in 1965, both awarded by the University of Iowa, and two post-doctoral fellowships — one at the University of Iowa for the year 1965-1966, and one at the Massachusetts Institute of Technology for the year 1969-1970. He served in the United States Marine Corps during the years 1957-1959.

Following his post-doctoral year at the University of Iowa Dr. Shriner was appointed Research Assistant Professor in the Children's Research Center, Department of Speech, University of Illinois. He held this position and rank until 1969. In 1970 he returned to Illinois from his post-doctoral year at MIT with the rank of Associate Professor in the Department of Speech. At Illinois he taught courses in Development of Spoken Language and Psychology of Speech and seminars in Language Development, Language Measurements, Auditory Cognition, and Language Research. Following the 1970-1971 academic year he left the University of Illinois to accept a position as Associate Professor and Director of the Infant Language Laboratory, Mailman Center for Child Development, University of Miami School of Medicine. In addition to his research activities as laboratory director, he taught courses in Linguistics: Science and Application and Special Studies in Speech in the Department of Speech and Hearing Sciences, University of Miami.

Although Dr. Shriner had doubtless acquired an interest in language behavior during his undergraduate studies with Dr. Ray Bontrager at California State College, his intense interest in the area of language development in infants and children apparently began while he was a graduate student at the University of Iowa. His doctoral dissertation, directed by Dr. Dorothy Sherman, was a report of research on the measurement of language development. His post-doctoral studies at both Iowa and MIT were devoted to continued development of his special research interest in language development.

It is probably significant that this interest in children's language had its early beginnings while he was a graduate student in a department that supported a substantial clinical program concerned with speech, language and hearing disorders, as well as extensive programs of research into the fundamental processes of speech, language and hearing and the disorders of speech, language and hearing. This context not only encouraged and fostered the development of his specialized interest in children's language, it did so as part of a broad program of studies in human communication processes and disorders. In this context Dr. Shriner had the opportunity to take courses and seminars which provided a broad background concerning both normal and abnormal speech and hearing processes as well as language, to engage in research and to interact directly, on a day-to-day basis, with fellow graduate students and with faculty who were involved both with research into these processes and with the clinical management of persons with disorders of speech, language and hearing. One of Dr. Shriner's earliest published papers was not a report of research on language, but was a collaboration with Dr. Kenneth L. Moll which reported research on an aspect of motor activity during speech production. He also served as a graduate assistant to Dr. Wendell Johnson, who was not only a pioneering researcher in the area of stuttering, but had broad interests and wrote extensively in the area of personal and social effects of language behavior. It is not too much to suggest that this broad exposure to many varied aspects of human communication provided Dr. Shriner with a particularly broad and rich context in which to develop his interests in language development and may have contributed to both the breadth of his scholarship and thinking with respect to more specifically linguistic processes and to his pragmatic approach to the analysis and understanding of issues in language behavior.

One of the most frequent comments concerning Tom Shriner's work both as a scholar and teacher, from both former students and colleagues, concerned the breadth of his interests in the total communication processes and his insistence that language processes could only be understood in a context which considered human communication as a total process. These comments indicate that this was a distinguishing characteristic that set him apart from many of his contemporaries who approach the study of language more narrowly. One of his former students, now a faculty member at a large state university, commented that he was one of the very early linguistic pragmatists, certainly the first such thinker with whom this person had come into contact. The breadth of his research and scholarly interests is clearly evident in the titles of his publications and convention papers, and it is appropriately reflected in the broad scope of the contributions to these memorial volumes.

Tom Shriner's record as a productive scholar is well documented by the pages of his publication in scientific journals and by published convention proceedings that reflect his contributions. In the all too brief time allotted to him he authored, or co-authored, more than twenty research articles and nearly as many convention papers. The quality of his work has been recognized, and its influence extended, by the reprinting of no less than five of these research articles in book collection form. He was an invited contributor to the Revised Handbook of Speech Pathology (1971). He served as an associate editor of the Journal of Speech and Hearing Research from 1969 to 1972, as a guest editor of the American Speech and Hearing Association Monograph Series, and as guest editor of the Bulletin of the Division for Children with Communication Disorders of the Council for Exceptional Children. He was invited to be a visiting professor at the University of Minnesota during the summer of 1969, and he was called on frequently as a lecturer and contributor to workshops in speech, hearing and language. All this and more in a brief post-doctoral career that spanned less than a decade and a half.

Finally, but perhaps most importantly, Tom Shriner was a superb teacher. He must have been, for during his brief tenure at the University of Illinois an amazing number of talented graduate students chose Dr. Shriner as the person with whom they wanted to work most closely. The record shows that during the short period of four years one Senior Honors thesis, two Master's theses and four doctoral dissertations were completed under Dr. Shriner's direction. In addition his influence was felt by the numerous students who enrolled in his courses and seminars, or who participated in many informal discussion groups.

Because my close personal contact with Tom Shriner came at an earlier time, while he was a graduate student at the University of Iowa, what follows is primarily based on comments of his former students. It is clear from their statements that his influence was profound. They express the highest respect for him as a scholar and thinker and deep affection for him as a person. They unanimously report that he was completely unselfish with his time, that he gave of himself unstintingly, that he was always available for counsel and discussion of problems. His relationships with students was never authoritarian. He seemed to them more like a fellow student sharing in their quest for knowledge than a mentor directing that quest. They never felt subordinate or dominated. And yet he was able to stimulate them with new ideas, challenge them to new ways of thinking, and to help them in the difficult process of learning to expose ideas and thinking to critical analysis and testing. Moreover, it is very evident from these former students' reports that he had the gift of making this challenge enjoyable, exciting and exhilarating. According to one former student, an important key to Dr. Shriner's teaching was his emphasis on the importance of learning how to ask questions, not just any questions, but the critical ones that would go to the core of an idea and test the validity of that idea or of a line of reasoning. Quite obviously he taught far more by example than by precept, and the example his students saw was that of a scholar, a disciplined, inquiring mind, tirelessly searching for new understanding, and having fun in the searching.

That he was a highly successful teacher cannot be doubted. Not only was he respected by both students and colleagues, but the successes enjoyed by his former students bears testimony to his teaching effectiveness. All four of the persons who completed Ph.D. degrees under his tutelage have gone on to achieve success as faculty members at major universities. Tom would have been justifiably proud of their accomplishments, but too humble to claim the share of credit that his students more than gladly accord him.

These three memorial volumes are eloquent testimony to the high regard in which Thomas H. Shriner was held by his students and colleagues and to the influence which he had on their thinking and development. The fact that some of the contributions in these volumes are the work of students of his students bear witness to the fact that this influence continues to be felt. Although he is no longer with us, Tom Shriner's example of dedication to his students and to his field of scholarship continues, and will continue, as it is repeated daily in the work of his former students and colleagues and their students.

James F. Curtis

# 1

# PRE-ASSESSMENT: A PROCEDURE FOR ACCOMMODATING LANGUAGE USE VARIABILITY

*Tanya M. Gallagher*
*The University of Michigan*

## Introduction

*T*hroughout the 1970's and early 1980's two facts about language performance have been highlighted — that language always occurs in a context and that contexts are not all the same. These obvious and potentially trivial facts have never really been at issue. Even the realization in the early 1970's that context was an interpretive aid for the child language investigator (Bloom, 1970; Brown, 1973), and probably for the child (Ervin-Tripp, 1973), posed no threat to the basic generative grammatical assumptions of the 1960's regarding spontaneous language sampling.

One of these assumptions was that if the language produced by the child was "spontaneous" (not elicited), contextual variables were relatively unimportant. In other words, any variation that resulted from contextual differences would be minimal. This acceptable range of variation therefore would not impair the investigator's or clinician's ability to represent the child's underlying grammar. A second assumption was that any specification or control of contextual variables during language sampling would influence all children equally. A third assumption was that standardized contexts would have not only uniform but predictable, specifiable influences on the language children produced.

The important issue relative to these assumptions is not that contexts exist or that they vary, but whether contexts are static backgrounds within which language occurs, "a 'label' for a cluster of extralinguistic or extra-grammatical factors . ." (Cook-Gumperz and Gumperz, 1978, p.5) or whether they are dynamic aspects of the message for both the encoder and the decoder. Pragmatic theories of language, those addressing language as it is used (Austin, 1962; Bates, 1976; Searle, 1969), characterize linguistic elements and contextual elements as forming an interactive communicative whole. The goal of these theories is to characterize communicative competence, not simply linguistic competence, and the basic unit of analysis is a communicative interaction. This view of language as performance assumes that language use will vary with contexts and that the contexts are dynamic. This assumption about language performance raises questions about some of the implicit generative grammatical assumptions regarding spontaneous language sampling, and it raises important issues for an applied discipline such as speech and language pathology. These questions include:

> What does a 'representative' sample mean if all samples are context bound?
> What does a "standardized language sampling context" mean and can the interactive effects of contextual variables be pre-defined?
> What interactive contexts will be most revealing of a child's underlying structural grammar?

The major response to these questions has been to continue relying heavily upon spontaneous language sampling but to recommend that samples be collected in more than one context. Sometimes specific contexts are identified as critical for various reasons, and sometimes "more than one context" is not defined. These recommendations begin to acknowledge the important impact language use variability has upon the formulation of language assessment procedures, but there is need for further refinement.

## The Spontaneous Language Sample

Spontaneous language sampling is the centerpiece of child language assessment. It has been recommended as one of the major sources of information about children's language from the 1930's (Davis, 1937; McCarthy, 1930) to the present (Aram and Nation, 1982; Bloom and Lahey, 1978; Johnson, Darley and Spriestersbach, 1963; Miller, 1981; Muma, 1978; Tyack and Gottsleben, 1974). A recent survey of 275 PSB accredited programs in the United States indicated that spontaneous language sampling was the most preferred method of language elicitation across five age groups from "toddler to adult" (Atkins and Cartwright, 1982).

Analysis procedures have changed over time. Early analyses computed the child's mean length of response (McCarthy, 1954), the mean of the five longest responses (Davis, 1937; Templin, 1957), and the Structural Complexity Score (Davis, 1937; McCarthy, 1930; Templin, 1957). These procedures later were criticized as inadequate (Shriner, 1967; 1969) and were replaced with analyses that computed mean length of utterance (Brown, 1973), Developmental Sentence Scores (Lee, 1974; Lee and Canter, 1971), and Developmental Sentence Types (Lee, 1966; 1974). Recently, more comprehensive form, function, and use analyses have been introduced (Bloom and Lahey, 1978; McLean and Snyder-McLean, 1978; Miller, 1981; Muma, 1978).

The procedures for obtaining a language sample, however, have remained relatively unchanged since they were first described by McCarthy in 1930. Stimulus materials generally have been toys and/or pictures, depending upon the children's preferences (McCarthy, 1930; Templin, 1957). Davis (1937), however, selected toys as stimulus materials and pictures were an alternative that was used as needed. Clinicians have been advised to establish good rapport with the child, to keep their remarks to a minimum, and to stimulate the child's talking by asking open-ended questions and using phrases such as "tell me about" (Davis, 1937).

These procedures are still the basic framework for clinician language sampling behavior and are frequently the suggestions made to parents, teachers, and other adults if they are going to participate in the language sampling. Current practice, however, incorporates in addition more specific guidelines regarding the use of parallel play and interactive play (Miller, 1981; Muma, 1978) and the use of nonstandardized elicitations of specific language structures (Bloom and Lahey, 1978; Lee, 1974; Leonard, Prutting, Perozzi, and Berkley, 1978).

The goal of language sampling also has remained essentially the same, to obtain a "representative" sample. The term "representative," however, has been used in three different senses in the literature: as "comprehensive" and as "idealized" and "typical" behavior.

Comprehensiveness is a universal standard. A representative sample must be large enough to be interpretable and reliable but of a reasonable length to be efficient. Since the term "comprehensive" entails all of these features, its operational definition has changed over time, reflecting changes in the subsequent analyses that were performed. McCarthy (1930) and Darley and Moll (1960) recommended a 50 utterance sample. Engler, Hannah, and Longhurst (1973), Tyack and Gottsleben (1974), Crystal, Fletcher, and Garman (1976), and Leonard (1972) recommended a 100 utterance sample. More recently, Bloom and Lahey (1978) have recommended a 200 or more utterance sample with a minimum sampling time of 30 minutes. Miller (1981) has suggested that 30 minutes of sampling should be sufficient.

"Representative" has also been used in the sense of idealized performance. McLean and Snyder-McLean (1978) suggest that language sampling should be designed to "optimize the child's performance and to evoke the best possible sample of his abilities" (p.127). There are cautions throughout every major textbook relating to language assessment against under-estimating or overestimating the child's language structural knowledge. A language sample is considered unrepresentative if it leads to an analysis that results in either one of these errors.

Although it has received differential emphasis throughout the years, "representative" has also been used to imply "typical." In this sense, a child's language sample is considered representative if it portrays his/her "usual," "habitual," "most frequent," or "daily" language performance. It has not been consistently and sufficiently made clear that one language sample may not be both an "idealized" representation and a "typical" representation of the child's language abilities. Even collecting more than one sample does not ensure that either of these kinds of representativeness will be realized.

In addition to the occasionally conflicting aims involved in the concept of representativeness, language assessment is complicated further by the fact that language use varies with context. Any language sample would be the interactive product of contextual variables and the child's language structural knowledge.

The major response to this dilemma has been to obtain language samples in more than one context. For example, Miller (1981) has recommended that three 15 minute language samples be obtained: one with the mother in free play, one with the clinician in free play, and one with the clinician "directing the child with questions and commands" (p.3). In addition, he suggested that a sample could be collected with a playmate or a sibling. Miller emphasized the mother-child language sample because it allowed the clinician to observe the mother's behavior as well as the child's. The samples could be taken in a number of settings including the home, the school, and the clinic, with their advisability being determined by the clinician's evaluation of their potential constraints.

McLean and Snyder-McLean (1978) have recommended that language samples be obtained in a "warm" atmosphere. This might be the home, the classroom, or a playroom with someone familiar to the child present. Potential conversational partners could be the clinician, if he/she has established good rapport with the child, or if not, the parent, a teacher, or an older sibling. They suggested that the assessment consist of three observation sessions over a number of days. These need not differ in terms of the communicative partner, materials, or setting.

Muma (1978) has also indicated that three language samples are needed. He suggested a peer, a sibling, and a parent in addition to the clinician as potential conversational partners and the home, school, and playground in addition to the clinic as potential interactional settings.

Similarly Bloom and Lahey (1978) have recommended that the child's language be sampled in more than one setting if that is possible. Potential conversational partners and settings suggested are similar to those indicated by Muma (1978).

There are three basic problems with this multiple context language sampling procedure as an accommodation to language use variability. First, the number of possible combinations of stimulus materials, conversational partners, and settings is infinite. Second, the selection of any combination of contextual variables is either arbitrary or the result of trial and error sampling of a pre-selected subset of possible combinations. Third, the assertion that multiple context language sampling effectively deals with the language assessment problems resulting from language use variability is questionable. It is predicated on the tenuous assumption that once a combination of contextual variables is selected, its effects on the child's behavior can be predicted and will be consistent across children. It is important to consider research on language use variability relative to these problems.

# Language Use Variability and Communicative Contexts

Studies of language development in normal and specifically language impaired children (Stark and Tallal, 1981) have demonstrated that there are several major contextual parameters that seem to be important for language assessment. These parameters lead to significant variations in children's language use. While the studies taken as a whole indicate that these parameters can affect language use significantly, the findings frequently conflict and some of the individual data differ from the group trends. Thus the potential influence of these parameters on the language performance of an individual child cannot be predicted at this time. The following is an illustrative review of that literature.

## The Communicative Partner

*Mother*

The influence of the mother as a communicative partner on the young child's language use has been the focus of several studies. Scott and Taylor (1978), Kramer, James, and Saxman (1979), and Olswang and Carpenter (1978) are examples of a line of research that compared children's language use with their mothers as partners to their language use with a trained clinician.

The subjects in Scott and Taylor's (1978) study were 12 normal middle class children aged 2;1 to 5;1 years. The children ranged in MLU values from 3.0 to 6.0. Language samples collected in the home with the mother were compared to language samples collected in the clinic with a clinician. Analysis of the average utterance length for each child revealed significant differences in favor of the mother-child home setting only for children with MLU's of 4.0 - 5.0. The data as a whole suggest individual differences. One child produced longer utterances in the clinic setting, seven children produced longer utterances in the home setting, and four children produced utterances of essentially equal length in both settings.

Kramer, James, and Saxman (1979) made similar comparisons with specifically language impaired subjects. Their subjects were 3 - 5 year old children who had speech and/or language problems "ranging from mild to severe" (p.323). Samples were collected of each child talking with his/her mother at home and with a clinician in a speech and language clinic. The results indicated that the children as a group produced significantly longer utterances in the home setting with their mothers than in the clinic with a clinician. Examination of the individual data, however, reveals that only eight of the 10 children were consistent with this group trend. Two children produced utterances of equal length in the two contexts. Differences in DSS scores were not significant; however, seven of the subjects had higher scores in the mother-child sample and three children had slightly higher scores in the clinician-child sample. The investigators highlight the clinical significance of the results by reporting that seven of the children would have been evaluated as being in Brown's Stage III (MLU 2.5 - 3.5 morphemes) based upon their clinician-child samples and in Brown's Stage V (MLU over 4.0 morphemes) based on their mother-child samples.

Olswang and Carpenter (1978) collected both their mother-child and clinician-child language samples in a clinic setting. Their subjects were nine children with language problems aged 3 - 6 years with MLU values of 1.5 - 3.0. Five of these children were normally intelligent, three were of borderline intelligence, and one was mildly retarded. Of the 21 measures of lexical, grammatical, and semantic characteristics of the two samples obtained, only the number of utterances produced in each context was significantly different. The mother-child samples contained more child utterances than the clinician-child samples.

These data seem to be at variance with the major trends of the Scott and Taylor (1978) study of normal children and the Kramer, James, and Saxman (1979) study of language impaired children. There were several research design differences, however, that may have contributed to the inconsistency. Olswang and Carpenter collected the mother-child samples in the clinic rather than in the home, as the other investigators had done, and their subjects, unlike those of the other studies, were not all normally intelligent.

Unfortunately, the consistency or inconsistency of individual data with the general trend, so revealing in the other two studies, was obscured in the Olswang and Carpenter study since no individual data were presented. It seems reasonable to assume, however, that the data of some of the subjects within each study would overlap across studies regardless of the major group trend.

Several studies of normal language development have compared mother-child speech to mother-adult speech and have concluded that there is a maternal speech adjustment when the mother is speaking to the child. This adjustment has been characterized as speech that is syntactically simple, highly redundant, fluent, and well formed (Snow, 1972; Phillips, 1973; Broen, 1972; Snow, 1977). Snow (1972) also reported these adjustments in adult-child speech as well as mother-child speech. Individual differences have been noted, however, that indicate that while maternal speech style may be a useful concept, maternal speech to children is variable across mothers (Dore, 1974; Lieven, 1978; Nelson, 1973). Lieven (1978), for example, reported marked differences in the conversational interactions of two mother-normal language child dyads. The interactions were taped over a six month period when the children, Beth and Kate, were approximately two years of age. Lieven described Kate's mother as highly responsive to her child, producing speech that was closely related to what her child had said. Beth's mother, on the other hand, failed to respond 54 percent of the time and her speech was less contingent on Beth's speech and less accepting of it. Lieven also noted differences in the children's speech styles and concluded that the "child by the way he/she talks may be influencing the way in which other people speak to her/him" (p. 185).

The contradictory results reported in studies of maternal speech to the language impaired child may support Lieven's conclusion. Millet and Newhoff (1978) compared the mother-child speech patterns with nine language impaired disordered children and nine normal children matched for MLU. They reported differences between the two groups, including the observation that mothers of language impaired children provided fewer elaborations of their child's comments than did mothers of normal children. Similarly, Friel-Patti's (1979) study of verbal and nonverbal behaviors in mother-child dyads indicated that mothers of language impaired children look at their children less frequently during interactive play than do mothers of normal children.

Lasky and Klopp (1982), however, recently reported that mother-child interactions with language impaired children did not differ significantly from those with normal language children. They compared mother-child interactions with seven specifically language impaired children, 27 - 45 months of age, to mother-child interactions with 10 normal language children, 12 - 39 months of age. Although they did not report individual data they found that mothers of children in the two groups did not differ in their frequencies of types of verbal or nonverbal interaction or in their mean length of utterance. The major trends of Macpherson and Weber-Olsen (1980) support these findings.

These studies indicate that there is no independently definable "mother style" that entails a predictable degree of speech adjustment and that exerts a predictable influence on a normal or language impaired child's language use. They also suggest, however, that the mother as a communicative partner can potentially affect a child's language performance significantly.

### Father

Many studies comparing the father to the mother as a conversational partner for the normal language child indicate that there are no significant differences between the parents' interactive styles (Berko-Gleason, 1975; Golinkoff and Ames, 1979; Smith and Daglish, 1977; Wilkinson, Hiebert, and Rembold, 1981). It has also been reported, however, that fathers introduce more rare vocabulary items into their parent-child interactions than mothers do (Gleason and Grief, 1979) and use shorter utterances (Rondal, 1980). Giattinno and Hogan (1975) in a study of one 36 month old normal language child and Newhoff, Silverman, and Millet (1980) in a study of normal language children approximately two years old and linguistically matched 3 to 5-year old language impaired children concluded that fathers used fewer semantically related responses than mothers did. Weintraub and Frankel (1977) suggest that there is a significant parent-sex $x$ child-sex interaction that should not be ignored in parent-child interaction studies. They observed that parents talked to and tended to play more with the same sexed than the opposite sexed child. Cherry and Lewis (1978) reported similar parent sex-child sex interactional differences. The girls' mothers talked more, asked more questions, repeated the child's utterances more often and had higher MLU values than boys' mothers. Phillips (1973) data, however, for 8, 18, and 28 month old children are not consistent with this pattern. No mother-son, mother-daughter differences were observed. Similarly, Pakizegi (1978) reported no significant qualitative and quantitative differences between mother-son and father-son interactions with their three-year-old children, and Cramblit and Siegel (1977) observed similar speech modifications for a four-year-old speech and language impaired boy by the child's mother, father, and 16-year-old aunt.

Triadic interactions seem to impose different constraints upon parent-child interactions than dyadic situations, however, and again the results across studies are inconsistent. Clarke-Stewart (1978) observed that in the presence of the father, the mother spoke less and became "less engaging, directive, reinforcing and responsive" (p. 476), while Golinkoff and Ames (1979) report that fathers spoke less than mothers in a triadic situation.

The studies as a whole indicate that the father, like the mother, can present a variable set of constraints as a communicative partner on the child's speech. The data suggest that there probably will be individual differences and that for some children the mother will be the most facilitating conversational partner and for others it will be the father, or both the mother and father, or perhaps neither.

## Peers

Several studies indicate that children's speech to peers differs from their speech to adults. Young children answer more questions posed by adults (Martlew, Connolly and McCleod, 1978) and inform adults more than they do their peers (Cooper, 1979). Children as young as two years old talked more to adults and adjusted their speech to adult listener needs more than they did for peers (Wellman and Lempers, 1977). Wilkinson, Hiebert, and Rembold (1981) reported that the speech of normal children approximately 30 months of age to their same aged peers include a "high degree of repetitions, attentionals, and directives" while parent-child interactions were "more structurally complex, fluent, and interactive..." (p. 387).

The language use of children is also influenced by the age of their peer interactants. Sachs and Devin (1976) and Shatz and Gelman (1973) have reported that normal language children as young as three and four years of age reduce the complexity of their speech for a younger peer. These adjustments can even be role played with dolls (Sachs and Devin, 1976; James, 1978).

A few studies also have reported that normal language children respond differentially to language impaired children (Wellen and Broen, 1982) and to children with limited syntactic abilities (Masur, 1978) than to their normal language peers. Wellen and Broen (1982) found that the older siblings of 4-year old language impaired and normal language children interrupted their younger siblings with similar frequency during an adult directed question and answer task. The responses of the two groups of older siblings, however, were qualitatively different. Unlike the older siblings of normal language children, the older siblings of language impaired children supplied answers more often rather than promptings or rephrasings of the questions.

Masur (1978) also found that four-year-olds adjusted their speech differently for two groups of two-year-olds, those with "high verbal" skills (MLU 1.8 - 4.0) and those with "low verbal" skills (MLU 1.0 - 1.5). She reported a strong relationship between several measures of "listener responsiveness" and the complexity of the four-year-olds' speech. Higher MLU's and more frequent complex sentences were obtained when the four-year-old's listener was more responsive.

Fey, Leonard, and Wilcox (1981) have reported that language impaired children also are capable of adjusting the complexity of their language relative to age of the communicative partner. Their six language impaired subjects, aged 4;3 to 6;5 with MLU values of at least 3.0, were paired with chronologically age matched normal language peers and with two - three year old MLU matched normal language peers. They found significant differences in mean pre-verb length, in the frequency of internal state questions, and in the frequency of "back channel" responses in the speech of the language impaired children in these two interactional contexts.

While it is not directly contradictory, a recent study by Van Kleeck and Frankel (1981) found that three to four-year-old language impaired children's use of focus and substitution discourse devices did not significantly vary in frequency with the mother or with a chronological peer as a discourse partner. Speech adjustments analogous to those reported by Fey, Leonard, and Wilcox (1981) for partners of different ages were not observed.

Both studies, however, underscore the importance of individual differences regardless of group trends. Within the Fey, Leonard, and Wilcox study, the frequency of internal state questions did not significantly vary for one of the six language impaired children (Subject 3). Similarly, Subject 5 whose frequency of back channel responses with a younger peer was 0 percent and with a same aged peer was 5 percent, seemed to be another exception to the group data.

Significant individual differences were also observed in Van Kleeck and Frankel's study. Although in general the mother-language impaired child and peer-language impaired child samples did not vary on the basis of conversational partner, one of the three subjects (Subject 2) "did not interact verbally with the other children even after efforts to encourage and facilitate such interaction" (p. 253). The other children's peer samples contained 123 utterances for Subject 1 and 120 utterances for Subject 3.

Some studies of normal children report similar individual variation. Lougee, Grueneich, and Hartup (1977), for example, obtained same-age and mixed-age dyadic samples from 54 children 3;4 to 5;4 years old. They reported "no consistent tendency" for either the younger or the older members of mixed-age dyads regarding utterance length or amount of social interaction. Lieberman (1977) also observed individual differences among the 40 three-year-olds she studied. She found that maternal attitudes toward children's expressions of aggression and the freedom they had to explore were significantly correlated with measures of peer interactive competence.

Familiarity seems to be one of the factors that can affect child-child interactions. There is a greater preference for interaction with a child after repeated exposure to him/her (Scholtz and Ellis, 1975), and there is more social and complex play if young children are familiar with each other (Doyle, Connolly and Rivest, 1980).

Child research indicates that child-child communicative behavior is not described sufficiently by reference to a single variable such as chronological age or structural linguistic knowledge. Individual differences suggest that a complex of variables whose effects are still not fully understood, such as personality, previous social experience, degrees of familiarity, birth order, sex, etc., interact significantly with a child's communicative behavior. Lougee et al. concluded that the term 'peer' should be used conservatively: "Peerlike behavior, it seems, is social activity in which the actions of one child represent a developmental status that is very similar to the developmental status of a companion...children may or may not be peers depending on the accommodation each makes to the immediate situation" (p. 1354). The influence that a "peer," with all of the various definitions of the term, has upon a normal and language impaired child's language use is no more predictable than is that of any of the other potential communicative partners described. The degree of influence, as various studies indicate, however, can be substantial.

## Physical Context Variables

The relationship between a variety of physical context variables and children's language use also has been investigated. Some of the studies have explored the possible differential effects of objects, primarily toys and pictures, and others have focused upon the effects of activities, how objects are used, and what tasks are involved.

Several studies have investigated the relative utility of different types of toys for language sampling. Within this variable, sex differences have been observed. For example, Smith and Daglish (1977) studied the play behaviors of 32 normal language children, 16 boys and 16 girls, aged one to two years. They found that boys showed a preference for more active play and for play with transportation toys while girls played more with soft toys and dolls.

It also has been observed that different toys elicit different types of communicative behavior from children. Rubin and Seibel (1979) observed a higher incidence of "sociodramatic" play when normal language preschool aged children played with house and vehicle toys than when they played with toys in other settings. Cook-Gumperz and Corsaro (1977) noted that the communicative demands on normal language three to four-year-olds varied when they played in a playhouse area, when they were engaged in fantasy play with a sandbox, and when they participated in adult directed arts and crafts projects. They reported that fantasy play was the most communicatively demanding situation.

Directly comparable data are not available for language impaired populations. Based upon their clinical experience assessing language disordered children, however, Bloom and Lahey (1978) suggest that a greater number of utterances and a greater variety of utterances can be obtained by structuring the clinician-child interaction "around a concrete activity" using science experiments, art projects, construction toys, etc. Miller (1981) similarly has noted through his experience that language disordered children tend to talk more about "new and unique toys."

The influence of pictures upon language samples also has been explored. While the use of pictures with clinical populations has been recommended (Engler, Hannah and Longhurst, 1973; Wilson, 1969), particularly for young school aged children (Lee, 1974; Lucas, 1980), studies of normal children suggest that there are significant differences in the effectiveness of various kinds of pictures for children within this age group (Cowen, Weber, Hoddinott, and Klein, 1967), and that there are individual differences across children (Longhurst and File, 1977).

Longhurst and File (1977) investigated the language performance of 20 children, 13 girls and 7 boys, enrolled in a Head Start program. The children were 3;11 to 5;0 years of age and were normally intelligent. Language samples were collected from each child in four adult-child conditions. The stimulus materials varied for each condition. In one condition the children were asked to talk about multi-object pictures, in another about toys that were provided, and in another about single object pictures. In one condition, "conversation," no stimulus materials were present, and the experimenter "elicited conversation about a variety of topics including family, school, television and familiar activities" (p. 58). The group data indicated that according to DSS scores conversation-elicited samples were the most complex, toy-elicited samples ranked second, and multi-object pictures and single object picture samples ranked third. Examination of the individual subject data, however, reveals that almost every possible ordering of the four conditions occurred, and that there were essentially no differences across conditions for three of the subjects, Subjects 3, 8, and 17. The magnitude of variability across conditions for some children, on the other hand, was large. Longhurst and File (1977) stressed the clinical significance of the kind of language use variability they observed by indicating that according to Lee's (1974) chart for estimating language delay, Subject 1 would have been considered 20 - 23 months language delayed on the basis of one sample and in the ninetieth percentile on the basis of another.

The data suggest that the materials which serve as a focus for an interaction can influence the communicative behavior of normal language children and probably of language impaired children, although the effects for an individual child are not predictable a priori. Language impaired children have not been investigated as extensively as normal language children, but since variability across children frequently characterizes this population, it seems reasonable to assume that there would be individual differences of at least the magnitude observed for normal language children.

The possible effects of activities and of how materials are used upon language use also have been examined. Fokes and Konefal (1981) reported that copying object manipulations of an examiner facilitated five to nine-year-old language impaired children's productions of agent + action + object + locative utterances more than observations of object manupulations did. Similar differences were not noted for three to six-year-old normal language children.

Stalnaker and Craighead (1982), however, found that 12 four to five-and-a-half-year-old normal children enrolled in a Head Start program produced the longest MLU's when they retold a story using toys to act it out, compared to two other toy manipulation conditions. In one of these conditions the child told the investigator what he/she was doing while playing with the toys and in the other the investigator asked questions about the toys while the child played with them. The conditions ranked in language structural complexity in the above order. Exceptions to these group trends were noted, however, and the investigators conclude that "The results of this study did not demonstrate that one method of obtaining a language sample was superior..." (p. 127).

Pictures also have been used in different ways. Several studies of normal children's language use indicate that three to six-year-old normal language children produce more complex utterances when their picture stimuli are not viewed jointly with the experimenter (Blank, 1975; Bokus and Shugar, 1979; Haynes, Purcell, and Haynes, 1979). These relationships within the speech of language impaired children have not been investigated sufficiently.

Dore (1978) and Hall and Cole (1978) examined the influence of two physical settings, a classroom and a supermarket, on the language use of three to four-year-old normal children attending a Head Start nursery. They found that a change in setting alone did not necessarily elicit more complex speech. The language used related to a number of variables including the "interactive style of participants and the task as it is mutually constructed by them" (Dore, 1978, p. 441).

Therefore, activities, like types of objects, can affect children's language. The complex interrelationships of these variables, however, are not sufficiently clear to allow prediction, and individual differences seem probable. The literature as a whole suggests that every aspect of physical context probably can, but will not necessarily, affect a particular child's language use.

There is extensive evidence, such as that reviewed above regarding significant inter-relationships between language use variability and selected contextual parameters. This evidence and the knowledge that there is no natural limit to the number of parameters that could be explored present criticial problems for the speech and language pathologist. It is clear that the number of contextual variables potentially influencing the child's language use is too great to suggest that all contexts should be sampled during language assessment. While this is obviously impossible, it would address the basic issue apparent in the literature previously reviewed. Individual differences in the interrelationships of language use variability and particular contextual variables would probably be complementary across all of the samplings for each child. The goal of attaining representativeness in the sense of comprehensive and idealized performance could then be met. Regardless of the use-context patterns that characterized each child's behavior, incorporating all possible contextual configurations would allow every child to perform in what to him or her were the most facilitating contexts.

Sampling across a limited number of contextual environments, however, meets the practical requirement of efficiency. The literature, unfortunately, does not specify a limited number of "standard" sampling contexts, contexts that will elicit child language samples meeting all three criteria for representativeness. It suggests instead that the effects on language performance cannot be predicted for an individual child nor can they be assumed to be consistent across children.

Based upon the current research literature, the goal of defining "standard contexts" in terms of environmental variables seems to be an unobtainable one. This may not always be the case. Efforts to define sub-groups within the category of language impaired children continue (see Aram and Nation, 1975 and Fey and Leonard, this volume), and when these definitions are sufficiently refined they may enable the clinician to make this kind of prediction. Currently, however, decisions regarding which configurations of contextual variables are to be used for a child's language assessment, because they cannot be empirically motivated, either are made arbitrarily or they are the result of trial and error sampling. One concern is that guidelines for these trial and error samplings of pre-selected subsets of contextual configurations have never been provided (e.g. how long they should be, what type and quantity of child behaviors indicate that a particular contextual configuration should be continued and used for the language sampling or replaced, etc.) What weakens this procedure even more critically, however, is that the pre-selected subset of possible contextual configurations to be sampled is itself arbitrary and subject to the same threats to representativeness as the alternative procedure (simply specifying the contexts for the language sampling).

What must be standardized across children is representativeness, which means that the language sampled must be comprehensive and must represent idealized and typical performance. Contexts, therefore, cannot be standardized. They must be prescribed for each child based upon his/her own pattern of language use variability. What is needed then is a procedure that enables the clinician to select a realistic number of contexts in which to sample the child's language and to ensure that these contexts reflect each child's individual use-context interactions. This procedure, which is a pre-assessment procedure, would provide critical information about the child's language use variability that can guide the clinician in the selection of those contextual configurations which should be used in the language assessment to sample each child's idealized and typical performance.

## Pre-Assessment

One means of obtaining the information needed is to interview the parents or other significant individuals in the child's life, such as relatives, teachers, and other professionals. Traditionally this has been a major source of information about children with language problems. Early parent interview procedures, such as the case history (Johnson, Darley and Spriestersbach, 1963), and social and verbal scales (Doll, 1965; Mecham, 1958) have been used to assess the nature and extent of the child's language problem. More recent scales, such as the *Oliver: Parent Administered Communicative Inventory* (MacDonald, 1978), not only ask the parents to describe the child's communicative behavior but suggest activities to be used in guiding their observations.

Historically, the parents or other significant individuals have been used as informants successfully and are being incorporated more and more as members of the language assessment team (see particularly McLean and Snyder-McLean, 1978). The problems inherent in prescribing critical language sampling contexts for each child assessed suggest that these two major sources of information about the child, the language sample and the parents or significant others as informants, should interact.

I have developed a Pre-Assessment questionnaire that attempts to incorporate these two major sources (see Appendix). We have used this questionnaire in the Developmental Language Programs, Communicative Disorders Clinics of the University of Michigan. The Pre-Assessment Questionnaire enables the clinician to individualize language sampling contexts by systematically obtaining information from the parents and/or other significant individuals who may be knowledgeable about the child's language use. The questionnaire is designed to elicit information about the child's communicative behavior and possible language variability relative to major contextual parameters. The form is best administered as an interview, because this allows the clinician to clarify the questions for the informant and to probe further when necessary to obtain the desired information. This questionnaire is a supplemental one for language assessements of children. Standard forms administered to all clients obtain other relevant information such as medical history, school history, etc.

The Pre-Assessment Questionnaire can be administered in person or by phone. In either case, if the informant is unsure of the answers to some of the questions, information is provided regarding critical variables to observe, and the informant is contacted again. Language sampling is not scheduled until information about the contextual configuration, which is most likely to reveal the child's idealized or best performance, and about the configuration which is most likely to reveal his typical performance is provided.

Two language sampling contexts are prescribed for each child according to this information. In addition, a third sample is obtained with the clinician as the conversational partner. For this sample contextual variables other than the communicative partner from the child's "best" context are held constant. This third sample enables the clinician to probe for specific language structures and to pursue tentative hypotheses regarding the child's language use.

There have been many examples within our clinical program of the important impact this type of contextual individualization has had upon the representativeness of the language assessment data obtained. One child who was particularly sensitive to the communicative partner had an MLU value of 1.6 in the clinician-child sample and an MLU of 3.96 when she talked with her brother. One boy produced his most structurally complex utterances while he was playing with water toys in a plastic pan filled with water, an activity his mother had indicated "he would talk most about." One boy's most structurally complex language performance was obtained when he played with a younger friend who was his neighbor. For one child, it was talking about pictures in a family album.

Idealized performance is not the only goal, however. The child's range of variability across contexts is a more comprehensive description of his/her language performance than any one particular value. Language use entails language variability across critical contexts, and this important aspect of the child's language performance should be assessed. For example, the language performance of the first child mentioned above is best described in terms of MLU values as a range of 1.6 - 3.36 with a specification of the configurations of contextual variables in which each value was obtained. The difference between the values obtained in the "best" context and those obtained in the "typical" context are particularly important for formalizing language intervention goals and for interpreting descriptions of the child's language behavior that suggest inconsistency. It is often possible to clarify behaviors that may appear inconsistent on the surface by interpreting them in terms of the language use variability patterns observed during the assessment.

The discussion of language use variability and the need for pre-assessment as a pre-requisite for defining critical language assessment contexts has focused primarily on language structural aspects of performance. These aspects of language performance were highlighted because they represent the most conservative case relative to the arguments presented. Other aspects of language performance that are defined as interactive, such as discourse regulation behaviors, would be even more sensitive to contextual variation.

## Summary

A modification of current language sampling procedures is proposed to accommodate language use variability. A pre-assessment interview of parents and/or other significant individuals regarding the influence of major contextual parameters upon the child's language use is necessary in order to achieve representativeness during language assessment. Information from this pre-assessment can be used to prescribe contextual configurations that will vary across children but will sample analogous types of language use variation. Individualizing contexts seems to be the most satisfactory answer to the individual patterns of language use reported in the literature.

## References

Aram D., & Nation, J. *Child language disorders.* St. Louis, MO: The C. V. Mosby Company, 1982.

Aram, D., & Nation, J. Patterns of language behavior in children with developmental disorders. *Journal of Speech and Hearing Research,* 1975, *18,* 229-241.

Atkins, C., & Cartwright, L. Preferred language elicitation procedures used in five age categories. *Asha,* 1982 *24*(5), 321-323.

Austin, J. *How to do things with words.* Cambridge: Oxford University Press, 1962.

Bates, E. Pragmatics and sociolinguistics in child language. In D. Morehead and A. Morehead (Eds.), *Normal and Deficient Child Language. Selected readings.* Baltimore: University Park Press, 1976.

Berko-Gleason, J. Fathers and other strangers: Men's speech to young children. In D. Dato (Ed.), *Georgetown University Roundtable on Language and Linguistics.* Washington, D.C., 1975.

Blank, M. Eliciting verbalization from young children in experimental tasks: a methodological note. *Child Development,* 1975, *46,* 254-257.

Bloom, L. *Language development: Form and function in emerging grammars.* Cambridge, MA: MIT Press, 1970.

Bloom, L., & Lahey, M. *Language development and language disorders.* New York: John Wiley and Sons, 1978.

Bokus, B., & Shugar, G. What will a three year old say? An experimental study of structural variation. In O. Garnica and M. King (Eds.), *Language, children and society.* New York: Pergamon Press, 1979.

Broen, P. The verbal environment of the language learning child. *American Speech and Hearing Association Monograph, 1972, 17.*

Brown, R. *A first language: The early stages.* Cambridge, MA: Harvard University Press, 1973.

Cherry, L., & Lewis, M. Differential socialization of girls and boys: Implications for sex differences in language development. In N. Waterson and C. Snow (Eds.), *The development of communication.* New York: John Wiley and Sons, Inc., 1978.

Clarke-Stewart, K. And daddy makes 3: the fathers impact on mother and the young child. *Child Development, 1978, 49,* 466-478.

Cook-Gumperz, J., & Corsaro, W. Social-ecological constraints on children's communication strategies. *Sociology, 1977, 11,* 411-434.

Cook-Gumperz, J., & Gumperz, J. Context in children's speech. In N. Waterson and C. Snow (Eds.), *The development of communication.* New York: John Wiley and Sons, Inc., 1978.

Cooper, M. Verbal interaction in nursery schools. *British Journal of Educational Psychology, 1979, 49,* 214-225.

Cowen, P., Weber, J., Hoddinott, B., & Klein, J. Mean length of spoken response as a function of stimulus, experimenter and subject. *Child Development, 1967, 38,* 191-203.

Cramblit, N., & Siegel, G. The verbal environment of a language impaired child. *Journal of Speech and Hearing Disorders, 1977, 42*(4), 474-482.

Crystal, D., Fletcher, P., & Garman, M. *The grammatical analysis of language disability: A procedure for assessment and remediation.* New York: Elsevier -North Holland Publishing Co., 1976.

Darley, F., & Moll, K. Reliability of language measures and size of language sample. *Journal of Speech and Hearing Research,* 1960, *3,* 166-173.

Davis, E. The development of linguistic skill in twins, singletons with siblings, and only children from age five to ten years. *Child Welfare Monographs,* 1937, *14.*

Doll, E. *Vineland social maturity scale.* Minneapolis: American Guidance Service, 1965.

Dore, J. A pragmatic description of early language development. *Journal of Psycholinguistic Research,* 1974, *3,* 343-350.

Dore, J. Variation in preschool children's conversational performances. In K. Nelson (Ed.), *Children's language* (Vol. 1). New York: Gardner Press, 1978.

Doyle, A., Connolly, J., & Revist, L. The effect of playmate familiarity on the social interactions of young children. *Child Development,* 1980, *51,* 217-223.

Engler, L., Hannah, E., & Longhurst, T. Linguistic analysis of speech samples: A practial guide for clinicians. *Journal of Speech and Hearing Disorders,* 1973, *38*(2), 192-204.

Ervin-Tripp, S. Some strategies for the first two years. In T. Moore (Ed.), *Cognitive development and the acquisition of language.* New York: Academic Press, 1973.

Fey, M., & Leonard, L. Pragmatic skills of children with specific language impairment. In T. Gallagher and C. Prutting (Eds.), *Pragmatic assessment and intervention issues in language.* San Diego: College Hill Press, 1982.

Fey, M., Leonard, L., & Wilcox, K. Speech style modifications of language impaired children. *Journal of Speech and Hearing Disorders,* 1981, *46*(1), 91-96.

Fokes, J., & Konefal, J. Children's use of four semantic cases in two conditions. *Journal of Communicative Disorders,* 1981, *14,* 497-506.

Friel-Patti, S. Mother-child dyads: Further exploration of verbal and nonverbal behaviors. Paper presented at the American Speech and Hearing Association Annual Convention, 1979.

Giattino, J., & Hogan, J. Analysis of a father's speech to his language learning child. *Journal of Speech and Hearing Disorders,* 1975, *40*(4), 524-537.

Gleason, J., & Grief, E. Hi, thanks and goodbye: Some more routine information. *Standford Child Language Forum,* 1979.

Golinkoff, R., & Ames, G. A comparison of fathers' and mothers' speech with their children. *Child Development,* 1979, *50,* 28-32.

Hall, W., & Cole, M. On participants' shaping of discourse through their understanding of the task. In K. Nelson (Ed.), *Children's language* (Vol. 1). New York: Gardner Press, 1978.

Haynes, W., Purcell, E., & Haynes, N. A pragmatic aspect of language sampling. *Language, Speech and Hearing Services in Schools,* 1979, *10,* 104-110.

James, S. Effect of listener age and situation on the politeness of children's directives. *Journal of Psycholinguistic Research,* 1978, *7*(4), 307-317.

Johnson, W., Darley, F., & Sprietstersbach, D. *Diagnostic methods in speech pathology.* New York: Harper and Row, 1963.

Kramer, C., James, S., & Saxman, J. A comparison of language samples elicited at home and in the clinic. *Journal of Speech and Hearing Disorders,* 1979, *44*(3), 321-330.

Lasky, E., & Klopp, K. Parent-child interaction in normal and language disordered children. *Journal of Speech and Hearing Disorders, 1982, 47,* 7-18.

Lee, L. *Developmental sentence analysis.* Evanston, IL: Northwestern University Press, 1974.

Lee, L. Developmental sentence types: a method for comparing normal and deviant syntactic development. *Journal of Speech and Hearing Disorders,* 1966, *31,* 311-330.

Lee, L., & Canter, S. Developmental sentence scoring: a clinical procedure for estimating syntactic development in the children's spontaneous speech. *Journal of Speech and Hearing Disorders,* 1977. *36,* 315-341.

Leonard, L. What is deviant language? *Journal of Speech and Hearing Disorders,* 1972, *37,* 427-447.

Leonard, L., Prutting, C., Perozzi, J., & Berkley, R. Nonstandardized approaches to the assessment of language behavior. *Asha,* 1978, *20,* 371-379.

Lieberman, A. Preschoolers' competence with a peer: relations with attachment and peer experience. *Child Devlopment,* 1977, *48,*(4), 1277-1287.

Lieven, E. Conversations between mothers and young children: Individual differences and their possible implication for the study of language learning. In N. Waterson and C. Snow (Eds.), *The development of communication.* New York: John Wiley and Sons, Inc., 1978.

Longhurst, T., & File, J. A comparison of developmental sentence scores from head start children collected in four conditions. *Language Speech and Hearing Services in Schools,* 1977, *8,* 54-64.

Lougee, M., Grueneich, R., & Hartup. W. Social interaction in same- and mixed-age dyads of preschool children. *Child Development,* 1977, *48,* 1353-1361.

Lucas, E. *Semantic and pragmantic language disorders.* Rockville: Aspen Publication Corporation, 1980.

Masur, E. Preschool boy's speech modifications: The effect of listeners' linguistic levels and conversational responsiveness. *Child Development,* 1978, *49,* 924-927.

McCarthy, D. Language development in children. In L. Carmichael (Ed.), *Manual of Child Psychology.* New York: Wiley and Sons, 1954.

McCarthy, D. *The language develpment of the preschool child.* (Institute of Child Welfare Monograph Series No. 4). Minneapolis: University of Minnesota Press, 1930.

MacDonald, J. *Oliver: Parent-administered communication inventory.* Columbus, OH: Charles E. Merrill Publishing Co., 1978.

McLean, J., & Snyder-McLean, L. *A transactional approach to early language training.* Columbus, OH: Charles E. Merrill Publishing Co., 1978.

Macpherson, C., & Weber-Olsen, M. Mother speech input to deficient and language normal children. *Proceedings from the first Wisconsin symposium on research in child language disorders.* Madison: University of Wisconsin Press, 1980.

Martlew, M., Connolly, K., & McCleod, C. Language use, role and context in a five year old. *Journal of Child Language,* 1978, *5,* 81-99.

Mecham, M. *Verbal language development scale.* Circle Pines, MN: American Guidance Service, 1958.

Miller, J. *Assessing language production in children: Experimental procedures.* Baltimore: University Park Press, 1981.

Millet, A., & Newhoff, M. Language disordered children: Language disordered mothers? Paper presented at the American Speech and Hearing Association Convention, San Francisco, 1978.

Muma, J. *Language handbook: Concepts, assessment and intervention.* Englewood Cliffs, NJ: Prentice-Hall, Inc., 1978.

Nelson, K. Structure and strategy in learning to talk. *Monographs of the Society for Research in Child Development,* 1973, *38.*

Newhoff, M., Silverman, L., & Millet, A. Linguistic differences in parents' speech to normal and language disordered children. *Proceedings from the first Wisconsin symposium on research in child language disorders.* Madison: University of Wisconsin Press, 1980.

Olswang, L., & Carpenter, R. Elicitor effects on the language obtained from young language-impaired children. *Journal of Speech and Hearing Disorders,* 1978, *43,* 76-88

Pakizegi, B. The interaction of mother and father with their sons. *Child Development,* 1978, *49,* 479-482.

Phillips, J. Syntax and vocabulary of mother's speech to young children: Age and sex comparisons. *Child Development,* 1973, *44,* 182-185.

Rondal, J. Father's and mother's speech in early language development. *Journal of Child Language,* 1980, *7,* 353-371.

Rubin, K., & Seibel, C. The effects of ecological settings on the cognitive and social play behaviors of preschoolers. Paper presented at the Annual Meeting of the American Educational Research Association, Atlanta, 1979.

Sachs, J., & Devin, J. Young children's use of appropriate speech styles in social interaction and role playing. *Journal of Child Language,* 1976, *3,* 81-98.

Scholtz, G., & Ellis, M. Repeated exposure to objects and peers in a play setting. *Journal of Experimental Child Psychology,* 1975, *19,* 448-445.

Scott, C., & Taylor, A. A comparison of home and clinic gathered language samples. *Journal of Speech and Hearing Disorders,* 1978, *43*(4), 482-495.

Searle, J. *Speech acts.* Cambridge: Harvard University Press, 1969.

Shatz, M., & Gelman, R. The development of communication skills: Modifications in the speech of young children as a function of listener. *Monographs of the Society for Research in Child Development,* 1973, *38.*

Shriner, T. A comparison of selected measures with psychological scale values of language development. *Journal of Speech and Hearing Research,* 1967, *10,* 828-835.

Shriner, T. A review of mean length of response as a measure of expressive language development in children. *Journal of Speech and Hearing Disorders,* 1969, *34,* 61-68.

Smith, P., & Daglish, L. Sex differences in parent and infant behavior in the home. *Child Development,* 1977, *48*(4), 1250-1254.

Snow, C. Mothers' speech research: From input to interaction. In C. Snow and C. Ferguson (Eds.), *Talking to children: Language input and acquisition.* Cambridge: Cambridge University Press, 1977.

Snow, C. Mother's speech to children learning language. *Child Development,* 1972, *43,* 549-565.

Stark, R., & Tallal, P. Selection of children with specific language deficits. *Journal of Speech and Hearing Disorders,* 1981, *46,* 114-122.

Stalmaker, L., & Craighead, N. An examination of language samples obtained under three experimental conditions. *Language Speech and Hearing Services in Schools,* 1982, *13*(2), 121-128.

Templin, M. *Certain language skills in children.* Minneapolis: University of Minnesota Press, 1957.

Tyack, D., & Gottsleben, R. *Language sampling, analysis and training: A handbook for teachers and clinicians.* Palo Alto: Consulting Psychological Press, 1974.

VanKleeck, A., & Frankel, T. Discourse devices used by language disordered children: a preliminary investigation. *Journal of Speech and Hearing Disorders,* 1981, *46*(3), 250-257.

Weintraub, M., & Frankel, J. Sex differences in parent-infant interaction during free play, departure and separation. *Child Development,* 1977, *48,* 1240-1249.

Wellen, C., & Broen, P. The interruption of young children's responses by older siblings. *Journal of Speech and Hearing Disorders,* 1982, *47*(2), 204-210.

Wellman, H., & Lempers, J. The naturalistic communicative abilities of two year olds. *Child Development,* 1977, *48,* 1052-1057.

Wilkinson, L., Heibert, E., & Rembold, K. Parents' and peers' communication to toddlers. *Journal of Speech and Hearing Research,* 1981, *24,* 383-388.

Wilson, M. A standardized method for obtaining a spoken language sample. *Journal of Speech and Hearing Research,* 1969, *12*(1), 95-102.

# Appendix

## Pre-Assessment Questionnaire

Tanya M. Gallagher

Developmental Language Programs
Communicative Disorders Clinic
The University of Michigan

(All information in this questionnaire will be considered confidential)

Child's  Name_____  Birthdate_____

Address_____  Sex_____

Name of person filling out questionnaire_____

Relationship to child_____

List children and adults who live in child's home other than the parents:

Name_____  Age_____  Relationship_____

Name_____  Age_____  Relationship_____

Name_____  Age_____  Relationship_____

Name_____  Age_____  Relationship_____

Who recommended that the child's communicative behavior be assessed?

Name_____  Relationship to child_____

How did the above person describe the child's communicative difficulties?

Have others commented upon the child's communicative difficulties? If so, what were these comments?

Have you consulted other professionals regarding the child's communicative difficulties?
Whom

What were the recommendations?

What things have you tried to change the child's communicative behavior? Describe:

Describe the child's communicative behavior as completely as possible:

Does the child's communicative behavior change relative to that description when he talks with:

1. A friend? Name_____ Age_____ What changes do you observe?

_____

2. A younger sibling? Name_____ Age_____ What changes do you observe?

3. An older sibling? Name_____ Age_____ What changes do you observe?

4. A teacher (or someone in authority)? What changes do you observe?_____

_____

_____

5. Mother? What changes do you observe?_____

_____

6. Father? What changes do you observe?_____

_____

7. Familiar adult (neighbor, grandparent, etc.)? What changes do you observe?_____

_____

8. Unfamiliar adult (sales persons, etc.)? What changes do you observe? _____

9. Small group? What changes do you observe? _____

Does the child's communicative behavior change relative to your original description when he talks about:

1. Things he has done? How? _____

2. Things he will do? How? _____

3. Things he is doing? How? _____

4. Things someone else is doing? How? _____

5. Familiar toys or activities? How? _____

6. Unfamiliar toys or activities? How? _____

7. What are your child's favorite playthings? _____

8. What activities does your child enjoy participating in? _____

9. Describe how your child plays with his favorite playmates: _____

Of the following, recommend what would probably be the child's best communicative situation:

Who _____

When (time of day) _____

Place _____

Activities _____

Objects _____

Other _____

Relative to the following, recommend what would probably be the child's most frequent communicative situation:

Who _____

When (time of day) _____

Place _____

Activities _____

Objects _____

Other _____

# 2

# APPLIED PRAGMATICS

*Carol A. Prutting*
and
*Diane M. Kirchner*
University of California at Santa Barbara


## Introduction

*A* paradigm shift has taken place which explains language as a theory of action (Austin, 1962; Searle, 1969). That is, words can effect change and make events happen. Steiner (1981) has spoken of the autonomous nature of language and how words are able to bless, heal, cripple, and kill. He mentions the inexhaustible way man can create as well as destroy with words. Steiner is fascinated with the idea that there are no brakes within us. In other words, there is nothing which cannot be said and, therefore, nothing which cannot be done with the power of words. Searle has asked: "How do words relate to the world? How is it possible that when a speaker stands before a hearer and emits an acoustic blast such remarkable things occur as: The speaker means something; the sounds he emits mean something; the hearer understands what is meant; the speaker makes a statement, asks a question, or gives an order?" (p. 3). Searle has discussed the four basic components of how understanding is accomplished: the utterance act (uttering words), the propositional act (referring and predicating), the illocutionary act (stating, questioning, asserting, etc.) and the perlocutionary act (effects such acts have on the thought, actions, beliefs, etc. of the hearer). So, basically there is a speech act. The speaker means something, the sentence means something and the hearer understands something. In addition, there are basic rules governing the linguistic elements. These are the basic components, or units, of the speech act. Somehow all of these aspects operate together and the communicative tasks between or among partners get accomplished.

In our prior formalistic linguistic paradigm, the rules for governing word order were of most import and what the rules did or did not accomplish was not addressed. In the functionalist paradigm the effects of sentence use in context are heightened. The shift has been from a formalist syntactically based theory to a functionalist pragmatically based theory (Bates and MacWhinney, in press). The issue is whether one views syntax as central and regulative to the language system or whether one views pragmatics as a framework from which to understand syntax and semantics. This shift should provide us with much research activity. As Kuhn suggests, "In learning a paradigm the scientist acquires theory, methods, and standards together, usually in an inextricable mixture. Therefore, when paradigms change, there are usually significant shifts in the criterion determining the legitimacy both of problems and of proposed solutions" (Kuhn, 1962, p. 109). He goes on to suggest that no paradigm solves all the problems; however, paradigm debates involve the question: "Which problems is it more significant to have solved?"

We have moved from being interested in the innate characteristics which permit an individual to know grammaticalness from ungrammaticalness. Today, the questions of interest have to do with the social and cognitive context in which structures develop and are used. It is interesting to note that our "new" theoretical framework was expounded in 1955 when Austin delivered the William James lectures at Harvard University. He delivered this address two years prior to the treatise, *Syntactic Structures,* which was primarily responsible for the linguistic revolution (Chomsky, 1957). Actually, Austin in his preface said, "The views which underlie these lectures were formed in 1939" (Austin, 1962, p. vi). However, Kuhn suggests a paradigm shift does not occur unless there is a consensus among the scientific community. Max Planck (1949) has stated, "a new scientific truth does not triumph by convincing its opponents and making them see the light, but rather because its opponents eventually die, and a new generation grows up that is familiar with it " (p. 150).   We are viewing our second contemporary paradigmatic shift in the past two and a half decades. There has been a displacement from viewing syntax as central to seeing pragmatics as the overall framework from which to study syntax and semantics.

Recently, there have been several attempts to provide clinicians with a useful way of incorporating pragmatics into our current assessment procedures (Damico and Braziel, 1981; Prutting, 1979; Rees and Wollner, 1981). Each of these investigators attempted to unravel the individual pragmatic behaviors and impose some type of systematic order to the data for clinical usage. All of the frameworks proposed are a result of the paradigm shift which has taken place in the field of child language and consequently applied to the field of Speech/Language Pathology.

Prutting (1979) suggested a developmental protocol which provides rough guidelines and sequencing of behaviors for remedial purposes. She extrapolated numerous behaviors across developmental levels which can be assessed in a natural setting. Rees and Wollner (1981) developed an extensive taxonomy of pragmatic abilities. Their taxonomy consists of the following conversational abilities: sequential organization of conversation, coherency of conversation, repair of conversation, establishment and variation of role with respect to the listener, and the production and comprehension of speech acts. Damico and Braziel (1981) included the following areas in their assessment procedures: illocutionary acts, conversational postulates, verbal error behaviors, and nonverbal error behaviors. Their procedure includes the evaluation of communicative interactions as well as noncommunicative acts.

The applied clinical frameworks (Damico and Braziel, 1981; Prutting, 1979; Rees and Wollner, 1981) developed as an outgrowth of the speech act paradigm. The authors have attempted to outline a strategy for assessment purposes. Clinical application using the various approaches should reveal their fruitfulness.

## The Pragmatic Behaviors

This section consists of organizing the pragmatic behaviors within a speech act framework. For us, it is important to utilize this framework since it provides the original theoretical model responsible for the shift. Our purpose is to include a representative sample of the behaviors discussed in the literature. All of the behaviors should be present in and used appropriately by school age children. Assessment protocols for the infant or young child should be based on other taxonomies which are presented in the literature (Bates, Benigni, Bretherton, Camaioni, and Volterra, 1979; Dore, 1975; Halliday, 1975). For this paper we have chosen to concentrate on assessment procedures for the school age and adult client.

### School Age and Adult Behaviors

Table 2-1 will describe the behaviors which may be included in an assessment of pragmatic abilities. The utterance act as extended here includes paralinguistic and nonverbal as well as verbal. These are the trappings by which the act is accomplished or the way in which the act is presented. The second broad area, propositional acts, consists of linguistic dimensions of the meaning of the sentence and serves to orient both speaker and listener. The illocutionary and perlocutionary acts are the shared dyadic behaviors regulated by the discourse partners. For the purpose of this presentation, they were positioned together. The illocutionary act is the speaker's intention while the perlocutionary act is the effects of the act on the listener. During a conversation these behaviors are reciprocal and are organized and executed in relationship to one another. The behaviors which follow are presented in terms of modality, description and coding, and references which may be helpful in understanding the behavior discussed. According to the developmental literature from which these behaviors were extrapolated, they are used appropriately, across contexts, by school age children. This pool of behaviors is intended to be used for assessment from school age through to the adult level.

**TABLE 2-1**
**Pool of Pragmatic Behaviors**

| Taxonomy | Modality | Description and Coding | References |
|---|---|---|---|
| *UTTERANCE ACT* | verbal/ paralinguistic/ | The trappings by which the act is accomplished | |
| 1. Intelligibility | | the extent to which the message is understood | |
| 2. Vocal intensity | | the loudness or softness of the message | |
| 3. Voice quality | | the resonance and or laryngeal characteristics of the vocal tract | |
| 4. Prosody | | the intonation and stress patterns of the message; variations of loudness, pitch and duration | |
| 5. Fluency | | the smoothness, consistency, and rate of the message | |

**TABLE 2-1 (continued)**

| Taxonomy | Modality | Description and Coding | References |
|---|---|---|---|
| 6. Physical proximity | nonverbal | the distance from which speaker and listener sit or stand from one another | for the nonverbal behaviors see these references: |
| 7. Physical contacts | | the number of times and placement of contacts between speaker and listener | R. Harper, A. Wiens, and J. Matarosso (Eds.), *Nonverbal communication: The state of the art.* New York: John Wiley and Sons, 1978. |
| 8. Body posture | | forward lean is when the speaker or listener moves away from a 90° angle toward other person; recline is when one party slouches down from waist to head and moves away from the partner; side to side is when a person moves to the right or left | B. Hoffer and R. St. Clair (Eds.). *Developmental kinesics: The emerging paradigm.* Baltimore: University Park Press, 1981. |
| 9. Foot/leg movements | | any movement of foot/leg | |
| 10. Hand/arm movements | | any movement with hand/arm (touching or moving an object or touching part of the body or clothing) | |

**TABLE 2-1 (continued)**

| Taxonomy | Modality | Description and Coding | References |
|---|---|---|---|
| UTTERANCE ACT (continued) | nonverbal (continued) | | |
| 11. Gestures | | any movements which support, complement or replace verbal behavior | |
| 12. Facial expression | | a positive expression is when the corners of the mouth are turned upward; negative is downward turn; neutral expression is when face is in a resting position | |
| 13. Eye gaze | | when one looks directly at the other's facial region; mutual gaze is when both members of the dyad look at each other | |
| PROPOSITIONAL ACT | verbal | linguistic dimensions of the meaning of the sentence | |
| 1. Lexical selection/use | | | |
| A. specificity/ accuracy | | lexical items of best fit considering the context | |

**TABLE 2-1 (continued)**

| Taxonomy | Modality | Description and Coding | References |
|---|---|---|---|
| PROPOSITIONAL ACT (continued) | verbal (continued) | | |
| 2. Specifying relationships between words | | | |
| A. Word order | | grammatical word order for conveying message | |
| B. Given and new information | | given information is that information already known to the listener — new information is information not already known to the listener. | B. Mac Whinney and E. Bates. Sequential devices for conveying givenness and newness: A cross-cultural development study. *Journal of Verbal Learning and Verbal behavior*, 1978. |
| a. Pronomin-alization | | pronouns permit the listener to identify the referent and is one of the devices used to mark givenness | |
| b. Ellipses | | given information may be deleted | |
| c. Emphatic stress | | new information may be marked by stressing various items | |

**TABLE 2-1 (continued)**

| *Taxonomy* | *Modality* | *Description and Coding* | *References* |
|---|---|---|---|
| PROPOSITIONAL ACT (continued) | verbal (continued) | | |
| d. Indefinite/ definite article | | if new information is signaled, the indefinite article is used; if old information, then the definite article is used | |
| e. Initial- ization | | given information is stated prior to new information | |
| 3. Stylistic variations A. the varying of communicative style | verbal, para- linguistic, non- verbal | adaptations used by the speaker under various dyadic conditions e.g. polite forms, different syntax, vocal quality changes | M. Shatz and R. Gelman. *The development of communication skills: Modification in the speech of young children as a function of the listener.* SRCD Monographs, 1973. |
| *ILLOCUTIONARY AND PERLOCUTIONARY ACTS* | verbal | illocutionary (intentions of the speaker) and perlocutionary (effects on the listener) | |
| 1. Speech act pair analysis | | the ability to take both speaker and listener role appropriate to the context | |

**TABLE 2-1 (continued)**

| Taxonomy | Modality | Description and Coding | References |
|---|---|---|---|
| ILLOCUTIONARY AND PERLOCUTIONARY ACTS (continued) | verbal (continued) | | |
| 1. Speech act pair analysis (continued) | | directive/compliance—personal need, imperatives, embedded imperatives, permissions, directives, questions directives, hints | |
| | | query/response—requests for confirmation, neutral requests for repetition, requests for specific constituent repetition | C. Garvey. Contingent queries. Unpublished master's thesis Johns Hopkins University, 1975. |
| | | | T. Gallagher. Revision behaviors in the speech of normal children developing language. *Journal of Speech and Hearing Research*, 1977. |

**TABLE 2-1 (continued)**

| Taxonomy | Modality | Description and Coding | References |
|---|---|---|---|
| ILLOCUTIONARY AND PERLOCUTIONARY ACTS (continued) | verbal (continued) | request/response—direct requests, indirect requests, inferred requests, request for clarification, acknowledgement of the request, perform the desired action | C. Mitchell-Kernan and K. Kernan. Pragmatics of directive choice among children. In S. Ervin-Tripp and C. Mitchell-Kernan (Eds.), *Child discourse.* New York: Academic Press, 1977. |
| | | comment/acknowledgement— descriptions of on-going activities of immediate subsequent activity, of state or condition of objects, persons, naming, acknowledgements which are positive, negative, expletive, indicative | |
| 2. Variety of Speech Acts | | the variety of speech acts or what one can do with their language such as: comment, assert, request, promise, etc. | J. Austin. *How to do things with words.* Cambridge: Harvard University Press, 1962. |

**TABLE 2-1 (continued)**

| Taxonomy | Modality | Description and Coding | References |
|---|---|---|---|
| ILLOCUTIONARY AND PERLOCUTIONARY ACTS (continued) | verbal (continued) | | |
| 2. Variety of Speech Acts (continued) | | | J. Searle. *Speech acts: An essay in the philosophy of language.* Cambridge: University Press, 1969. |
| A. Topic a. Selection | | the selection of a topic appropriate to the context | E. Keenan, and B. Schieffelin (Eds.), Topic as a discourse notion A study of topic in the conversations of children and adults. In C. Li (Ed.) *Subject and topic.* New York: Academic Press, 1976. |
| b. Introduction | | introduction of a new topic in the discourse | |
| c. Maintenance | | maintenance of topic across the discourse | |

**TABLE 2-1 (continued)**

| Taxonomy | Modality | Description and Coding | References |
|---|---|---|---|
| ILLOCUTIONARY AND PERLOCUTIONARY ACTS (continued) | verbal (continued) | | H. Sacks, E. Schegloff, and G. Jefferson. A simplest systematics for the organization of turn taking for conversation. In J. Schenkein (Ed.), *Studies in the organization of conversational ambiguity.* New York: Academic Press, 1978. |
| d. Change | | change of topic in the discourse | |
| B. Turntaking | | smooth interchanges between speaker and listener | |
| a. Initiation | | initiation of speech acts. | |
| b. Response | | the responding as a listener to speech acts | |
| c. Repair/revision | | the ability to repair a conversation when a break down occurs and the ability to ask for a repair when misunderstanding, ambiguity etc. has occurred. | |

**TABLE 2-1 (continued)**

| Taxonomy | Modality | Description and Coding | References |
|---|---|---|---|
| ILLOCUTIONARY AND PERLOCUTIONARY ACTS (continued) | verbal (continued) | | |
| d. Pause Time | | when pause time is excessive or too short between words or in response to a question or between sentences | |
| e. Interruption/ overlap | | interruptions between speaker and listener; overlap is when two people talk at the same time | |
| f. Feedback to speaker | | verbal behavior to give the speaker feedback such as "yea," "really"; nonverbal behavior such as head nods up and down, can be positive; side by side can express negative affect or disbelief | S. Dunkin and D. Fiske. *Face to face interaction* New Gersen: Earlbaum 1977. |
| g. Adjacency | | utterances which occur immediately after the partner's utterance | L. Bloom, L. Rocissano, and L. Hood. Adult-child discourse: |
| h. Contingency | | utterances which share the same topic with the preceding utterance and which add information to the prior communicative act | Developmental interaction between information processing and linguistic knowledge. *Cognitive Psychology,* 1976. |

**TABLE 2-1 (continued)**

| Taxonomy | Modality | Description and Coding | References |
|---|---|---|---|
| ILLOCUTIONARY AND-<br>PERLOCUTIONARY ACTS<br>(continued) | verbal<br>(continued) | | |
| i. Quantity/<br>conciseness | | the contribution should be as<br>informative as required, but not<br>too informative. | H. Grice. Logic and<br>conversation. In P.<br>Cole and J. Morgan (Eds.),<br>*Syntax and semantics*.<br>New York: Academic Press<br>1975. |

# The Measurements

Researchers and clinicians studying communicative development are no longer satisfied exclusively with the structural analysis of the sentence. Rather, with the current interest in pragmatics, the shift is away from studying the sentence to the analysis of how larger units function in discourse. As a result, many researchers are focusing on the dynamic aspects of conversational discourse — "the rights, obligations, and expectations underlying its maintenance " (Ochs and Schieffelin, 1979, p. 324).

The conceptual shift, emphasizing the sociolinguistic aspects of language use, has methodological consequences for researchers and clinicians studying language from this perspective. Previously, the field has been occupied with measures that document type and frequency of various topographies at the syntactic, semantic, and phonological levels. Taken alone, this type of analysis does not address the dynamic processes of communication and is less sensitive to the interactional aspects of the communicative situation. Researchers and clinicians operating from a pragmatic framework suggest that the utterance or sentence may not always be the most distinguishing unit of analysis in the interaction. Instead, the unit of analysis is variable depending on the communcative behavior being studied. The smallest unit of measurement, however, in conversational analysis is the dyad.

No single method of measurement is appropriate to all types of data and all clinical and research questions. The analysis and collection of data is an infinitely extendable notion. The method employed depends on the theoretical perspective from which one operates, the behaviors one chooses to identify, and the aspects of the interaction one thinks are important. The options available for selection of appropriate coding systems and measurement parameters are many and the final decision is an important one. "The specific structure of the system and the form in which the events are recorded place rigid limitations on the types of questions that can be answered and the kinds of analyses which can be conducted " (Patterson and Moore, 1979, p. 77). In any given situation, the experimental question and purpose of the assessment will dictate the unit of measurement and level of analysis.

Cairns (1979) warns investigators to be cautious in their use of methodology employing fine, molecular procedures. He suggests that, in doing so, the investigator may destroy the integrity of the behaviors under study. "The burden lies with the investigator to keep in focus the essential coherence of the system while, simultaneously, dissecting its parts " (Cairns, 1979, p. 4). The question remains: How specific or global should the measurement parameters for assessment or research purposes be? In general, the level of analysis should be fine enough to detail the information important to the assessment question. However, the analysis should not be so extensive that major trends or patterns are lost and bringing the data back together for interpretation is no longer possible.

Lamb (1979) suggests that behavioral units should be roughly equivalent to the unit of meaning, not necessarily the smallest unit of meaning. That is, researchers and clinicians should not make finer discriminations or categorize the behaviors more finely than the interactants do. To make a similar point, Patterson and Moore (1979) suggest that the investigator search for functional units of behavior to answer questions about the interaction under study. To do so, one may apply a series of progressively finer filters to isolate smaller units as necessary. Meanwhile, existing taxonomies are not imposed on a corpus if they do not characterize the important components of the data. In some instances, the analysis of the structural components of individual sentences may be sufficient to answer a particular assessment question. However, in many cases, it is necessary to examine larger sequences of the interaction (e.g. two- and three-turn exchanges) to gain meaningful information about a particular communicative process.

Analysis can be conducted at two different levels. A molar analysis consists of a global appraisal of the client's system while a molecular approach is a fine grain analysis of the client's behavior. If we operate on the premise that assessment is conducted for the purpose of designing intervention programs, then the level of assessment for the client should be no finer than would be functional in a therapeutic sense.

## Molar Analysis

It is sometimes advantageous to employ a molar analysis of pragmatic behaviors. Clinicians can use an observational protocol, such as the one included here, to make judgments about the appropriateness and inappropriateness of behaviors exhibited. The judgment clinicians make is whether or not the behavior is penalizing to the client. If perceived as penalizing, the clinician then marks the behavior as inappropriate. Observations of the clients in various settings can be made on line or can be videotaped and judgments made at a later time. These appraisals can be made by clinicians with a high degree of inter-observer reliability. In addition, the procedure does not require an extensive amount of time. Judgments can be made across the behaviors with a small but representative sample of data in a relatively short period of time. This seems to be the case since most of the behaviors are present during ongoing conversational interactions. We make these observations based on our experience using the protocol at the University of California Speech and Hearing Center.

We have come from a period whereby each utterance or linguistic act was quantified. As with any behavior, one may quantify but at some point in time the clinician will have to interpret the number in some way. As Gould (1981) has commented, we live in an era where numbers are king. Gould suggests that the quantification of behavior and science, in general, is a social act like any human activity and at its core is subjectivity. In other words, there is nothing less objective in a molar analysis compared to a molecular analysis. In the end, someone must also interpret a number and decide what it represents. Table 2-2 presents an observational protocol which has been developed for the assessment of pragmatic behaviors.

## TABLE 2-2
## Pragmatic Protocol

Name:_____     Date:_____

Communicative                    Communicative
Setting Observed:  _____  Partners' Relationship  _____

| Communicative Act | Appropriate | Inappropriate | No Opportunity to Observe |
|---|---|---|---|
| *UTTERANCE ACT* | | | |
| A. Verbal/ Paralinguistic | | | |
| 1. Intelligibility | | | |
| 2. Vocal intensity | | | |
| 3. Voice quality | | | |
| 4. Prosody | | | |
| 5. Fluency | | | |
| B. Nonverbal | | | |
| 1. Physical proximity | | | |
| 2. Physical contacts | | | |
| 3. Body posture | | | |
| 4. Foot/leg movements | | | |
| 5. Hand/arm movements | | | |
| 6. Gestures | | | |
| 7. Facial Expression | | | |
| 8. Eye gaze | | | |

## TABLE 2-2 (continued)

| Communicative Act | Appropriate | Inappropriate | No Opportunity to Observe |
|---|---|---|---|
| *PROPOSITIONAL ACT* | | | |
| A. Lexical selection/Use | | | |
| 1. Specificity/ accuracy | | | |
| B. Specifying relationships between words | | | |
| 1. Word order | | | |
| 2. Given and new information | | | |
| C. Stylistic variations | | | |
| 1. The varying of communicative style | | | |
| *ILLOCUTIONARY ACTS AND PER-LOCUTIONARY* | | | |
| A. Speech acts | | | |
| 1. Speech act pair analysis | | | |
| 2. Variety of speech acts | | | |
| B. Topic | | | |
| 1. Selection | | | |
| 2. Introduction | | | |
| 3. Maintenance | | | |
| 4. Change | | | |

**TABLE 2-2 (continued)**

| Communicative Act | Appropriate | Inappropriate | No Opportunity to Observe |
|---|---|---|---|
| C. Turntaking | | | |
| 1. Initiation | | | |
| 2. Response | | | |
| 3. Repair/revision | | | |
| 4. Pause time | | | |
| 5. Interruption/ overlap | | | |
| 6. Feedback to speakers | | | |
| 7. Adjacency | | | |
| 8. Contingency | | | |
| 9. Quantity/con- ciseness | | | |

C.A. Prutting
University of California
Santa Barbara
1982

This protocol is organized around four broad areas: the utterance act, the propositional act, the illocutionary and the perlocutionary act. These categories can serve as clinical indicators as to where the problem exists. It may be at any one of the levels or across levels. For instance, a problem at the propositional level (problems in the linguistic dimensions or the meaning of the sentence) may affect conversational interaction differently than a problem at the utterance act (trappings by which the act is accomplished.) Therefore, the breakdown serves to demonstrate at which particular level the problem surfaces.

Regardless of the type of communicative problem, a pragmatic deficit may exist in combination with linguistic and cognitive deficits or exist separate from them. As yet, we do not have a clear understanding of the incidence of pragmatic deficits either independent of or in addition to other deficits. There seems to be some question as to whether a pragmatic deficit alone qualifies as a legitimate problem under our current clinicial classification system. When we moved from the area of phonology to the clinical treatment of syntax and semantics, this very same issue was addressed. New advances always require a respect for time in order to fit them into our existing schemas.

## Molecular Analysis

While a more global or molar kind of analysis is useful in the clinical setting, many occasions arise where the researcher and clinician must perform a more in-depth analysis. In the following pages, six potential measurement parameters are defined with examples of application to the assessment of pragmatic behaviors. These parameters are designed to be used with written transcripts from audio and/or video-taped segments of communicative behavior. Employing measures of this type will enable the researcher or clinician to obtain a molecular or fine grained analysis of communicative interactions. In some instances, one parameter may be sufficient to characterize the important aspects of a given interaction. In other cases, it may be necessary to apply multiple measures to the data set, each reflecting variable degrees of analytic detail. Above all, the behavioral units and measurement parameters applied to a particular set of data should remain flexibile and interpreted in relationship to each other.

*Measurement Parameters for Pragmatic Behaviors\**

1. Frequency

2. Latency

3. Duration

4. Density

5. Amplitude

6. Sequence

**1. Frequency** - Frequency refers to the number of times a particular behavior occurs and is the parameter from which rate measures are often derived. Frequency measures are used to determine the presence or absence of a particular behavior, to calculate relative proportions of behaviors fitting into several taxonomic categories  and are often correlated with the strength of a behavior.

Taken from:
\*W. Hartup. Levels of analysis in the study of social interaction: An historical perspective. In M. Lamb, S. Suomi, and G. Stephenson. (Eds.), *Social Interaction Analysis: Methodological Issues*. Madison: University of Wisconsin Press, 1979.

*Examples of Application to Assessment of Pragmatic Behavior:*

*Contingency* — Contingent speech, defined by Bloom, Rocissano, and Hood (1976) is that speech which both shares the same topic with the preceding utterance and which adds information to the prior communicative act. A measure of contingency quantifiable in a percentage point provides information regarding the general notion of relatedness. Percent contingent responses provides a gross measure of the notion while specific adjacency pairs may be analyzed in a "fine grain" sense as a more precise way of looking at the same issue. Bloom et al. (1976) give the following examples of contingent speech:

Eric (Stage 2)  *I see two*

*I see two bus come here*

Kathryn (Stage 2)

*I'm gonna build a*
*high house.*

*I wanna build a high house too.*

In their research, Bloom et al. (1976) found that the frequency of contingent speech increased developmentally, particularly linguistically contingent speech. This type of utterance is one which expands the verb relation of the prior adult utterance with added or replaced constituents within a clause.

*Initiation* — Frequency data can be used to count the number of topic initiations on the part of either speaker in the interaction.

(Both are seated at a small table and chairs looking at a book. Another book and some small toys are resting on the table.)

| **Adult** | **Child** |
|---|---|
| (Pointing to a picture in the book.) "Look, the baby is tired so her mother put her to bed." | |
| | (Turning the pages of the book.) "Doggie. Where doggie?" |

"Yes, we saw a doggie on the
other page."

(Picks up another book from the
table and points to the cover.)
"Truck. Big truck" "Daddy's
truck"

"Yes, that looks like Daddy's
truck."

(Picking up toys from the
table.)
"Lookit blocks"
"More blocks"

In this example, the child introduces a topic with each utterance. Even though the child remains contingent to his own topic for two or three consecutive utterances he is unable to form a contingent utterance to a topic introduced by his communicative partner.


*Taxonomic Categorizaton* — Calculation of the frequency of communicated acts in a particular category (pragmatic, semantic, syntactic, or phonological) can be used to calculate the percentage or proportion of the total sample within each category. Frequency distributions are often used in the assessment of language behaviors and may lead to patterns reflective of interactive style and linguistic sophistication.


**2. Latency** — Latency refers to the span of time in which an individual does not engage in an appropriate or inappropriate behavior.

*Examples of Application to Assessment of Pragmatic Behavior:*

*Timing Relationships* — Adjacent and nonadjacent speech is differentiated by pause time (Bloom, Rocissano, & Hood, 1976). The intent in measuring adjacent and nonadjacent speech is to examine only a specific contingency relationship. That is, to what extent does a child's single communicative act occur in the time-space context of a prior adult act? Bloom et al. (1976) give the following example of adjacent and nonadjacent speech.

|                  Adult                  |                  Child                  |
|-----------------------------------------|-----------------------------------------|

Adult and child sit on the floor;
child picks up block.

(i) Here a block
(Non-adjacent)

"Let's build a bridge."

(ii) A big bridge
(Adjacent)

Child and adult build; child
picks up a block.

(iii) This block
(Non-adjacent)

The authors report that the first utterance is nonadjacent since it occurred without a previous adult utterance. The second utterance, by contrast, is adjacent to the adult utterance "Let's build a bridge." Finally the child's third utterance is nonadjacent as it occurred following a pause during which there was also a shift in focus on the part of the child.

*Pauses and Hesitations* — Ochs (1979) suggests that pauses and hesitations in utterances may reveal trouble sources for a child related to the complexity of the idea to be conveyed, the structure of the expression, or situational difficulties (e.g. accommodation to the listener's knowledge). She provides the following example:

|  | David |  | Toby |
|---|---|---|---|
| Nonverbal | Verbal | Nonverbal | Verbal |
| Moves rabbit to right | mm/ (High) OH!/ | Holds monkey still then moves it down right | |
| | We got to..... (Pause .4 sec) | to bed and looks at David. | |
| | We have to get (/staps/)* | | |
| | | | (Very high) should we?/ |
| | Yeah | | |
| | | | Should we |
| *"shops" (?) | | | Could we go |
| **"store" (?) | | | (/ sərəl /)?/** |

In this example David says "We got to....", pauses for .4 seconds and, then says "We have to get (/staps/)." Ochs (1979) suggests that the second utterance appears to be a reformation of the preceding expression and indicates that this child is able to modify his utterance to one of greater syntactic sophistication. Ochs (1979) also suggests that gaps within utterance may be evidence that the child is aware of missing constituents. If this is the case, then a gap in an utterance where a constituent would normally be placed may indicate that a child's linguistic knowledge is greater than can be realized in the surface structure of his utterance.

*Contingency* — Frequency data may indicate that a child can be contingent 100% of the time required in a conversation, but the more sensitive assessment may be how long it takes the child to be contingent by measuring latency.

(Child and adult are seated on the floor with a box of blocks and another box of cars and trucks.)

| **Adult** | **Child** |
|---|---|
| (Putting blocks away) "Let's put the blocks away and play with the cars now." | (Helping the clinician put the toys away.) |
| "We'll have to put the blocks back in the box before we put them away." | |

| **Adult** | **Child** |
|---|---|
| | "Let's play with the cars in the garage." |
| | (Latency 6.8 seconds) |
| "Alright. We better make sure the cars have enough gas first." | |
| | (Taking cars out of the toy box.) |
| (Clinician assembles a pretend garage from the box while putting toy people in the cars. Begins pushing them around on top of the table.) | |
| | "That man put some gas in my car." |
| | (Latency 30.5 seconds) |

In this example, the issue is not whether the child can be contingent to a prior adult communicative act. The child does respond verbally to both suggestions from the clinician — to play with the cars instead of the blocks and to put gas in the cars. However, response latency is as much as 30 seconds in one case. In some instances, another act may intervene from the adult before the child responds contingently.

**3. Duration** — Duration refers to the length of time it takes for a behavior to "run off," or proportion of observed time in which a subject engages in a designated class of behavior. A behavior may occur with the same frequency on two different measurements, while the parameter which provides the more meaningful interpretation and a more sensitive index of severity may be the duration associated with the behavior.

*Examples of Application to Assessment of Pragmatic Behavior:*

*Gaze* — Gaze has a regulatory function in communicative interaction serving to coordinate conversation, allocate turn exchanges, and gain attention (Craig, 1979). However, for excessively long duration gaze may be an inappropriate communication behavior.

This example from Craig is a segment of communicative behavior in a triadic interaction. Utterances are in quotation marks and nonverbal behaviors, gaze loci, and gaze shifts are in parentheses.

| A: | B: | C: |
|---|---|---|
| (holds full grocery bag; looks at B) | (extends hand holding can toward C; looks at C) | (holds purse; looks at can/ B's act) |

| A: | B: | C: |
|---|---|---|
| (continues holding bag; looks at bag C) | (continues holding can, on "I" lowers arm; looks at can/ self) | "No I wanta do that" (holds purse on "I" turns toward shopping cart; looks at shopping cart) |

If gaze behavior is too long (e.g. duration) the conversational relevance of gaze shifts may be weakened. If gaze shifts do not occur within a reasonable temporal span of conversation, gaze may not be a successful device for turn allocation.

*Turntaking* — In verbal turntaking, duration measures may provide information regarding the appropriateness of overlap time and gaps between speakers (Ervin-Tripp, 1979). The following example from Ervin-Tripp shows inappropriate interruptions in lines 3 and 5 with one joint start at a sentence boundary in line 4. Ervin-Tripp suggests that, even with such overlaps, these children are reciprocal and monitor the conversational mutually. Still, she suggests that there is a greater chance of overlap in a triadic interaction.

| 1. E: 2:8 Where's Daddy? | | He's not here? | | Home? |
|---|---|---|---|---|
| J : 3:1 | At home | | No. At home | |
| 2. E: | Home? | Oh. (To third person) | | Daddy's |
| J : Uh. at home. | | Yeah. | | |
| 3. E: home. My daddy's not here | (Shaking head) | And these is nuts not here. (Steps to | |
| J : | My daddy's | third person) | |
| 4. E: | My daddy's | not here. | |
| J : My daddy's not here | He's at home. | | |
| 5. E: | At - not till night | | The next days I go to Maria's |
| J : My daddy's | not at - My daddy's | at home | (To third person) |

Overlap which is excessive or of unreasonable length may interfere with a successful conversation exchange. Appropriate timing of overlap which allows a speaker to enter and leave a conversation smoothly tends to increase with age (Ervin-Tripp, 1979).

**4. Density** - Density is the measurement of the number of times a particular behavior occurs per unit of time.

*Examples of Application to Assessment of Pragmatic Behavior:*

*Topic* — For a child who has demonstrated the ability to introduce new topics into a conversation, the sensitive measure may be number of topic introductions per a specified unit of time. Introduction of new topic fifteen times within a 10 minute span of time may be reflective of an inappropriate conversational style.

*Linguistic Structures* — Frequency of the WH-question per unit of time could be the significant variable for a child who uses that form twenty-five times within a five minute sample of conversation. In this case, the presence or absence of the interrogative form structurally is not so important as how it is used.

**5. Amplitude/Intensity** - Measures of response magnitude are a way of measuring the intensity of behavior. Frequently this measurement is best accomplished on a scale or semantic differential type of measurement. Objective techniques for making decisions about the intensity of a behavior are not always available, but meaningful measurements which are helpful clinically can be obtained using unbiased observers and reliability measurements.

*Examples of Application to Assessment of Pragmatic Behaviors:*

*Verbal/Vocal Measurements* — Assessment of the child with an adequate semantic, syntactic, and phonological system, but whose verbal behavior is loud and aggressive with peers may be important. Reactions of strangers, classmates, and/or teachers on dimensional scales can be used to make judgments about the appropriateness of a child's communicative interactions. Improvement on the dimension of intensity may be the most meaningful way of making judgments about the social acceptability of the child as judged by his/her communication.

**6. Sequence** - Measurement of sequences of behavior within the ongoing behavior stream may be a meaningful assessment tool. In one form, the measure consists of counting instances in which particular behavior sequences occur within a given time. Or, the analysis of events following each other in ordinal sequences without a particular unit of time in mind may also be a useful measure. Numerous properties of the communication situation cannot be studied without attention to sequential order. Natural conditions associated with eliciting and terminating responses can be studied. In this case the unit of analysis is extended beyond the utterance to adjacency pairs or longer communicative sequences.

*Examples of Application to Assessment of Pragmatic Behavior:*

*Propositions Across Speech Acts and Speakers* — To evaluate the child's strategies for linguistically encoding an idea or proposition, sequences of communicative behavior may be the appropriate unit of analysis. The assessment question is: Is the idea encoded in the space of a single utterance through syntactic means or is the proposition conveyed through a sequence of two or more utterances? In the latter the discourse rather than the sentence is the vehicle for expressing propositions. The unit of analysis becomes the proposition rather than the utterance. The ability to express a proposition syntactically within an utterance is generally considered more advanced behavior than to express the proposition sequentially (Ochs, Schieffelin and Platt, 1979). Ochs et al. (1979) use this example from Bloom (1973) to illustrate the sequential expression of an idea.

Allison III: 20 months, 3 weeks
(Mother had suggested taking off
Allison's coat)

(Allison pointing to her neck)          up/up/

M: What?

                                         neck/up/

M: Neck? What do you want?
   What?

                                         neck/

M: What's on your neck?
   (Allison pointing to zipper
   and lifting her chin up)

                                         zip/zip/zip/

In summary, while observational methods have long been used to study communicative behavior, the unit of analysis has largely been the utterance and the measure is usually frequency. Now that the field has shifted its theoretical and research focus to include the study of language in context, it has become necessary to seek comparable advances in the means whereby data are gathered and reduced. Such methodology should employ a broader range of assessment parameters than those traditionally used as well as provide a means to analyze data at multiple levels. Meanwhile, existing taxonomies are not necessarily imposed on the data if they do not characterize the interesting components accurately. Such an approach suggests that coding systems should remain flexible, allowing for selection of multiple measures with varying degrees of analytic detail depending on the assessment question of interest. Thus, the level of analysis is adapted to the data rather than data adapted to available methods.

## Pragmatics and Language Disordered Children

Bates' 1976 work is exemplary of those researchers attempting to delineate a theory of language in context. Such a theory maintains that "language is acquired and used in a social context" (Bates, 1976, p. 412) and, therefore, should be studied as such. The majority of research in the area of pragmatics has been conducted with young children developing language normally. Studies exist that focus on the interactive aspects of communication in disordered populations. The majority of studies investigating pragmatic abilities of language disordered children suggest that these children follow the same developmental sequence and exhibit the same range of pragmatic strategies as do normal children in a comparable linguistic stage. (Bricker and Carlson, 1980; Fey, Leonard, and Wilcox, 1981; Gaines, 1981; Gallagher and Darnton, 1978; Shatz, Shulman, and Bernstein, 1980; Skarakis and Greenfield, in press; Snyder, 1975; Van Kleeck and Frankel, 1981). Evidence suggests the same is true for children with language disorders as a result of impaired hearing. (Curtiss, Prutting, and Lowell, 1979). However, serveral researchers (Gallagher and Darnton, 1978; Skarakis and Greenfield, 1982) have also reported that differences in the proportional use of those strategies exist as well, suggesting a qualitatively distinct pattern of communicative behavior. Further, Gaines (1981) found that on various dimensions of social and non-social tool use, Down's Syndrome infants use some strategies which reflect delayed development, some strategies which are the same as normal children, and some strategies which are unlike normal children and reflect a qualitatively different course of development. Therefore, with regard to the use of various pragmatic abilities and certain cognitive precursors to language development, it may be erroneous to only assume that language disordered children are delayed compared to normals; although delay may be one of the profiles.

This relatively small body of research has described pragmatic as well as several early cognitive skills in language disordered children. Still, the field is in need of incidence studies that will carefully document the range of pragmatic deficits in a larger sample of children with language disorders. Prutting, Kirchner, Hassan, and Buen (forthcoming) have implemented a study to address this issue using the pragmatic protocol. However, the research to date along with clinical observations suggest possible subgroups of children with pragmatic disorders. One might hypothesize that these groups could be separated on the basis of an inability to use and organize the multiple dimensions of context — social, cognitive, linguistic.

The first group of children might be those who appear to lack sensitivity to the various dimensions of social context. The child may not be sensitive to the rules of conversation and dimensions of social interaction. As such, he/she may not acknowledge the partnership of interaction, may not show conversational reciprocity or contingency, and may not be sensitive to those aspects of intervention which delineate socially appropriate communicative behavior (e.g. variations in speech style depending on the listener).

In the second group of children, cognitive deficits delimit or place a boundary condition on the potential level of communicative competence that an individual can achieve. It has been hypothesized that the language disordered child who lacks early cognitive prerequisites to communication typically exhibits a delay in onset, rate, or sequence of language acquisition (Bates et al., 1979). Still another profile exists representing the child who possesses basic communicative skills but whose cognitive limitations result in restricted lexical repertoire and poor comprehension of language. These restrictions may limit his/her ability to establish and maintain topic, make appropriate lexical choices, identify and establish referents, etc.

The third, and final group of children, might exhibit certain pragmatic deficits as a result of the interaction between constraints imposed by linguistic context (e.g. rules of conversation) with a restricted range of options available. In other words, given that conversation is organized and maintained sequentially, each communicative act is dependent on the previous or prior utterance. (e.g. reciprocal contingency relationships or sequential organization of turns.) In this way, the rules of conversation and social interaction serve to constrain the type and form of successive utterances. Even though a child may acknowledge the partnership of a communicative interaction and is relatively sensitive to his/her obligations as a participant, what continues to interfere with communication are those higher level linguistic operations which overlap with usage. The children Gallagher and Darnton (1978) studied are representative of this group as well as those of Skarakis and Greenfield (in press).

One result of the paradigm shift in this field of Speech Language Pathology has been marked growth in the understanding of the rules which govern the use of language in context. It is apparent, from the literature focusing on the pragmatic aspects of communication that competencies exist at the level of discourse as well as at the level of the utterance; to date, clinical observations and research have permitted the authors to suggest how pragmatic deficits might manifest themselves in subgroups of language disordered children. However, the process of subgrouping is always difficult to some extent. Children may be assigned to a subgroup based on the primary characteristics of their communicative profile. But, since the various dimensions of context are interdependent, social, cognitive, and linguistic deficits may exist separately or in combination with one another within a single child or across children. Still, it is instructive to speculate until future research and clinical validation of the proposed subgroups prove their usefulness.

To determine exactly how much certain pragmatic deficits restrict the range of communicative behavior in an individual, the most important assessment may be that which focuses on the dynamics of conversational discourse. A child may exhibit a sophisticated and relatively intact linguistic system but pragmatic deficits may impair the overall level of communicative comptence. A linguistic profile alone does not necessarily predict the child's effectiveness as a social interactant. Thus, identification of pragmatic deficits assists the speech-language clinician in selecting remediation goals which will increase the overall effectiveness of the child's communication. Clearly, then, there is good reason for identifying pragmatic deficits in the language disordered child. It is also apparent that the speech-language clinician should assess the pragmatic strengths of the same child as well. Developmentally, there is a continuum from reliance on discourse to maintain conversation to a greater reliance on formal linguistic devices to achieve the same goal. As forms increase in structural sophistication, the child begins to rely less on discourse support systems and moves toward greater reliance on syntactic devices to do the same work (Ochs, Schieffelin, and Platt, 1979). Still, few of the notions seem to require syntactic sophistication for their execution. As such, the language disordered child may be able to improve the quality of his/her communication by relying on pragmatic strengths to compensate for linguistic deficits.

For example, repetition (Keenan, 1977) is a functional means of participating in a conversation which can serve a number of communicative needs given limited syntactic ability. Directives (Ervin-Tripp, 1977) are first accomplished gesturally and the ability to share referent in the form of a topic is evidenced even at the single word level (Greenfield, 1979). Thus, simply because the child does not possess linguistic/structural sophistication does not mean that the child does not acknowledge the partnership and meet the obligations of the conversaton. Even when the disordered communicator cannot give the exact linguistic response, he/she may know that an answer was required and can be cooperative. In fact, given a restricted range of linguistic options, the disordered communicator may be forced to rely on a pragmatic strength to engage in cooperative conversation as a means of sustaining social interaction. In other words, some language disordered clients may exhibit intact pragmatic systems using relatively unsophisticated linguistic means. If this is the case, pragmatic assets may permit the language disordered individual to attain some higher level of communicative competence in the context of otherwise limited ability. What the disordered communicator strives for is a level of functional adaptation within the limits of the disorder. Hence, communicative strengths allow these individuals to interact with greater effectiveness than their purely linguistic performance would suggest.

With this paradigm shift a different clinical perspective has emerged. There are now pragmatic behaviors to assess and remediate, new procedures for assessing and remediating the behaviors as well as a more complete understanding of the disordered language system. In the field of Speech/Language Pathology there has been a shift to place language within the context of socialization (Prutting, 1982). We have treated the pragmatics of language as a legitimate and justified area within the communicative system. Pragmatics should not be dealt with as peripheral, global, or nebulous. Indeed, it is a pervasive aspect of language which affects the entire communicative system. Pragmatics need no longer be considered the weak sister to syntax and semantics.

What appears to be important in the development and understanding of phenomena, is the careful integration of theory with practice. Theoretical explication makes it possible to reconstruct the problems at hand. Clinicians who make use of theoretical principles in their applied work are equipped to participate in the growth of professional knowledge (Volpe, 1981). The focus of our paper has been to merge theory with practice.

# References

Austin, J. *How to do things with words.* Cambridge: Harvard University Press, 1962.

Bates, E. *Language in context.* New York: Academic Press, 1976.

Bates, E., L. Benigni, I. Bretherton, L. Camaioni, & V. Volterra. *The emergence of symbols.* New York: Academic Press, 1979.

Bates, E., & MacWhinney, B. Functionalist approaches to grammar. In L. Gleitman and E.Wanner (Eds.), *Language acquisition: The state of the art.* New York: Cambridge University Press (in press).

Bloom, L. *One word at a time.* The Hague: Mouton, 1973.

Bloom, L. Rocissano, & L. Hood. Adult-child discourse: developmental interaction between information processing and linguistic knowledge. *Cognitive Psychology,* 1976, *8,* 521-522.

Bricker, D., & Carlson, L. The relationship of object and prelinguistic social-communicative schemes to the acquisition of early linguistic skills in developmentally delayed infants. Paper presented at the Conference on Handicapped and At-Risk Infants: Research and Application, Asilomar, CA, April 29-May 2, 1980.

Cairns, R. (Ed.). *The analysis of social interaction: Methods, issues, and illustrations.* New York: John Wiley and Sons, 1979.

Chomsky, N. *Syntactic structures.* The Hague: Mouton, 1957.

Craig, H. A comparison of three-party and two-party conversations of normal children: an examination of increased social complexitiy. Unpublished doctoral dissertation, University of Michigan, Ann Arbor, 1979.

Curtiss, S., Prutting, C., and Lowell, E. Pragmatic and semantic development in young children with impaired hearing, *Journal of Speech and Hearing Research,* 1979, *22,* No. 3, 534-552.

Damico, J., & Braziel, K. Systematic observation of communicative interaction: A naturalistic language assessment technique. Paper presented at American Speech-Language-Hearing Association, Los Angeles, CA, 1981.

Dore, J. Holophrase, speech acts, and language universals. *Journal of Child Language,* 1975, *2,* 21-40.

Dunkin, S., & Fiske, D. *Face-to-face interaction.* New Gersen: Earlbaum, 1977.

Ervin-Tripp, S. Wait For me roller-skate. In S. Ervin-Tripp and C. Mitchell-Kernan (Eds.), *Child discourse.* New York: Academic Press, 1977, 165-188.

Ervin-Tripp, S. Children's verbal turntaking. In E. Ochs (Ed.), *Developmental pragmatics.* New York: Academic Press, 1979, 391-414.

Fey, M., Leonard, L., & Wilcox, K. Speech-style modifications of language-impaired children. *Journal of Speech and Hearing Disorders, 46,* 1981, 91-97.

Gaines, B. Nonsocial and social tool use ability of Down's Syndrome and normal infants at the prelinguistic stage of development. Unpublished master's thesis, University of California, Santa Barbara, 1981.

Gallagher, T., & Darnton, B. Conversational aspects of the speech of language disordered children: Revision behaviors. *Journal of Speech and Hearing Research,* 1978, *21,* 118-135.

Garvey, C. Contingent queries. Unpublished master's thesis, Johns Hopkins University, 1975.

Gould, S. *The mismeasure of man.* New York: W.W. Norton and Co., 1981.

Greenfield, P. Informativeness, presupposition, and semantic choice in single word utterances. In E. Ochs and B. Schieffelin (Eds.), *Developmental pragmatics.* New York: Academic Press, 159-166, 1979.

Grice, H.P. Logic and conversation. In P. Cole and J. Morgan (Eds.), *Studies in syntax and semantics, speech acts.* (Vol. 3). New York: Academic Press, 1975.

Halliday, M. *Learning how to mean.* London: Edward Arnold, 1975.

Harper, R. Wiens, A. & Matarazzo, J. *Nonverbal Communicaton: The state of the art.* New York: John Wiley and Sons, 1978.

Hartup, W. Levels of analysis in the study of social interaction: An historical perspective. In S. Lamb, S. Suomi, and G. Stephensen (Eds.), *Social interaction analysis - methodological issues.* Madison: University of Wisconsin Press, 1979, 11-31.

Hoffer, B., & St. Clair, R. (Eds.). *Developmental kinesics: The emerging paradigm.* Baltimore: University Park Press, 1981.

Keenan, E., & Schieffelin, B. Topic as a discourse notion. In C. Li (Ed.), *Subject and topic.* New York: Academic Press, 1976, 337-384.

Keenan, E. Making it last: Repetition in children's discourse. In S. Ervin-Tripp and C. Mitchell-Kernan (Eds.), *Child discourse.* New York: Academic Press, 1977.

Kuhn, T.S. *The structure of scientific revolution.* Chicago: University of Chicago Press, 1962.

Lamb, S. Issues in the study of social interaction: an introduction. In S. Lamb, S. Suomi, and G. Stephenson (Eds.), *Social interaction analysis - methodological issues.* Madison: University of Wisconsin Press, 1979, 1-10.

MacWhinney, B., & Bates, E. Sequential devices for conveying giveness and newness, a cross-cultural developmental study. *Journal of Verbal Learning and Verbal Behavior,* 1978, *17.*

Mitchell-Kernan, C., & Kernan, K. Pragmatics of directive choice among children. In S. Ervin-Tripp and C. Mitchell Kernan (Eds.), *Child discourse.* New York: Academic Press, 1977.

Ochs, E., & Schieffelin, B. (Eds.).*Developmental pragmatics.* New York: Academic Press, 1979, 324.

Ochs, E., Schieffelin, B., & Platt, M. Propositions across utterances and speakers. In E. Ochs (Ed.), *Developmental pragmatics.* New York: Academic Press, 1979, 251-268.

Ochs, E. Transcription as theory. In E. Ochs (Ed.), *Developmental pragmatics.* New York: Academic Press, 1979, 43-72.

Patterson, G., & Moore, D. Interactive patterns as units of behavior. In S. Lamb, S. Suomi, and G. Stephenson (Eds.), *Social interaction analysis - methodological issues.* Madison: University of Wisconsin Press, 1979, 77-96.

Planck, M. *Scientific autobiography and other papers,* translated by F. Gaylor, New York, 1949.

Prutting, C. Process/pra/ , ses/n: The action of moving forward progressively from one point to another on the way to completion. *Journal of Speech and Hearing Disorders,* 1979, *44,* 3-30.

Prutting, C. Pragmatics as social competence. *Journal of Speech and Hearing Disorders,* 1982, *47,* 123-133.

Prutting, C. Observational protocol for pragmatic behaviors. Developed for the University of California Speech and Hearing Clinic, Clinic Manual, 1982.

Prutting, C., Kirchner, D., Hassan, P., & Buen, P. The clinical appraisal of pragmatic behaviors, (forthcoming).

Rees, N. & Wollner, S.G. A taxonomy of pragmatic abilities: The use of language in conversation. Paper presented at convention of the American-Speech-Language-Hearing Association, Los Angeles, 1981.

Sacks, H., Schegloff, E., & Jefferson, G. A simplest systematics for the organization of turn taking for conversation. In J. Schenkein (Ed.), *Studies in the organization of conversational interaction.* New York: Academic Press, 1978.

Searle, J. *Speech Acts: An essay in the philosophy of language.* Cambridge: University Press, 1969.

Shatz, M., & Gelman, M. The development of communication skills: Modifications in the speech of young children as a function of the listener. *SRCD Monographs,* 1973.

Shatz, M., Shulman, M., & Bernstein, D. The responses of language disordered children to indirect directives in varying contexts. *Journal of Applied Psycholinguistics,* 1980, *1,* 295-306.

Skarakis, E., & Greenfield, P. The role of new and old information in the verbal expression of language disabled children, *Journal of Speech and Hearing Research* (In press).

Snyder, L. Pragmatics in language disabled children: Their prelinguistic and early verbal performatives and suppositions. Unpublished Ph.D. dissertation, University of Colorado, 1975.

Steiner, G. *The portage to San Cristóbal of A.H.* New York: Simon and Schuster, 1981.

Van Kleeck, A. and Frankel, T. Discourse devices used by language disordered children: A preliminary investigation. *Journal of Speech and Hearing Disorders,* 1981, *46,* 250-257.

Volpe, R. Knowledge from theory and practice. *Oxford Review of Education,* 1981, *7,* 41-51.

# 3

# PRAGMATIC SKILLS OF CHILDREN WITH SPECIFIC LANGUAGE IMPAIRMENT

*Marc E. Fey*
University of Western Ontario

*Laurence B. Leonard*
Purdue University

## Introduction

Specific language impairment is a condition characterized by a pronounced deficit in the comprehension and/or expression of language in the relative absence of impairments in other areas of development (Johnston, 1982; Leonard, 1979; Snyder, in press; Stark and Tallal, 1981; Weiner, 1980). Traditionally, children with specific language impairment have been identified on the basis of deficits in lexical and syntactic development, and studies attempting to provide a description of these deficits have focused on such factors as the modality which is most affected in these children (e.g. comprehension or production, Ingram, 1972; Stark and Tallal, 1981; Wolfus, Moskovitch, and Kinsbourne, 1980) and the structural level at which difficulties are most apparent (e.g. sentential, clausal, phrasal, or morphological; Crystal, Fletcher, and Garman, 1976).

Although the lexical and syntactic abilities of specifically language impaired (SLI) children are still a major concern, investigators recently have broadened their perspective on language impairment to include not only considerations of linguistic form, but also of the ways in which SLI children put language to use, i.e. their pragmatic abilities. The study of pragmatic skills among SLI children is only in its infancy. This is illustrated clearly by the large number of recent investigations cited in this chapter which have not yet appeared in the professional literature. Because so many studies have come forth over such a short period of time, and because much work in the area must be viewed as preliminary in nature, there is a need to examine this body of research critically.

Unfortunately, the results of the investigations performed to date lead to a somewhat confusing picture. In this paper, we will carefully examine and evaluate these investigations in five related areas of pragmatics: conversational participation, discourse regulation, speech acts, code-switching, and referential skills. Our evaluation will place special emphasis on differences among studies in the subjects tested, the task performed, the individuals with whom the subjects interacted during the task, and the procedures used to analyze the data. This evaluation will enable us to come to some general conclusions about the performance of SLI children in social contexts.

# Pragmatic Skills In SLI Children

## Conversational Participation

Conversational participation is a rather broad category that includes a number of social and linguistic skills. Studies that are included in this area generally have examined the ability of SLI children to appreciate the reciprocal nature of conversation, i.e. to play active roles both as speaker-initiator and as listener-respondent.

Wulbert, Inglis, Kriegsmann, and Mills (1975) examined the home environments of SLI children aged 2;6 - 6;0, using the Caldwell Inventory of Home Stimulation (Caldwell, Heider, and Kaplan). This instrument is designed to evaluate the adequacy of several aspects of the home environment, including the mother's involvement with the child. Results revealed that the home environments provided by the mothers of SLI children were significantly less conducive to mutual involvement with their children than were the environments provided by mothers of same-age normal language (NL) children or Down's Syndrome children. It was also noted, however, that the SLI children, most of whom had receptive and expressive delays of at least one year, were generally unresponsive to their mothers and produced behaviors that tended to discourage their mothers' interactive efforts. These children seemed unwilling to assume either the role of initiator or the role of respondent in interactions with their mothers. This type of behavior was not observed among the NL or Down's Syndrome children.

This report suggests that SLI children may have pervasive social impairments affecting performance in all areas of social interaction. It is important to recognize that some SLI children may exhibit this pattern. At this time, however, we must view this report with caution. The Caldwell Inventory is not designed to provide a fine-grained analysis of conversation. Therefore, the report of interactive failures due to a general lack of responsiveness in the SLI children is not well quantified and is largely impressionistic.

Much more evidence can be marshalled to support the view that relative to same-age NL children, SLI children are not generally socially impaired but may be markedly deficient as the initiators of social-conversational interaction. For example, Stein (1976) observed SLI subjects aged 3;11 - 5;11 in storytelling and blockbuilding tasks with parents. Most of the children had 10 - 25 month delays on the Peabody Picture Vocabulary Test (PPVT) (Dunn, 1965). The same data were examined by Watson (1977). These investigators noted that relative to same-age NL subjects, the SLI subjects appeared to be overly reliant on the use of back channel communication devices. These include all verbal and non-verbal efforts by a listener to indicate to a speaker the degree to which messages are being understood. Sheppard (1980) also reported excessive use of back channel responses in SLI children between the ages of 4;2 and 7;7. These children had marked expressive delays, judging from their MLUs of 2.09 to 2.30. Interestingly, high rates of back channel responses were observed in single-role monologue "conversations" with a pretend partner as well as in dialogue with the experimenter.

The frequent use of back channel devices by the SLI children in these studies implies that they were willing to participate in conversations. Given the severity of their language impairments, it seems possible that these SLI children found the use of back channel communication the most efficient means of maintaining social contact in conversations.

Inordinate use of back channel communication may enable SLI children to participate in conversations while avoiding the use of topic initiations and elaborations. This issue was explored by Stein (1976), whose study included an examination of several "main channel" behaviors. She observed that her SLI subjects used fewer attention-orienting responses, fewer speech acts that pointed out parental errors, and fewer expansions and semantic extensions of adult utterances than did the group of NL controls. Thus, while SLI children may be socially responsive, they seem to do little compared to their NL counterparts to initiate topics or elaborate upon those already established.

This view is supported strongly by the findings of Siegel, Cunningham, and van der Spuy (1979). These investigators studied SLI children with a mean age of 3;9 and mean delays of 10 and 11 months in comprehension and expression, respectively. Though they state that their findings indicated a lower level of responsiveness and a lack of assertiveness in the SLI children, only the latter characterization is well supported. In interactions with their mothers, the SLI children were significantly less likely to initiate interactions than were the same-age NL controls. This tendency was especially marked following lapses of social contact. The SLI children seemed, in such cases, to depend upon their mothers to initiate interaction. This finding has been replicated in subsequent unpublished experiments by these same investigators (Cunningham, personal communication, 1981). In each case, the lack of assertiveness tended to encourage the partners of the SLI children to assume dominant roles in the conversation. This more thoroughly commits the SLI children to roles as junior partners.

That some SLI children are less assertive than same-age NL children seems to be an incontrovertible fact. The pattern has shown up in relatively structured tasks with parents (Stein, 1976; Watson, 1977) and in free play dyadic interactions with mothers (Siegel et al., 1979), with an investigator (Sheppard, 1980), and with peers (Cunningham, Siegel, and van der Spuy, 1978, cited in Siegel et al., 1979). However, two studies have indicated that the well-documented failure of SLI children to assume the role of conversation-initiator may be limited to certain social contexts. For example, Fey, Leonard, and Wilcox's (1981) subjects aged 4;3 - 6;5 produced fewer back channel responses with younger NL partners who had similar linguistic skills than with same-age NL mates. Jacobs (1981) reported that school-aged SLI children talked more frequently and produced more behaviors characterized as dominant when they interacted with other SLI children than when they addressed NL mates.

Although subjects have not always been described in the detail necessary to make comparisons with confidence, the subjects in the studies of Fey et al. (1981) and Jacobs (1981) do not appear to have been as significantly impaired expressively or receptively as the subjects of the studies reported above. This difference, if it is real and not just apparent, might have had a significant impact on the outcomes of these investigations. Studies which carefully describe the SLI subjects and observe them in a number of social contexts are needed to determine whether a lack of conversational assertiveness is a general characteristic of some SLI children or whether it characterizes their behavior only with certain conversational partners.

There is some evidence that if the investigations which suggest that SLI children are conversationally nonassertive had included a control group of younger NL children with language skills equivalent to those of the SLI children, no impairments may have been noted. For example, Prelock, Messick, Schwartz, and Terrell (1981) studied a group of pre-syntactic SLI children with a mean age of 2;10 in interactions with their mothers. They found no differences in the number of conversational turns taken, the number of topics initiated or responded to, or in the overall number of communicative acts performed by the SLI children relative to the performance of a group of language-matched NL controls. Similarly, Van Kleeck and Frankel (1981) examined the patterns of contingent responses produced by SLI children aged 2;0 - 4;0 with 9- to 21-month delays in expressive and receptive skills. They observed patterns which parallel those for NL children at similar stages of linguistic development as determined by MLU.

It would be reasonable to assume that, had Prelock et al. (1981) and Van Kleeck and Frankel (1981) also used age-matched NL children as controls, such children would have exhibited more sophisticated conversational behavior than did the SLI children. However, findings reported by Fey (1981) indicate that this is not always the case. Fey compared SLI children aged 4;7 - 6;2, language-matched NL children, and age-matched NL children in their interactions with unfamiliar adults, peers, and babies. Not only were the SLI children superior to the language-matched NL children on a number of conversational measures, but no differences between the SLI and the same-age NL children were noted in the use of acknowledgments (a back channel device) or in any measure of conversational assertiveness, such as the rate of utterance production, the ratio of speaker-to-listener utterances, or the use of imperatives or questions in any listener context.

There seem to be few differences in the ages of the subjects, the tasks, or the measures used for analysis to explain why Fey's (1981) results differ so significantly from those of other studies. We suggest two possible explanations that deserve experimental attention. First, although the average expressive delay of the subjects in Fey's (1981) study was 2½ years, the mean comprehension delay of these children was only 5 months. Average delays in comprehension where reported in other studies ranged from 10 months (Siegel et al., 1979) to roughly 15 months (Stein, 1976). It seems possible that children with marked comprehension deficits also exhibit commensurate deficits in their ability to take part in conversations. Such children probably have difficulty understanding the messages of their partners. Yet a semantic/syntactic representation of antecedent messages serves as the very basis for the formulation of semantically and syntactically contingent responses. Perhaps these children recognize this difficulty and attempt to compensate by using an abundance of corroborating and acknowledging reponses (e.g. "yeah," "okay," "uh-huh"), thus giving the impression that they understand the speaker.

There is some converging evidence on comprehension delays that makes this hypothesis seem even more plausible. Wolfus, Moskovitch, and Kinsbourne (1980) found that SLI children with comprehension deficits also exhibited significant semantic impairments. This pattern was not observed among children with expressive delays only. It seems that children with significant deficits in comprehension are more generally impaired than are children with less notable comprehension difficulties. A general impairment in comprehension of language form and content may result in the child's assumption of a relatively passive role in conversations. Whether or not this issue is studied directly, we feel that the possibility that deficits in conversational participation covary with impairments in comprehension of language structure and content makes explicit description of SLI children's comprehension abilities essential in future investigations of SLI children.

A second possible explanation for the differences between the findings of Fey (1981) and those of other investigations is that the divergent pattern of results may reflect discrete clinical patterns. That is, some SLI children may be characterized justifiably as inactive or nonassertive conversational partners, while others displaying similar profiles of syntactic and semantic skills may be essentially unimpaired in conversational assertiveness. There are two important implications of this hypothesis if it can be shown to be true. First, it would represent evidence that despite an obvious interdependence between structural and conversational abilities, social, cognitive, personality, and environmental factors may enable some SLI children to play a more assertive role in conversation than others. Second, if this hypothesis is shown to be valid, it will be quite clear that traditional research designs which group children according to their structural linguistic skills may yield results which are confounded by this factor. Both of these implications underscore the need for empirical tests of this hypothesis.

## Discourse Regulation

The smooth flow of connected discourse depends on the listener's ability to monitor the speaker's messages and to provide feedback to the speaker concerning their effectiveness. The speaker, on the other hand, must be sensitive to cues provided by the listener and respond by repeating and/or modifying messages when necessary. Moves by both the initiator and the respondent in these repair sequences require a number of social, cognitive, and linguistic skills. Therefore, the ability of SLI children to make use of and to respond to such regulatory devices has been of interest to several researchers.

Gallagher and Darnton (1978) reported that SLI children aged 3;6 - 5;4 at each of Brown's Stages I, II, and III responded to non-specific requests to repeat messages (e.g. "what?") as frequently as did NL children at the same syntactic stages. The forms of the repairs produced by the two groups of children, however, differed significantly. The NL children exhibited a clear developmental progression from a predominant use of phonetic revisions and constituent elaborations in Stage I to a more frequent use of constituent reductions and substitutions at Stage III (Gallagher, 1977). No such developmental pattern was exhibited by the SLI children. Constituent substitutions were infrequent at all three developmental levels and other types of revisions were constant across all three stages. These findings were interpreted as evidence that SLI children are deficient in their knowledge of alternate codings to express equivalent meanings.

Stein (1976) made an observation that supports this interpretation. An analysis of her subjects' self-repetitions indicated that the SLI children produced more simple repetitions of part or all of the original utterance and fewer repetitions containing word substitutions than did the NL children.

If SLI children have difficulty using different words to express similar meanings, their ability to paraphrase sentences would be expected to be similarly impaired. Hoar (1977) found this to be the case in her study of SLI and NL children in grades 1 through 7. In an experimental task, each child was asked to paraphrase a number of test sentences. The SLI children produced more errors than the NL children at each grade level. They made more frequent use of simple repetition, lexical substitution, and antonymic responses in which sentence constituents were inappropriately inverted or a word was replaced by its antonym. Appropriate syntactic reformulations were rare in the responses of the SLI children. The frequent use of lexical substitution in this study may indicate that school-aged SLI children are beginning to appreciate ways in which different forms can be used to express similar meanings. This flexibility is apparently not extended to include alternations in syntactic form until a later age, however.

Watson (1977) reported that the same subjects studied by Stein (1976) made less frequent use of requests for clarification than did the same-age NL subjects. This finding, taken with those of Gallagher and Darnton (1978), suggests that SLI children may be deficient in both the ability to produce and the ability to respond to requests for clarification.

Fey (1981) presented evidence that conflicts with Watson's (1977) results. He noted that regardless of the age of the conversational partner, SLI children produced requests for clarification as frequently as did their same-age NL counterparts. It is significant, perhaps, that the highest proportions of clarification requests were addressed to peers and babies rather than to adults. Watson's findings may be at least a partial reflection of the infrequency with which contingent queries typically occur in interactions with adults. The influence of the social partner cannot account completely for Watson's findings, however, since her NL subjects used requests for clarification significantly more frequently than did the SLI subjects under similar social circumstances.

Griffin's (1979) results both corroborate and extend Fey's (1981) findings. He compared SLI children aged 4;8 - 6;1 who were delayed at least 18 months according to Developmental Sentence Analysis (Lee, 1974) with same-age NL children with respect to their ability to generate clarification requests. The SLI children not only produced these requests as frequently as did the same-age NL children, they also produced the same types of queries with equivalent frequencies.

SLI children's production of requests for clarification was also the focus of an investigation by Gale, Liebergott, and Griffin (1981). These investigators compared the requests of SLI children (mean age 3;10) with those of MLU-matched NL children. The mean MLUs for the two groups were 2.52 and 2.50 morphemes, respectively. Although the SLI and NL children were equivalent in the frequency with which they requested clarification, the SLI children were more likely to request it through nonverbal means. Such differences in request types were less apparent in a comparison of SLI and NL children at somewhat older ages (mean age 5;4).

The findings of Gallagher and Darnton (1978), Hoar (1977), and Stein (1976) indicate that SLI children are sensitive to listener requests for clarification. Their impairments seem to rest in a restriction in the means by which they modify their speech in response to such requests.

The differences between Watson's results (1977) and those of Fey (1981), Griffin (1979), and Gale, Liebergott and Griffin (1981) with respect to the initiation of requests for clarification may stem from the relative conversational assertiveness of children in each study. Requests for clarification seem to be assertive moves, since these interrupt the development of the topic and place restrictions on the manner in which the speaker can respond appropriately. If Watson's subjects were generally nonassertive and Fey's subjects showed no signs of this nonassertiveness, as was claimed in the last section, the pattern of results on requests for clarification in these studies is predictable. That is, the infrequent use of contingent queries may constitute another symptom of nonassertiveness. Had the studies of Gale, Liebergott, and Griffin (1981) or Griffin (1979) included a wider range of conversational measures, it might have been possible to determine whether their findings on requests for clarification were consistent with this assertiveness account.

## Speech Acts

Speech acts refer to the functions that utterances are intended to serve. The study of speech acts in the population of SLI children is of special interest because of the partial independence between a speech act and the linguistic forms with which it can be expressed. For example, while the use of an interrogative request for action requires some knowledge of question formation, a simple imperative can do just as well to indicate requestive intent. It is possible, then, that SLI children may show no impairments in their performance of speech acts despite significant limitations in formal linguistic skills.

Evidence contrary to this possibility was presented by Geller and Wollner (1976), who studied three SLI children aged 3;0 - 5;0 with MLUs of 1.1 to 1.6. The speech act repertoires of these children were compared with those of the 3-year-old subjects reported by Dore (1977). The SLI children were shown to be markedly deficient in the range of speech acts that they employed. This finding suggests the possibility that SLI children may be significantly impaired not only in the formal aspects of language but in their intent to communicate as well.

The investigations of Fey, Leonard, Fey, and O'Connor (1978) and Ball and Cross (1980) produced results that conflict with the results and interpretations of Geller and Wollner (1976). The subjects of Fey et al. ranged in age from 4;3 to 6;5 and had MLUs of 3.0 to 4.8. Ball and Cross's subjects averaged 6 years of age with mean MLUs of 3.8 and mean comprehension ages of approximately 3;10. These investigators compared the speech acts performed by their SLI subjects with those produced by both age- and language-matched NL controls. Although deficits were noted relative to the same-age NL groups, no differences were observed in comparisons of children at similar linguistic levels. In the study of Fey et al., SLI children were observed to produce significantly fewer rules than the same-age NL children. Rules frequently require complex modal notions such as necessity and obligation (e.g. "You hafta stay over there"). Children with syntactic impairments might be expected to have difficulty employing speech acts that require such complex semantic-syntactic operations.

An inspection of the Dore (1977) speech act categories, which served as the basis for the comparison in the Geller and Wollner (1976) study, suggests that the SLI children in the Geller and Wollner study did not have sufficient syntactic ability to produce many of the speech acts used by the 3-year-olds studied by Dore. The set of primitive speech acts described by Dore (1974) or the communicative functions of Halliday (1975), based on younger, less linguistically advanced NL children, might have been a more realistic standard for Geller and Wollner's severely impaired subjects.

Geller and Wollner (1976) are not the only investigators who have reported differences in the speech act behaviors of SLI and language-matched NL children. Snyder (1978) compared SLI children at the single-word stage with MLU-matched NL children in the use of communicative behaviors expressing declarative and imperative functions. Although the two groups were equivalent in their tendency to communicate with declarative and imperative intent, the SLI children were far less likely than the NL children to express these early intentions linguistically. Thus, even when there was reason to assume that they had the requisite language forms at their disposal, the SLI children failed to make use of them in the service of early communicative functions.

Rowan and Leonard (1981) presented evidence consistent with Fey et al. (1978) and Ball and Cross (1980) but which is at odds with Snyder's (1978) results. They noted the possibility that even though Snyder's SLI and NL children both were at the single-word stage of development, their knowledge of the test words may not have been the same. For example, the size of the children's lexicons in Snyder's study (14-30 words) was determined by sampling the children's spontaneous word usage pre-experimentally as well as by soliciting maternal reports. It is possible that the criteria for reporting that a child possessed a given word varied from mother to mother. Some words may have been comprehended or produced infrequently while others may have been common in the children's expressive repertoires. Any such discrepancies might have influenced the results. Further, with such small vocabularies, it seems likely that some of the children were expected to use general non-specific words (e.g. "that," "more") to refer to some of the test referents. Whether use of these words in the contexts studied by Snyder is the same as the use of words that identify the test referent specifically is not clear. Therefore, Rowan and Leonard carefully controlled the children's expressive command over the requisite vocabulary in their experiment. SLI and language-matched NL children at the single-word utterance stage served as subjects; however, it should be stressed that the cognitive abilities and lexicon sizes of the children were higher than those of Snyder's subjects. The same tasks as those introduced by Snyder were used. The results revealed no differences between SLI and NL children in the use of words to express declarative and imperative intent. Whether differences in expressive mastery of the words tested, in cognitive abilities, in lexicon size, or in some combination of these factors can account for the differences in the results of these two studies cannot be determined conclusively.

Another investigation reporting differences between SLI and language-matched NL children was reported by Morehead and Ingram (1973). They performed syntactic analyses on the language samples of SLI children aged 3;6 - 9;6 who fell into Brown's Stages I through V based on MLU. Samples were collected in free play with the experimenter or parent and in two elicitation tasks. Morehead and Ingram observed significant deficits in the production of questions by the SLI children. These children rarely produced questions of any type. Since the same children showed evidence of other equally or more complex transformations in their speech, Morehead and Ingram suggested that they might have assumed "a general sociolinguistic posture which is antithetical to seeking information by linguistic code" (p. 342).

In contrast to the findings of Morehead and Ingram (1973), Fey (1981) noted no differences between SLI and same-age NL children in the frequency with which questions were produced in interactions with adults, peers, or babies. The only obvious experimental difference between Fey's study and that of Morehead and Ingram that might have resulted in this discrepancy is the manner in which the language samples were collected. Fey observed larger proportions of questions by both SLI and NL children when they addressed peers and babies than when they talked to adults. Therefore, Morehead and Ingram may have sampled question production in the context least likely to elicit questions, that is, with adults. However, the possibility that the overall frequency of question usage was minimized for both groups of subjects in the Morehead and Ingram study cannot explain the observed differences between their SLI and NL subjects under the same eliciting conditions.

Prinz (1977) compared the requests conveyed by SLI children aged 5;0 - 7;0 to those of NL children aged 3;0 - 5;0. The degree to which the children in the two groups were comparable in general linguistic ability is unclear. In addition, the pattern of results reported in this study is difficult to interpret. For example, while the SLI children used fewer declarative and imperative requests than the NL children, they produced many indirect requests. According to the literature, the use of indirect requests represents a more sophisticated level of requesting than does the use of imperatives and of at least some forms of declarative requests (Ervin-Tripp, 1977). More recently, Prinz (in press) has provided a descriptive report of the request behaviors of SLI children aged 3;6 - 8;10. Somewhat surprisingly, the children at each successive age level produced a greater number of direct requests than did children at younger age levels. Snyder (in press) has speculated that this finding may be due to the older children's use of a doctor kit to play the role of a doctor in this condition. Thus, the older children's more frequent use of direct requests as doctor may reflect a developing awareness of status and the manner in which status influences requesting behavior.

In both Prinz (1977, in press) studies, the subjects also participated in an experimental task in which they judged the politeness of utterances addressed to puppets representing different ages. Relative to NL children, the SLI children had difficulty making appropriate judgments of politeness.

Shatz, Bernstein, and Shulman (1980) examined the abilities of SLI children aged 5;0 - 6;0 to respond to indirect requests. The children's MLUs ranged from 1.5 to 4.0. Like the 2-year-old NL subjects of Shatz (1978), the SLI children in a first experiment made use of an action response strategy in complying with several different types of requests in neutral contexts. In a subsequent experiment, the investigators attempted to condition the children to provide informing responses ("yes" or "no"). They introduced ambiguous test questions (e.g. "Can you talk on the telephone?") after the presentation of four unambiguous requests for information. Unlike the NL children, the SLI children continued to provide action responses even after these efforts were made to "set" the children for producing informing responses. The production of an appropriate informing response required the children to make inferences about the interrelatedness of utterances from previous discourse. The SLI children were notably impaired in their ability to use antecedent discourse in generating a response.

## Code-Switching

It was shown above that many SLI children can produce a wide variety of speech acts when they possess the requisite syntactic skills. The degree to which they can produce stylistic variations in the form or frequency of specific acts to meet situational requirements has not yet been discussed. The difficulties of SLI children in producing semantically equivalent responses with different forms (Gallagher and Darnton, 1978; Hoar, 1977; Stein, 1976) suggest that they might show similar limitations in their ability to alter their speech to suit the social situation.

Fey, Leonard, and Wilcox (1981) demonstrated that SLI children can make significant stylistic speech modifications based on the age and/or linguistic status of their listeners. Their subjects used greater mean pre-verb lengths (MPL), more back channel responses, and fewer questions concerning the internal state of the listener when talking to age level partners than when talking to MLU-matched partners. Yet no differences were observed on five other measures which typically reflect stylistic adjustments of NL 4-year-olds when talking to adults versus babies (see Shatz and Gelman, 1973; Sachs and Devin, 1976). The design of the Fey et al. study, which included neither an age- nor an MLU-matched NL control group, severely limits the interpretability of these findings.

Fey (1981) remedied this major shortcoming by observing groups of SLI children, same-age NL children, and language-equivalent NL children in play interactions with unfamiliar adults, peers, and babies. The SLI children were observed to make statistically significant adjustments in their use of contingent queries, self-repetitions, imperatives, total number of questions, and internal state questions which were always in the same direction as those of the same-age NL children. With the exception of internal state questions, their adaptations were also of the same magnitude as those of the same-age NL children. The only measures on which the same-age NL children adapted their speech while the SLI children did not were general measures of syntactic ability: MLU and MPL. The SLI children were identified as language impaired on the basis of their performance on tests of syntax. Therefore, it is not particularly surprising that these children exhibited a lack of flexibility in their use of syntactic structures. It was shown that the mean MLU of the SLI children when talking to adults (where MLU was highest) was not as great as that of the same-age NL children when talking to babies (where MLU was lowest). Thus, the task of appropriately modifying syntactic complexity in conversations with partners of different ages seemed to place too great a demand on these SLI children's area of greatest weakness, syntactic production.

Messick and Newhoff (1979) observed SLI children aged 4;6 - 7;10 and MLU-matched NL children in a role-play task. The subjects had MLUs ranging from 3.4 to 4.8. Each child was asked to request a drink while playing in the role of a mother, a father, an adult female, a girl, and a baby. No differences between groups were noted in the number of request variations produced across the different roles. Although these findings seem generally consistent with those of Fey (1981), the nature of the speech modifications involved in each study is fundamentally different from that of the other. Messick and Newhoff were concerned with their subjects' ability to use socially appropriate alternate forms of a single speech act. Fey, on the other hand, observed differences in the frequency with which a number of different speech acts occurred across listener conditions. Speech modifications of this type do not require variations in the form of any particular act. This type of modification places less of a strain on the children's formal linguistic skills than does the former type.

Messick and Newhoff (1979) also employed a judgment task in their study in which the children were to assign each of a number of different request forms to the picture of the most likely recipient (adults, a girl, and a baby). The SLI subjects made random judgments on this task while the NL subjects gave simple imperatives most frequently to the baby and imperatives with an adjoining explanation or politeness marker ("please") to adults.

## Referential Skills

Making reference involves the use of language to point out or delineate an object, action, or idea from a set of alternatives. Since many SLI children are late in acquiring their first words and are typically slow in moving from their first words to the onset of syntax (see Leonard and Fey, 1979), they might be expected to exhibit delays in referential abilities from the outset of language use.

In an investigation of the ability of SLI children to encode that element of context which carries the greatest informational load, Snyder (1978) observed that such problems do indeed exist. Her SLI subjects were significantly less likely than language-matched NL children to name the new object in the experimental context despite their frequent non-linguistic encoding of these same objects.

An attempt by Rowan and Leonard (1981) to replicate this finding yielded conflicting results. The SLI subjects in this study encoded the most informative referent linguistically just as often as the NL children did when the children's expressive command over the lexical items tested was controlled carefully. As noted above, however, there were lexical and cognitive differences between the SLI children in the Snyder (1978) and Rowan and Leonard studies that may have contributed to the discrepant findings.

Two studies of older, more linguistically advanced SLI children indicate that these children at times may outperform language-matched peers on tasks of referential skill. Skarakis and Greenfield (1979) observed SLI children age 4;0-6;7. All of these children exhibited at least a 1-year delay in syntactic expression and a 1- to 2-year delay in comprehension. It was noted that while the SLI and the MLU-matched NL children were equal in their ability to encode new information in the experimental condition, the SLI children were more likely to use anaphoric pronouns to refer to established referents.

Meline (1978) found converging results in a classical referential communication task. The subjects were SLI children with an average age of 8;6 and MLUs of 4.5 to 5.5. A group of younger NL children at the same MLU levels also participated. The task was for each child to describe novel geometric shapes to a naive listener. The descriptions produced by the SLI children were interpreted more accurately by a group of adult listeners than were the messages of the NL children. Meline also reported some tentative findings on comparisons on these same SLI children with same-age NL controls. Although the SLI children were superior on this task relative to MLU peers, their performance was surpassed by the same-age NL peers. Perhaps a similar pattern would have emerged in the Skarakis and Greenfield study (1979) if they had included same-age NL controls.

The results of Skarakis and Greenfield (1979) and Meline (1978) provide important corroborating evidence for the hypothesis that language form and use are at least partially independent of one another. Ultimately, how a child performs in a conversational context will depend on the social, cognitive, and linguistic abilities which the child brings to the social situation. Given that SLI children, by virtue of their age, have had greater experience in the social world than younger NL children with similar structural skills and often show cognitive abilities in advance of these younger children (Camarata, Newhoff, and Rugg, 1981; Kamhi, 1981), it seems reasonable that they may be expected to perform at higher levels than NL children at similar stages of syntactic development, at least on those communication tasks that do not severely tax areas of language form.

## Summary and Conclusions

In this chapter, we have compared and contrasted the studies on pragmatic skills in SLI children. As we have shown, there are a number of variables that make comparisons among studies difficult. A valid comparison of the results of any two studies depends on consideration of the similarities and differences between the studies on factors such as the subjects and the persons with whom they interact, the task, the behaviors being analyzed, and the procedures used for analysis. We have examined each of these factors in considerable detail and can now come to some tentative conclusions.

The most general conclusion to be reached from our evaluation is that the population of SLI children is no more homogeneous with respect to pragmatic skills than it is with respect to semantic, syntactic, or phonological abilities. The question then arises as to how the pragmatic skills of different SLI children can be described best. The three patterns of conversational participation that we have identified appear to hold considerable promise as a means of characterizing subgroups of SLI children along pragmatic parameters.

Children whose behavior is consistent with the first pattern are generally unresponsive in all types of social interaction relative to same-age NL children. These children may be regarded as having general pragmatic impairments since their unwillingness or inability to engage in conversations has a profound influence on all areas of language use. This pattern is not well documented. However, it is possible that the experimental designs traditionally used to study SLI children have effectively masked its presence. In these designs, children described by this pattern would have been grouped together with children exhibiting other patterns of conversational participation. Their particular social-interactional profiles may then have been obscured in reports of overall group performance.

More evidence exists for a second behavioral pattern. Children who fit the second pattern are more responsive to their social partners than are the children in pattern one. In fact, they make frequent use of back channel behaviors that serve to maintain social contact with their partners and at the same time enable them to avoid taking the conversational floor. These children can be described as responsive but nonassertive. They do not have general pragmatic impairments but show selective pragmatic deficits that often seem to reflect the severity of their impairments in the comprehension and production of syntax.

Based on our discussion of discourse regulation, speech acts, code-switching, and referential skills, we can make some comments about how children displaying the second pattern can be expected to perform on other pragmatic variables. Since requests for clarification are assertive acts, children exhibiting the second pattern will produce them infrequently. These same children can be expected to respond reliably to requests for clarification. The type of revisions they provide upon request, however, are not likely to include many lexical substitutions because of the difficulties they seem to have in generating alternate forms to express similar meanings. During the elementary school years, lexical substitutions may be used more frequently but alternation of syntactic forms to yield equivalent meanings will be slow to emerge.

The speech act repertoires of these children are likely to reflect deficiencies in their ability to produce requests for action and information. Futher, the range of linguistic forms they can employ to perform any individual speech act will be limited. The information we have on referential skills in SLI children does not enable us to predict how children who exhibit the second pattern would fare in this area. One might speculate, however, that they would be somewhat deficient in their use of anaphoric pronouns to encode previously established referents.

Pattern three describes the behavior of SLI children who assume the roles of both speaker-initiator and listener-respondent in a manner not unlike NL children their own age. These children cannot necessarily be described as pragmatically unimpaired, however. For example, while they produce requests for clarification with frequencies similar to same-age NL children, they may, at least in the early pre-school years, rely more on non-verbal means of encoding such results than do NL children with equivalent MLUs. Although we can be certain that these SLI children will provide responses to requests for clarification, there is no evidence to indicate whether they can respond with the same distribution of revision types as do MLU-matched NL children.

Unlike the children exhibiting patterns one and two, these children have speech act repertoires similar to children with equal levels of syntactic abilities. They seem to be limited only by their lack of the specific linguistic forms required to produce certain speech acts, such as the assertion of rules. Although they may exhibit some limitations in the range of syntactic variants they can use to serve individual speech functions, they can modify the frequency and the content of a number of speech acts to suit the requirements of different conversational situations. Finally, these children can be expected to perform at least as well as NL children with similar formal linguistic abilities on tasks involving referential skills.

It is clear that further investigations are needed to document the existence of these three behavioral patterns. If they are shown to be valid, studies should be undertaken to specify further the set of pragmatic and structural abilities that correlate with each. Clinical studies testing the efficacy of different intervention programs for these children could then be initiated on a sound empirical basis. Johnston (1982) has suggested that a major objective of studies of SLI children is to describe more adequately their characteristics so that programs for intervention can be developed to suit their specific needs. Further investigations into the pragmatic skills of SLI children such as those we have suggested should be viewed as major steps toward reaching that objective.

# References

Ball, J., & Cross, F. Formal and pragmatic factors in childhood autism and aphasia. Paper presented at Symposium on Research in Child Language Disorders, Madison, WI, 1981.

Caldwell, E.M., Heider, J., & Kaplan, B. The inventory of home stimulation (pre-school revision). Unpublished manuscript. (Available from Susan Inglis, [Child Development and Mental Retardation Center. WJ-10. University of Washington, Seattle, WA].)

Camarata, S., Newhoff, M., & Rugg, B. Perspective taking in normal and language disordered children. Paper presented at University of Wisconsin Symposium on Research in Child Language Disorders, Madison, WI, 1981.

Crystal, D., Fletcher, P., & Garman, M. *The grammatical analysis of language disability.* London: Edward Arnold, 1976.

Cunningham, C. Personal communication, 1981.

Dore, J. A pragmatic description of early language development. *Journal of Psycholinguistic Research,* 1974, *3,* 343-350.

Dore, J. Oh them sheriff: A pragmatic analysis of children's responses to questions. In S. Ervin-Tripp & C. Mitchell-Kernan (Eds.), *Child discourse,* New York: Academic Press, 1977.

Dunn, L. Peabody Picture Vocabulary Test. Circle Pines, Minnesota: American Guidance Service, 1965.

Ervin-Tripp, S. Wait for me, roller skate! In S. Ervin-Tripp and C. Mitchell-Kernan (Eds.), *Child discourse,* New York: Academic Press, 1977.

Fey, M. Stylistic speech adjustments of language-impaired and normal-language children. Unpublished doctoral dissertation, Purdue University, 1981.

Fey, M., Leonard, L., Fey, S., & O'Connor, K. The intent to communicate in language-impaired children. Paper presented at Third Annual Boston University Conference on Language Development, Boston, 1978.

Fey, M., Leonard L., & Wilcox, K. Speech-style modifications of language-impaired children. *Journal of Speech and Hearing Disorders,* 1981, *46,* 91-97.

Gale, D., Liebergott, J., & Griffin, S. Getting it: Children's requests for clarification. Paper presented to American Speech-Language-Hearing Association, Los Angeles, 1981.

Gallagher, T. Revision behaviors in the speech of normal children developing language. *Journal of Speech and Hearing Research,* 1977, *20,* 303-318.

Gallagher, T. and Darnton, B. Conversational aspects of the speech of language disordered children: Revision behaviors. *Journal of Speech and Hearing Research.* 1978, *21,* 118-135.

Geller, E. and Wollner, S. A preliminary investigation of the communicative competence of three linguistically impaired children. Paper presented to New York State Speech and Hearing Association, Grossingers, 1976.

Griffin, S. Requests for clarification made by normal and language impaired children. Unpublished master's thesis, Emerson College, 1979.

Halliday, M. *Learning how to mean.* London: Edward Arnold, 1975.

Hoar, N. Paraphrase capabilities of language impaired children. Paper presented at Second Annual Boston University Conference on Language Development, Boston, 1977.

Ingram, T. The classification of speech and language disorders in young children. In M. Rutter & J. Martin (Eds.), *The child with delayed speech.* Clinics in Developmental Medicine No. 43, Philadelphia: J.B. Lippincott, 1972.

Jacobs, T. Verbal dominance, complexity and quantity of speech in pairs of language-disabled and normal children. Unpublished doctoral dissertation, University of Southern California, 1981.

Johnston, J. The language disordered child. In N. Lass, L. McReynolds, J. Northern, & D. Yoder (Eds.), *Speech, language and hearing,* (Vol. 2). Philadelphia: W.B. Saunders Co., 1982.

Kamhi, A. Nonlinguistic symbolic and conceptual abilities of language-impaired and normally developing children. *Journal of Speech and Hearing Research,* 1981, *3,* 446-453.

Lee, L. *Developmental sentence analysis.* Evanston, IL: Northwestern University Press, 1974.

Leonard, L. Linguistic impairment in children. *Merrill-Palmer Quarterly,* 1979, *25,* 205-232.

Leonard, L., & Fey, M. The early lexicons of normal and language disordered children: Developmental and training considerations. In N. Lass (Ed.), *Speech and language (Vol. 2).* New York: Academic Press, 1979.

Meline, T. Referential communication by normal- and deficient-language children. Paper presented to American Speech and Hearing Association, San Francisco, 1978.

Messick, C., & Newhoff, M. Request form: Does the language-impaired child consider the listener? Paper presented to American Speech and Hearing Association, Atlanta, 1979.

Morehead, D., & Ingram, D. The develoment of base syntax in normal and linguistically deviant children. *Journal of Speech and Hearing Research*, 1973, *16*, 330-352.

Prelock, P., Messick, C., Schwartz, R., & Terrell, B. Mother-child discourse during the one-word stage. Paper presented at University of Wisconsin Symposium on Research in Child Language Disorders, Madison, WI, 1981.

Prinz, P. Comprehension and production of requests in language-disordered children. Paper presented to Second Annual Boston University Conference of Language Develoment, Boston, 1977.

Prinz, P. Requesting in normal and language disordered children. In K. Nelson (Ed.), *Children's language, (Vol. 3)*. New York: Gardner Press, In press.

Rowan L., & Leonard, L. Performative and presuppositional skills in language disordered and normal children. Paper presented to American Speech-Language-Hearing Association, Los Angeles, 1981.

Sachs, J., & Devin, J. Young children's use of age-appropriate speech styles in social interaction and role-playing. *Journal of Child Language*, 1976. *3*, 81-98.

Shatz, M. On the development of communicative understandings: An early strategy for interpreting and responding messages. *Cognitive Psychology*, 1978, *10*, 271-301.

Shatz, M., Bernstein, D., & Shulman, M. The responsiveness of language disordered children to indirect directiveness in varying contexts. *Applied Psycholinguistics*, 1980, *1*, 295-306.

Shatz, M., & Gelman, R. The development of communication skills: Modification in the speech of young children as a function of the listener. *Monographs of the Society for Research in Child Development*, 1973, *38*.

Sheppard, A. Monologue and dialogue speech of language-impaired children in clinic and home settings: Semantic, conversational and syntactic characteristics. Unpublished master's thesis, Univeristy of Western Ontario, 1980.

Siegel, L., Cunningham, C., & van der Spuy, H. Interaction of language delayed and normal preschool children and their mothers. Paper presented to Society of Research in Child Development, San Francisco, 1979.

Skarakis, E., & Greenfield, P. The role of new and old information in the verbal expression of language disabled children. Paper presented at Fourth Annual Boston University Conference on Language Development, Boston, 1979.

Snyder, L. Communicative and cognitive abilities and disabilities in the sensorimotor period. *Merrill-Palmer Quarterly,* 1978, *24,* 161-180.

Snyder, L. Communicative competence in children with delayed language development. In R. Schiefelbusch and C. Pickar (Eds.), *Communicative competence: Acquisition and intervention,* Baltimore, MD: University Park Press, In press.

Stark, R., & Tallal, P. Selection of children with specific language deficits, *Journal of Speech and Hearing Disorders,* 1981, *46,* 114-122.

Stein, A. A comparison of mothers' and fathers' language to normal and language deficient children. Unpublished doctoral dissertation, Boston University, 1976.

Van Kleeck, A., & Frankel, T. Discourse devices used by language disordered children: a preliminary investigation. *Journal of Speech and Hearing Disorders,* 1981, *46,* 250-257.

Watson, L. Conversational participation by language deficient and normal children. Paper presented to American Speech and Hearing Association, Chicago, 1977.

Weiner, P. Developmental language disorders. In H. Rie & E. Rie (Eds.), *Handbook of minimal brain dysfunction.* New York: Wiley, 1980.

Wolfus, B., Moskovitch, M., & Kinsbourne, M. Subgroups of developmental language impairment. *Brain and Language,* 1980, *10,* 152-171.

Wulbert, M., Inglis, S., Kriegsmann, E., & Mills, B. Language delay and associated mother-child interactions. *Developmental Psychology,* 1975, *11,* 61-70.

# 4

# LANGUAGE PROCESSING AND GEODESIC DOMES

## Judith F. Duchan
*State University of New York at Buffalo*

## Introduction

*I* remember Tom Shriner sitting crosslegged on the desk in front of us talking about Buckminister Fuller's geodesic domes and likening them to a structural model of language. What was bothering him was people's artificial sense of language as being made up of a set of boxes or levels with different aspects of a message being processed at the different levels. A prevailing idea then was that processing language was something like sending a linguistic package up and down a freight elevator in a multilevel, rectilinear building. That is still a prevailing view.

In those days I had only a beginning sense of what Shriner was talking about. I have spent the last ten years studying and thinking about what kinds of knowledge go in and out of the linguistic freight elevator as it stops at each level. Only now can I really appreciate Shriner's conception of how those levels might be modeled differently. What I would like to do in this chapter, as a tribute to his foresight, is to pursue that geodesic dome idea and to entertain others as well. My hope is to arrive at a model, or way of modeling, which will best fit what we have learned about how both normal and abnormal people know and process their language, and to apply this knowledge clinically.

## The Psychological Reality of Multistory Models

If we take a look around our literature and our clinic shelves, we find that the same terms keep popping up. In language pathology those terms are of at least two general types: those having to do with language knowledge, and those having to do with how that knowledge is processed. The language knowledge list of terms is organized into what have been called language levels: phonology, morphology, syntax, and semantics. These levels have crept into our books as chapter headings (Lund and Duchan, in press Palermo, 1978), into our assessment techniques (Prutting, 1979), and into our minds as a mental checklist for what we need to know about our children's language. Sometimes the list is organized into related steps by having knowledge at one level lead to another; other times the model building effort is spent on specifying what goes on inside each level.

The language processing lists are usually in different books from the ones organized by language level (Levinson & Sloan, 1980; Sanders, 1977). Those processing lists set up a different framework for our test construction and assessment procedures (Duchan and Katz, 1982; Rees, 1973, 1981). The categories in the list either combine in the same boxes with language knowledge categories (Butler, 1981; Wiig and Semel, 1976), or occur in separate boxes in our mental checklists (Cromer, 1981). This language processing framework is not like the tidy four tiers of the language knowledge framework, but is more open ended and may include selective attention, sensory processing, speech perception, memory processes, and perceptual strategies.

Although the lists are different in what they represent, the form of the models containing them are comparable. Both models are organized into labeled boxes, sometimes with arrows leading from one box to others. It is the familiar flow diagram, the freight elevator going up or down the rectilinear building.

We were all working happily within these two frameworks, some in one, some in the other, and some across several levels. Then, something called "pragmatics" hit the academic scene. It raised new concerns which showed that our units operated differently in different contexts. Indeed, the context variability was so great, the form of the units came under question. Somehow, the shake-up had to be handled. At a minimum, the context variability had to be represented in the old models.

The language knowledge model builders sometimes put pragmatics down as a fifth box or level or area (Cromer, 1981; Prutting, 1979) but without arrows and without specifying the units within the box. Other language knowledge modelers placed pragmatics in a separate domain from the language knowledge domain (Blank, Gessner, and Esposito, 1979; Rees, 1978). Those who felt the influence of pragmatics most strongly advocated new frameworks, such as eliminating flow diagrams and conceiving of something else that was more fluid in form and not boxlike in its representation at all (Bates and MacWhinney, 1979; Greenfield and Dent, 1979).

Meanwhile those who were building language processing models were less influenced by the pragmatics revolution unless the context influences seemed to locate within a particular processing stage. In these cases, the contents of those boxes changed somewhat. If context variability minimally affected what went on during the processing stages, the process model remained unscathed.

What has become apparent for all of us involved in the pragmatics upheaval is that we need to build new kinds of models or to devise ways to decide among existing and proliferating models. Before discussing how we might go about testing the various models, let me elaborate more on the precariousness of the models we are currently using. I will first look at the language knowledge levels, then the models of language processing stages, then models combining the two.

## Language Knowledge Levels

From the very beginning of the study of language knowledge, theoreticians were aware that the language level divisions they were making had fuzzy boundaries, where units and operations within one level required knowledge of units or operations at another level. We have long known, for example, that there is a fuzzy interface between phonology and morphology and have called it morphophonology. Morphophonemic rules contain within them information about morphemes and phonemes, so the morphological form for plurality has phonological representation. The variation between /s/, /z/, and /əz/ depends upon the phonological form of the noun being pluralized. The rule is a morphophonemic one because it contains both morphological and phonological information.

An even more dramatic cross level representation which has been with us for awhile is that which occurs in the lexicon. The lexicon is theoretically depicted as a dictionary which is organized by morphemes, the smallest units of meaning. Each morpheme is specified in terms of its general phonological shape, its capability for making combinations with other units, and its meaning. Morphology, phonology, syntax, and semantics sit all together here in the same place, in one box.

In the above mergers of levels, the knowledge from the different levels are together in the same representation but maintain their original identity. That is to say, the "morpho" part of morphophonology is still about morphemes, the phonology is about the way those morphemes are phonetically or phonologically organized. There are other kinds of mergers where the contents lose their level identity. One example of such a conflation of levels is in the area of intonation.

Intonation has often been treated strictly as an aspect of phonology, probably because it has to do with how language is pronounced. Certain aspects of intonation do, indeed, come from what we have traditionally thought of as phonology. For example, users of a language need to know how to assign relative stress to the different syllables of a word. However, there are other aspects of intonation that seem more to do with syntax. Relative and subordinate clauses, for example, are indicated intonationally by pauses and pitch changes. *Yes-no* questions are indicated by rising pitch at the end, and statements by falling pitch. Adjective and noun relationships are usually manifested by a relative weak-strong stress pattern, compound words by spondaic stress.

Intonation also reflects semantic information, but in a more opaque way. For example, Sag and Liberman (1975) found that there are pitch contours which indicate that the speaker is contradicting something or someone. Other than a few examples such as these, there is no one-to-one correspondence between semantics and intonation

Finally, intonation has recently come to the forefront by virtue of its ties with pragmatics. Specifically, it is studied for how it is used by speakers to keep listeners abreast of what is important about what they are saying. For example, speakers highlight new information by contrastive stress, and old information by lesser stress.

What makes intonation patterns so unique is that they have in them information which comes from different levels of language. Actually, they have in them even more than this. For example, in English intonation patterns are also structured into a rhythmic beat which builds on stressed syllables. Pike (1945) has called this isochrony and describes it as a tendency toward placing equal temporal distance between the most stressed syllables of a sentence or sequence of sentences. In my work with J. Oliva (Duchan & Oliva, 1979; Oliva & Duchan, 1976; Duchan, Oliva, & Lindner, 1979) we have taken issue with Pike's formulation and see the beat structure as including juncture as well as stress. We observed equal beats within each spoken measure in normal speakers, and we noted a departure from this rhythmic sequence in a dysarthric speaker, not in an autistic speaker. What was pertinent here about our data is that the beat structure in both speakers sometimes overrode the linguistic intonational indicators resulting in sing-song intonation which violated rules of contrastive and lexical stress. Our evidence from abnormal speakers suggests that for them we may need both types of formulations, one which ties to the linguistic knowledge at different levels, and a second more surface level which can override the first and which controls the rhythmic beat.

The intonation research points out that the same indicators, i.e., alterations in stress, pitch, and juncture can be responsive to the various levels of linguistic knowledge and temporal structuring. This leads logically to a sense that information from linguistic levels  feeds into a more surface interpretive intonation level. To model this level we would need to add another box to the flow diagram, an intonation box which receives information from other levels, or we would need to put an intonation compartment into each of the levels informing the speaker at each level of processing about how to indicate the information at that level intonationally.

The pragmatic literature presents a comparable dilemma to that witnessed for intonation. That is, the influences of varying contextual factors are felt at each language level and can be represented by adding more to the contents of the boxes of each level, or by placing the information all together in a pragmatics box. In this case, unlike intonation, the new box would need to be before the other levels since pragmatic knowledge leads to the choice of linguistic structures and not to their packaging.

Bates and MacWhinney (1980) have discussed this sense of pragmatics as the deepest level or activity in language production. That is, they see it as providing a foundation for choosing linguistic forms from the different linguistic boxes. They call their conceptualization functionalist because they are primarily concerned with underlying purposes which guide speakers in their selection of linguistic form. They see language forms as the tools used by speakers to carry out their intentions.

The reason Bates and MacWhinney call their formulation functionalism is to distinguish it from structuralism. They do not see these intents as being located in another box in a structural model of language knowledge. Instead, they depict the whole linguistic endeavor as being one where language knowledge ties closely to the speaker's intent. They describe the structures which have been traditionally organized into separate boxes as forms which compete in parallel fashion with one another for how best to express a speaker's intent. For example, the authors feel that syntactic forms are determined and maintained by communicative functions and processing constraints. Let us now proceed with Bates and MacWhinney's line of thinking by looking specifically at performatives - those nonverbal and verbal forms which directly express children's intentions.

Children who have not yet developed language can express their wants through action. One finds them reaching, grasping, and pushing things away. A particular action such as a reach may differ dramatically from the next in its shape, direction, velocity; but reaches deserve to be classified together because of their common purpose. The form of a purposeful action can be evaluated only in light of how well it functions; that is, whether it accomplishes the goal for which it was intended.

The reach can serve us as an idealized example of an act whose form and meaning is inextricably tied to its intent. To classify the forms of reaches into types of reach shapes, or into reaches of different velocities or directions is to disregard this sense that they are reaches. It is only in the context of their function that the form of the reach can be made relevant. Reaches that are too fast to achieve their purpose, or ones whose misdirection or poor contour blocks them from achieving their purpose, deserve being talked about in terms of their shape, velocity, or direction.

Functionalism, as it applies to reaches, can also be applied to language, except that for language the form may be less directly tied to the intent. For example, Barry Prizant and I (1981) studied the functions of echolalia in autistic children and found that many of the echoes were linguistically empty. They were, nonetheless, meaningful because they were expressions of children's intents. We found behavioral and contextual evidence that the children were using the echoes to express a variety of intentions, and the difference between these children and normal children is that the linguistic forms used by normal language users have closer semantic ties to the intent. Normal children, for example, accept an offer framed in a question (Do you want....?) by answering (Yes). Autistic children who are echolalic might express their acceptance by repeating part or all of the question.

This movement from seeing language form as primary to seeing the intent behind the form as more significant, has in it the arguments for moving away from a structuralist multilevel sense of language to a functionalist paradigm. In the functionalist perspective, the levels of form such as phonology, morphology, and syntax would be deemphasized and the structures within and across levels would be classed together in terms of the functions they can serve.

This reorganization of a structural model to bring together the forms which serve the same function is reminiscent of the line of thinking which Chomsky (1972) used to support his generative theory. Both reorganizations ask that we make a surface-deep structure distinction. The attempt is to have us disregard unimportant surface differences when comparing structures and look at their deeper similarities. Chomsky contended that active and passive sentences can state the same meaning, so they must have a similar deep structure. Functionalists contend that different surface forms which serve the same underlying function must have a deep structure similarity. So, requests for example, can be carried out nonverbally, or through direct verbal statements, or by indirect hints, and request makers need to have that knowledge about functional alliances between request forms in order to carry out their intent.

Before going on to language processing models, let me synopsize where we have been. I began this section on language knowledge levels by mentioning places where most agree that the ordinary separation between levels become something like an emulsion, one was where morphology and phonology touch in morphophonological representations, another was the multiple level indexing which happens in the lexicon. Then I pointed to things going on in intonation and pragmatics which displayed the level merger more like an alloy than an emulsion because the influence of the separate levels of ingredients were harder to identify in the final product. Finally, I suggested that the functionalist views might move us away from considering levels so important by either viewing them as interpretive or derivational or as artifactual. This would cast them as a by-product, playing a more secondary role than that which is entailed in being part of an emulsion or alloy.

## Language Processing Stages

While language knowledge models often seem to be about sentence building necessary for language production, language processing models typically assume a focus on language comprehension or even more particularly on verbal memory (Butler, 1981).

One commonly cited model of stages in language processing is that designed by Atkinson and Shriffrin (1968) for displaying stages of verbal memory. The model begins with a box for the environmental input, indicating there is something (a sentence, say) which is present in the person's environment to be processed. The sentence proceeds to a sensory register where it is recorded by the system; from there to a short term memory box where it is scanned and sometimes rehearsed or forgotten; and, if it makes it, it moves on to a long term memory box where it is permanently stored or perhaps forgotten.

This model, even more than the language level ones discussed above, assumes a unidirectional serial order which begins with the signal and then moves straight through the three storage boxes without jumping ahead or looking backward. Because it proceeds from the signal unidirectionally to the meaning interpretation, it has been called a "bottom up" model.

There have been some criticisms of this neat three-step progression. The most often cited is the criticism of Craik and Lockhart (1972) who argue that language processing must be more continuous than shown in these discrete boxes and that the temporally organized boxes are hiding the fact that there are different sorts of processing going on at each stage. Their depth of processing model converts the memory stores to processing steps; namely, sensory analysis, pattern recognition, and stimulus elaboration.

A second problem with Atkinson and Schriffrin's model is its assumption that language processing is a serially ordered set of operations. It assumes that the signal is first processed for one type of information, and then for another, and then another. Marlsen-Wilson (1975) and Studdert-Kennedy (1976) have demonstrated that processing systems are capable of carrying out information processing at several levels simultaneously. That is to say, an incoming signal can set up a reverberation through the entire system with different boxes resonating to its different contents. In the case of Atkinson and Schriffrin, for example, long term memory can be working on sentence analyses at the same time things are being processed in short term memory; in the Craik and Lockhart model, sensory analysis can co-occur with stimulus elaboration. This has come to be known as a parallel processing argument, and it counters the serial processing view of the box and stage models.

A third problem with those box and stage processing models, and one linked to the notion of parallel processing, is that processing models envision that the job of each box is to process the information which is contained in the signal. The box does this by carrying on according to a prescribed set of procedures. There is, however, a counter literature which offers evidence that language processing is a more active and creative process than the passive mechanical one forwarded by the multistory boxes (See Fodor, Bever, and Garrett, 1974, for a review). For example, listeners actively create meaning even before the signal is presented. These meanings include the listener's ongoing sense of the situation and they are constructed from the person's background knowledge of the world. It is in this rich meaning context that verbal stimuli are selected and understood.

This meaning context criticism is an example from what has been called the "top down" approach, countering the bottom up, signal to meaning, view of language processing. It raises again the pragmatics sensibility that people understand and produce language in light of the contexts in which they are embedded. And, once again, we see that embracing pragmatics sensibility leads to a discomfort with those context stripped, boxy, and serially ordered models such as the memory stores suggested by Atkinson and Schriffrin.

Summarizing, typical language processing models have deficiencies because they incorrectly assume that listeners begin by hearing the signal and then, in a step-like manner, continue through and passively process until an interpretation is made. Instead, perhaps even before the signal is introduced, there is an active higher order processing going on which selects the relevant signals and processes their contents in parallel fashion. The listener uses both signal and higher order knowledge in the effort to make sense of what is going on and to fulfill particular needs. Some who have recognized these deficiencies in traditional models have tried to remedy them. I will now proceed to a description of a few of these remedies.

## Combined Models—Language Knowledge and Its Processing

Some recent attempts have been made to combine the language processing and language knowledge models into a single framework. Sometimes this is done by putting knowledge boxes inside the processing boxes, showing that different kinds of knowledge are being processed at different points up the line. Craik and Lockhart (1972) hint at this approach in their depth of processing model, which places phonological processing in the first stage and semantic in the third. Norman (1976) has hypothesized this same sort of coalescence of the two models. The result of both Craik and Lockhart and Norman's amalgamation is a bottom up processing model, beginning with the processing of phonological information and ending with the semantic interpretation. It is also a model of language comprehension and memory, and not of language production.

Cromer (1981) has arrived at a less synthetic and more additive approach. His model contains the two frameworks as disparate descriptions of language-impaired children. Specifically, he has us ask whether a language-impaired child's primary deficit is one of knowledge or one of processing, and suggests we design diagnostic approaches for determining what box or "area of deficit" most contributes to the child's language problem.

Since Cromer's emphasis is on isolating areas of deficit, he does not address the issue of how breakdowns in one box lead to or stem from problems in another. It is also the case that Cromer is trying to combine a set of top-down boxes designed to model production, with a second set, this time a bottom-up set designed to model comprehension and memory.

Strait (1980) differs from Cromer in that he sees need for separate models of language comprehension and language production. His position is more radical than most because he holds that not only are different psychological processes involved in speech perception and production, but so are different linguistic knowledges. His "processual" theory, as he calls it, has in it an auditory phonology for analyzing information presented in the acoustic signal, and an articulatory phonology for producing speech. Strait makes his case from examples from child phonology which show discrepancies between children's perception and articulation of features, onset of acquisition of phonological processes, and feedback mechanisms. Strait concedes that there could be places where there is interaction between the two phonological systems—places where they seem to be in conspiracy, but he does not thereby relinquish his separatist position.

While most would not agree with Strait that we need two theories of knowledge, most would agree that different process models are required for comprehension and production. It is in this sense that Cromer's simple additive approach offers problems. He makes knowledge and processing into one model without indicating the differences. As the saying goes, "You can't add apples and oranges," or is it apples and peaches?

My colleague, Jack Katz, and I have tried to deal with this symptom of processing schizophrenia which combines comprehension with production models by confining ourselves to conceptualizing the processes involved just in language comprehension (Duchan and Katz, 1982). We also indirectly handle the serial ordering problem implied by stacked box descriptions by not having distinct processing stages. Finally, we emphasize in our framework, that top-down and bottom-up processing can be going on simultaneously with some tasks requiring more signal processing than others.

A failure of all the combined models is that they are, as yet, highly unspecified. Further, they still commit the error that Tom Shriner was complaining about all those years ago—that is, that they fail to show how the various aspects of language processing become integrated. I call this a problem in appreciating processing conspiracies, and will end this section discussing the way the box models fail to display the processing conspiracies which go on between different parts of the model.

Using the freight elevator metaphor, the processing conspiracies would occur when various levels need to share resources such as electricity or space. The conspiracies would become even more apparent when resources become scarce. For language processing, processing conspiracies can be seen in literature discussions of attention, cognitive load, working memory constraints, comprehension strategies, real-time constraints, or knowledge conspiracies. This criticism of the step-by-step processing models is that they fail to emphasize in their design that resources can be limited, and that extra resources used at one level of processing can deplete those needed at another. Similarly, the knowledge components of these combination models fail to display the way the different levels work together to serve the same underlying function, nor do fixed knowledge components capture the way listeners alter their language interpretations to make them compatible with what they know about the world (Duchan, 1980b; Duchan and Siegel, 1979).

## Geodesic Dome as a Model of Language Processing

In light of all this we can now think about Shriner's attraction to the geodesic dome as a way to think about language processing. What Shriner felt was important about Fuller's conceptualization of the dome was that it, as a system of units, did more than any or all of its component parts. Prutting and Elliott (1979) have recently discussed this gestalt which Fuller, and Shriner after him, called synergy. In their discussion of synergy in language, Prutting and Elliott convincingly show that the additive models with separable levels fail to demonstrate that the levels work together. Also, the models fail to show that the system can do more than is represented by adding together each of the separate contributions made by components within it.

Thus, the geodesic dome is not intended as a model after all, but a simile which Fuller and Shriner have used to show how insufficient it is to depict systems as a straightforward sum of their subsystems. The geodesic dome fails as a model of language processing because it does not contain temporality or directionality, nor does it stipulate the units and their interrelatedness. It also fails in principle because the structures by their spatial equivalence are portrayed as having equal importance, and identical to one another. This is certainly not the case for units involved in language processing either for production or comprehension.

I would like now to move to the clinical relevance of model building and argue that it is premature and probably wrongheaded to want to build general models of language processing like those I have been discussing. Instead we would do better to think carefully about models which represent particular children's error patterns and their performance on particular tasks (see also Duchan 1982).

## Clinical Relevance of Model Building

I have been concentrating on general models of adults' language comprehension. How do these general models aid us in our clinical assessment and intervention approaches? In this section, I would like to suggest that they do not, since what they are modeling is a summary of information gleaned from many studies in the psycholinguistic literature. Rather, clinical models will need to be of the language and thought which particular children bring to bear on their performance on particular tasks, in order for us to make specific use of them.

I have come to this for several reasons. First, I submit that the generalized box models as guides to our assessment methodology are susceptible to the same criticism which I presented in the foregoing sections. Cromer (1981) and Wiig and Semel (1976) have suggested that we use the combined box models to guide our assessment of language disordered children. They proceed by having us examine the child's ability within each of the areas depicted by the different boxes. This clinical approach overlooks the conspiracies problem, and it fails to separate processes involved, comprehension, and production. Finally, it denies the importance of depicting processing as parallel and topdown, by virtue of concentration on the bottom-up and serial organization.

There have been some recent attempts to argue for the clinical separability of different aspects of language knowledge and processing. For example, Curtiss, Franklin and Yamada et al. (1978) have reported on the unfortunate and fascinating child, Genie, who was confined and isolated in a single room for most of her first 13 years. She had problems with syntax, but not as much with semantics or language production. They also report that a second child whom they studied, child A., had a reverse pattern of high skill in syntactic and morphological structures and low in semantics. Results from Curtiss et al. (1978) lead to their advocating a separation between semantics and the grammatical knowledge involved in syntax and morphology. Blank et al. (1979) have reported on a child whose grammar was at age level, but whose language was inappropriate for the situation. Blank et al. (1979) use these results to argue for a level model which separates pragmatics from semantics and the grammatical knowledge involved in syntax and morphology. If we examine these authors' reports of the three children more carefully, with an eye toward conspiracies across levels rather than their separation, we can better evaluate their separatist conclusions.

Genie and the child referred to as A. were administered a series of tests designed to measure age equivalency for semantics and syntax, and for various types of memory and cognitive skills. The experimental procedure was to compare the children's performance with normal children on the different measures and the results of the comparisons were that the two children departed in different ways from the norms. Genie was better on semantics than syntax; A. was better on syntax than semantics.

Unfortunately, the authors did not describe their semantic measures, so I am unable to evaluate what they take to be semantics apart from syntax. They seem to be assuming that syntax has to do with word order, clause order, embedding, and that semantics is lexical and rational meaning interpreted through the syntax structure. Of course, this puts us in the middle of the prolific debate among generative semanticists such as McCawley (1968) and interpretive transformationalists such as Chomsky (1972). Does semantics derive from syntax as argued by Chomsky or does syntax interpret deeper meaning, as is held by Chomsky's adversaries? Whatever your conclusion, Curtiss et al. fail to address the intertwined nature of the levels and instead assume a separateness that denies the obvious complexity of the debate and the inextricable aspects of the two levels of knowledge.

Blank et al. (1979) present us with further modeling difficulties. In the case of their child, John, the issue is whether the child displays a separation of pragmatic and other linguistic knowledge. Do John's errors show pragmatic incorrectness, but semantic and syntactic sophistication as is claimed by Blank and her co-authors? I submit that John's pragmatic errors can be described as "opposite talk". If I am right, they can be seen as semantic-syntactic play fused with a social-pragmatic one. Let me explain.

John's errors look as if he has assigned himself the role of being in opposition to the ongoing event and the people in it. Rather than complying with what is expected, he takes as his goal not to do what is asked. Below are examples stated by Blank, which are expressions of his oppositions to the information in the preceding proposition:

1. When asked to imitate "I want the green one," John said:
   "I want the yellow one"
   and, "I want the green candy"
   and, "I don't want the green one"
2. In response to "Let's go to Pat's new house" he answered:
   "Pat's old house"

His oppositions were also expressed by offering a counter to the information presupposed in the preceding utterance, and to the understanding of the situation. If the adult talked about what was in the book, John replied about what was on the cover; when the adult referred to someone being home, John assumed she wasn't. Examples of the oppositions to presupposed information were:

3. Father (referring to a stroller in a book): "Who's in there?"
   John: "Read it again."
4. Father: "O.K. What do you want to read?"
   John (turning over the book and pointing to the cover):

"What's that?"

5. John (in the middle of a game): "That's the end."

My reinterpretation of Blank et al. argues against their separation of levels. For the "opposite talk" explanation, one needs to integrate the pragmatic, semantic, and syntactic levels and place them as co-conspirators in achieving the goal of making oppositions. John's oppositons are against the situational and logical presuppositions, the semantic content of the preceding propositions, and are expressed using different syntactic forms. This interpretation contains a synergistic, functional sensibility, not an additive multistory one.

The above discussions of Genie, A., and John suggest that we will need to devise separate models to explain the competencies and incompetencies of different children. However, even this degree of individualization is likely to be insufficient. The pragmatic literature makes it apparent that we must acknowledge the fact that children will use knowledge differently in different situations. Since one cannot predict particular performances on a task by looking at a general model of a child's performance, we will need different models for competencies involved in different tasks. So, not only will models be different for the different children, but the rules, the strategies, and the knowledge which a particular child uses will be different in different situations.

Let me illustrate these various knowledge and process relationships by describing an autistic child I have been studying over the last five years. (Duchan, 1980a, 1981; Duchan, Silverman, and Evans, 1978). Robbie, now 13 years old, is a severely retarded autistic child whose language and cognitive processing are unlike normal children. A model with labeled boxes which is developed from studies of normal adults and children does not capture either his language knowledge or processing, or his sense of the world.

For example, in typical psycholinguistic models, there is one phonological representation unless the modeler is representing style or dialect of speakers. In Strait's (1980) model, there are two phonological systems, one for comprehension and one for production. Silverman, Evans and I (Duchan, et al. 1978) studied Robbie's phonological system and found there were four involved in his production. These were not reflective of cultural style or dialect, but rather, depended upon the speech event in which Robbie was engaged.

Robbie also differs from normal speakers in his use of intonation. Whereas intonation usually works as an interpretive system which reflects various levels of linguistic knowledge, Robbie's was not interpretive. For him intonation was tied more closely to semantics or pragmatics than is ordinarily the case. An example of what I mean is that his response to his teachers's correction of an answer was to offer the same answer but change the intonation contour. It was as if he felt the correct answer lay in presenting the correct intonation contour.

What cued us to Robbie's unusual sense of intonation was its invariant quality. The same stereotyped melody recurred as in a song, lacking the normal flexibility allowable for intonation contours. This exactitude of intonation has been reported by others who have studied autistic children. For example, Park (1967) has vividly depicted her autistic daughter's use of what she calls leitmotifs. Park's description follows:

We became aware that this strange child who could not take in the simplest work could absorb a tune and make it do duty for an idea. Tunes became words for Elly. "Ring around a rosy" was the first. She was three and three quarters that spring, and she had been playing the game for many months. Now her new musical alertness picked up the tune. As soon as it did, she extended it spontaneously to a picture of children in a ring, then to a garland of flowers, and finally to the unadorned figure of a circle. The song—shortened to its first few notes—for more than a year remained her word for "circle"and the cluster of ideas around it, functioning far more reliably than any of her actual words (pp. 83-4).

Robbie's leitmotifs were several, and when I first met him they comprised the only examples of multiple morpheme utterances. He sometimes initiated the phrase "I want X." He also responded with "This is an X" to the question "What is this?" and with "You play with an X" in response to "What do you do with this?". These leitmotifs had lexical inserts for X, and those Xs were more carefully articulated than the rest of the phrase. They were also recipients of either primary or secondary stress.

I suspect that for Robbie these leitmotifs have no syntax. Although he could say the phrase, "This is a X," or "We play with a X" according to a script, his sense of what was important was the melody, with a secondary emphasis on segmental phonology and a nonemphasis on phrase structure.

Besides emphasizing intonation, Robbie paid attention to the turn-taking rituals involved in the leitmotif. His teacher's modus operandi with him was to tell him an answer or part of one and then ask him for that answer. The repeated sequence was of the form (1) teacher tells answer; (2) teacher asks for the answer; (3) Robbie repeats what the teacher said in (1). Robbie understood what was expected of him. He could respond in the format offered him by echoing the utterance before the question which was put to him. An example where he responded correctly was:

    Teacher:    This is a book
    Teacher:    What is this?
    Robbie:     This is a book

But there were instances where Robbie was wrong. He eloquently showed us his reliance on the turn-taking format of the routine rather than its meaning in the following sequence:

    Teacher:    Wipe our mouth
                and our hand
                when we eat

    Teacher:    What do we do with
                a napkin, Rob?

    Robbie:     When we eat

Even today, although his language is more versatile, Robbie still will initiate a request on occasion by offering something to himself in the form of a verbal "Do you want X?" and accept his own offer by taking what he wants and answering

"Yes." Robbie carries out both portions of the ritualized exchange. This suggests to me that a basic unit for Robbie is what Sacks, Schegloff, and Jefferson (1974) have called an adjacency pair, and that different paired sequences are functionally motivated. They are either ways to get things or to answer someone.

If I were to build a lexicon underlying Robbie's leitmofifs, it would contain these adjacency pairs as basic units. I would mark each phonologically and intonationally, but not syntactically. The semantics would be elaborated for the morphemes which fill the X slots, and could be separated from the routines themselves. The routine packages are able to carry out only one of two functions: either requesting or answering someone.

Finally, it is hard to determine how his knowledge of routines differs from his comprehension and production, since he could take either turn in the routine sequence. Unfortunately, except for his initiated routines which serve to request what he wants, there is very little structure involved in either and therefore a high degree of similarity between the two. Strait's convincing arguments for ordinary speakers do not apply to Robbie's system.

One last comment on Robbie's language processing is that language is not a primary system for him. If we can believe his actions, he would prefer to spend his time with other things. For example, he can spend hours picking lint from objects around him and watching the pieces float to the floor, through the air currents which he sets up with his deft fingers. These self-stimulatory behaviors always seems to be competing for language processing space, so that one gets the impression that not only does Robbie have a very different sense of what language is about, but also that he has a hard time even keeping his mind on that aspect of his world.

What I am suggesting then, as a model for Robbie's adjacency pairs is a base structure consisting of language functions and speech events and a limited or perhaps memorized set of surface structures which are inextricably associated with those particular context bound routines. His four phonologies, his stereotyped intonation patterns, are surface manifestations of his two-level language processing system. All of this goes on in a context which relegates it to a secondary status, secondary to his interest in self-stimulatory activities, eating, etc.

Thus we find once again that attempts to use rectilinear models which separate knowledge may be clinically inappropriate. Children like Robbie with language problems need to be evaluated on their own terms. Otherwise we may find ourselves imposing our level categories on the child's performance and arriving at an artificial separation, such as the one which sees the child's use of semantics separate from syntax (Curtiss et al., 1978) or pragmatics separate from semantics (Blank et al., 1979).

# Conclusion

I have argued in this paper that rectilinear buildings and geodesic domes are not proper depictions of language knowledge processing in normal as well as abnormal people. To what architectural metaphor might we turn as a better representation? Perhaps we can find it in Frank Lloyd Wright prairie homes; those split level structures with different entries leading to different levels, or with open expanses that have no levels, and with entries offering top down passages to lower levels. The choice of entry can be motivated by different needs or intents, and the listener or speaker will actively select passages to lead to those intended destinations. Wright's homes offer a proper metaphor for conspiracies, as well as processing flexibility, in that he designs structures to fit contours which are offered by the contextual surrounds. Indeed, he even suggests, as I have, that the edifice should be different depending upon the idiosyncracies of the contours to which it is designed to fit.

Whether or not you like my particular architectural solution, I offer the metaphoric properties as a way to guide us in understanding what language-impaired children know about their language and their world, and how they use that knowledge to process their language.

# References

Atkinson, R., & Shriffrin, R. Human memory: A proposed system and its control processes. In K. Spence and J. Spence (Eds.), *The psychology of learning and motivation* (Vol. 2). New York: Academic Press, 1968.

Bates, E., & MacWhinney, B. A functionalist approach to the acquisition of grammar. In E. Ochs and B. Schieffelin (Eds.), *Developmental pragmatics.* New York: Academic Press, 1979.

Blank, M., Gessner, M., & Esposito, A. Language without communication: A case study. *Journal of Child Language, 1979, 6,* 329-352.

Butler, K. Language processing disorder: Factors in diagnosis and remediation. In R. Keith (Ed.), *Central auditory and language disorders in children.* San Diego: College Hill Press, 1981.

Chomsky, N. *Studies on semantics in generative grammer.* Paris: Mouton, 1972.

Craik, F., & Lockhart, R. Levels of processing: A framework for memory research. *Journal of Verbal Learning and Verbal Behavior, 1972, 11,* 671-684.

Cromer, R. Reconceptualizing language acquisition and cognitive development. In R. Schiefelbusch and D. Bricker (Eds.), *Early language: Acquisition and intervention.* Baltimore: University Park Press, 1981, 51-138.

Curtiss, S., Franklin, V., & Yamada, J. The independance of language as a cognitive system. Paper presented at the First International Congress of Child Language. Tokyo, August 1978.

Duchan, J. Elephants are soft and mushy: Problems in assessing children's language. In N. Lass, L. McReynolds, J. Northern, and D. Yoder (Eds.), *Speech language and hearing*. Philadelphia: W. B. Saunders, 1982, 741-760.

Duchan, J. Interactions with an autistic child. In H. Giles, W. Robinson, and P. Smith (Eds.), *Language: Social psychological perspectives*. New York: Pergamon Press, 1980a.

Duchan, J. Temporal aspects of self-stimulating behaviors in abnormal speakers. In M. Davis (Ed.) *Interaction rhythms*. New York: Harkavy, 1981.

Duchan, J. The effect of cognitive bias on children's early interpretation of locative commands. *Language Science,* 1980b, *2,* 246-259.

Duchan, J., & Katz, J. Top down plus bottom up: Exposing the whole truth about children's language and learning difficulties. In E. Lasky and J. Katz (Eds.), *Auditory processing and language*. New York: Grune and Stratton, 1982.

Duchan, J., & Oliva, J. Using intonation to determine psycholinguistic structuring of a child's early multisyllable utterances. *Language Sciences,* 1979, *1,* 26-34.

Duchan, J., Olivia, J., & Lindner, R. Performative acts defined by synchrony among intonation, verbal, and nonverbal systems in a one and a half year old child. *Sign Language Studies,* 1979, *22,* 75-88.

Duchan, J., & Siegel, L. Incorrect responses to locative commands: A case study. *Language Speech and Hearing Services in the Schools,* 1979, *10,* 99-103.

Duchan, J., Silverman, C., & Evans, K. Four phonological systems in the speech of an autistic child. Paper presented at New York Speech and Hearing Association Convention, 1978.

Fodor, J., Bever, T., & Garrett, M. *The psychology of language*. New York: McGraw-Hill, 1974.

Greenfield, P. and Dent, Syntax *vs* pragmatics: A psychological account of coordinate structures in child language. *Papers and Reports on Child Language Development,* 1979, *19,* 65-72.

Levinson, P., & Sloan, C. (Eds.), *Auditory processing and language.* New York: Grune and Stratton, 1980.

Lund, N., & Duchan, J. *Assessing children's language in naturalistic contexts.* Englewood Cliffs, New Jersey: Prentice-Hall, in press.

Marlsen-Wilson, W. Sentence perception as an interactive parallel process. *Science,* 1975, *189,* 189-191.

McCawley, J. The role of semantics in grammar. In E. Bach and T. Harms (Eds.), *Universals in linguistic theory.* New York: Holt, Rinehart and Winston, 1968, 91-122.

Norman, D. *Memory and attention: An introduction to human processing.* New York: Wiley and Sons, 1976.

Oliva, J., & Duchan, J. Structural regularities in the intonation of an abnormal speaker: Psycholinguistic implications. In P. Reich (Ed.), *The second lacus forum.* Columbia, SC: Hornbeam Press, 1976, 120-128.

Palermo, D. *Psychology of language.* Glenview, IL. Scott Foresman, 1978.

Park, C. C. *The siege.* Boston: Little, Brown and Co., 1967.

Pike, K. *The intonation of American English.* Ann Arbor: University of Michigan, 1945.

Prizant, B., & Duchan, J. The functions of immediate echolalia in autistic children. *Journal of Speech and Hearing Disorders,* 1981.

Prutting, C. Process /pra/ses/n: The action of moving forward progressively from one point to another on the way to completion. *Journal of Speech and Hearing Disorders,* 1979, *44,* 3-30.

Prutting, C., & Elliott, J. Synergy: Toward a model of language. In N. Lass (Ed.), *Speech and language: Advances in basic research and practice.* (Vol. 1). New York: Academic Press, 1979.

Rees, N.S. Saying more than we know: Is auditory processing disorder a meaningful concept? In R. W. Keith (Ed.), *Central auditory and language disorders in children.* San Diego: College-Hill Press, 1981, 94-120.

Rees, N. Pragmatics of language. In R. Schiefelbusch (Ed.), *Bases of language intervention*. Baltimore: University Park Press, 1978.

Rees, N.S. Auditory processing factors in language disorders: The view from Procrustes' bed. *Journal of Speech and Hearing Disorders,* 1973, *38,* 304-15.

Sag, I., & Liberman, M. An intonational disambiguation of indirect speech acts. *Chicago Linguistics Society,* 11, 1975.

Sanders, D. *Auditory perception of speech.* Englewood Cliffs, NJ: Prentice-Hall, 1977.

Strait, S. Auditory *vs* articulatory phonological processes and their development in children. In G. Yeni-Komshian, J. Kavanagh, and C. Ferguson (Eds.), *Child phonology* (Vol. 1). New York: Academic Press, 1980, 43-68.

Studdert-Kennedy, M. Speech perception. In N. Lass (Ed.), *Contemporary issues in experimental phonetics.* New York: Academic Press, 1976.

Sacks, H., Shegloff, E., & Jefferson, G. A simplest systematics for the organization of turn-taking in conversation. *Language,* 1974, *50,* 696-735.

Wiig, E., & Semel, E. *Language disabilities in children and adolescents.* Columbus, OH: Charles Merrill, 1976.

# 5

# APPLICATIONS OF PRAGMATIC LANGUAGE MODELS FOR INTERVENTION

*Holly K. Craig*
*The University of Michigan*

## Introduction

O nce the presence of a language problem has been documented, the clinical processes of assessment and intervention can be conceptualized as a recycling series of interlocking steps between goal-setting and goal-attainment. Goal-setting depends upon careful description of the child's present speech and language behaviors while goal-attainment relates to the selection of appropriate remedial procedures. This perspective contrasts sharply with more traditional viewpoints that have dichotomized these clinical processes into separate diagnostic-identification and treatment-management functions. Since the 1960's, however, speech-language pathologists have relied less on these traditonal medical service models and increasingly have viewed assessment and intervention as integrally related and psycholinguistically based (Launer & Lahey, 1981; Muma, 1978).

During the late 1970's and early 1980's, the study of normal and disordered child language has been undergoing a theoretical shift toward pragmatic models of child language acquisition. Although this new perspective has had tremendous impact upon our descriptions of child language, the clinical impact of this new paradigm remains largely unexplored. In particular, the current literature suggests that pragmatics will influence intervention goal-setting in major ways, but the implications of the theory change for selecting the remedial procedures that underlie goal-attainment are not as readily discernible.

## Implications of Pragmatic Theory for Intervention

Pragmatic theory implies changes in both the goal-statement and procedural selection aspects of intervention. A more narrow interpretation of pragmatic theory would circumscribe its effects. In this more limited sense, pragmatics might be conceptualized simply as another set of language skills (for example, turn-taking, clarification, etc.) that the child acquires during development. Pragmatic rules might be viewed, therefore, as separate from syntactic and semantic rules, as though children acquire structural knowledge and then learn how to use this knowledge in societally accepted ways. On the surface, this interpretation appears consistent with Morris' (1946) division of language into syntactics (the relations among signs), semantics (the relations among signs and referents) and pragmatics (the relations among signs and their users). Alternatively, however, this tripartite division can be viewed as an analytical convenience rather than a theoretical statement. As MacNamara (1972) states:

"Meaning and the linguistic code are best treated as though they were elements of a compound, much in the way that oxygen and hydrogen are the separate elements which combine to form molecules of water. That is, the two are not usually experienced separately, though they are distinguishable" (page 3).

and, as Bates (1976) notes, within child language:

"At first, it seemed that pragmatic information was ancillary to the rest of semantics, something that could be added on or studied separately. It is now far less clear that this is the case...it does not define a separate kind of linguistic structure or 'object.' Rather, all of language is pragmatic to begin with " (page 420).

This issue is not a minor one for our field. Our assumptions about the relationship among syntax, semantics, and pragmatics will determine the pervasiveness of our theoretical applications. If we assume that structural and conversational taxonomies represent separate rule systems and that their relationship consequently is additive, then our definitions of language will be extended but our procedures largely unaffected. In other words, a restricted interpretation of pragmatics might suggest ways to specify goal-statements better and perhaps carryover variables for intervention, but would essentially place little demand for change on our present procedures. Indeed, a few programs have already been developed for the mentally retarded that have added "use" as a level of formulation within goal statements but still maintain operant conditioning as the procedural framework for intervention (Guess, Sailor, and Baer, 1978; Waryas and Stremel-Campbell, 1978).

Limiting pragmatic applications to definitional issues is inconsistent with the proposals formulated by the major theorists and ignores much of the clinical promise of pragmatics. Interpreted more expansively and perhaps more validly, pragmatics addresses issues central to both language definitions and developmental processes. Fundamentally, language is viewed as an integration rather than an addition of structural and conversational knowledge (Searle, 1969). This broader interpretation does not imply that pragmatics is merely another language taxonomy but proposes a radically different overview of language. Proponents of this broader perspective argue that communication functions are the principal motivation for language growth (Halliday, 1975; MacNamara, 1972; Miller, 1970; Corsaro, 1981). The communicative purposes provide the basic framework for language acquisition and the verbal code develops to mark these functions in socially negotiable ways (Bates, 1976; Bruner, 1975; Dore, 1975; Gallagher, 1977; Stern, Jaffe, Beebe, & Bennett, 1975). In this sense, conversational and structural development are distinguishable but functionally inseparable, and pragmatics is the new theoretical overview. Ervin-Tripp and Mitchell-Kernan (1977) describe the critical dependence of the one on the other during development, as follows:

"The child's language faculty is engaged only when the child needs to communicate. Language could not be learned if children did not, at the beginning, construe meanings from context. In this view, natural language learning has as a basic and necessary feature the dependence of the learner on communication " (page 6).

The present paper will begin to address these issues as they relate to intervention planning for children identified as "Specifically Language Impaired" (Stark & Tallal, 1981). Both goal-setting and goal-attainment will be examined by posing the following questions.

1) How have the goal-setting aspects of intervention program planning accommodated past changes in theory?
2) Have past changes in theory influenced procedures?
3) Are there comparable procedural accommodations suggested by the present pragmatic paradigm?

## The Impact of Theory Changes on Goal-Setting

Our definition of language determines what behaviors are considered critical for assessment and ultimately what behaviors constitute goals for intervention. Definitions of language are theoretically based. Therefore, theories that emphasize descriptions of language per se potentially have more impact upon intervention goal statements, while theories that emphasize the process of acquiring the described behavior have more potential impact upon intervention procedures. The following major theories have contributed to intervention goal-setting: behaviorism, generative syntax and semantics, and pragmatics.

*Behaviorism,* prominent in the 1950's, was a psychological theory that emphasized less the content of language learning and more the process by which that content is acquired. Definitions of language were not the primary concern; language was considered to be behavior like any other behavior. The major assumptions of the general psychological theory proposed by Skinner (1954; 1968) were applicable, therefore, to the study of children's language. These assumptions include: (1) all behavior, including language, can be observed, described, and characterized in peripheral terms without involving the mind or central behavior; (2) complex behaviors are the sum of a set of simple behaviors;

and (3) learning is the relationship between time and response strength (Holland, 1960; Holland & Skinner, 1961; Skinner, 1954; 1968). Translation of the theory's basic principles into a view of child language resulted in a concern for the quantification of language behaviors, such as vocabulary size or number of correct articulations in children's speech, as a function of age (McCarthy, 1954; Templin, 1957).

Language problems were assumed to be the result of incorrect relationships between the child and the environment and were best assessed in terms of quantitative differences from the normal child (for example: Darley & Moll, 1960; Dunn, 1959; Johnson, Darley & Spriestersbach, 1952). Intervention goals, developed primarily for mentally retarded individuals, attempted to increase the frequency of occurrence of vocabulary items and specific parts of speech (for example: Bricker & Bricker, 1970; Kent, 1972; Lovaas, Berberich, Perloff, & Schaeffer, 1966).

Both the general theory and the behavioral view of language were criticized in the late 1950's. Behavioral perspectives on child language accordingly were deemphasized in favor of generative syntactic theories of language acquisition.

*Generative syntactic theories,* prominent during the 1960's, were linguistic theories that attempted to formalize language as grammars (Braine, 1963; Brown & Fraser, 1964; Chomsky, 1957; Chomsky & Miller, 1963; Lenneberg, 1967; McNeill, 1966; Menyuk, 1964; Miller & Ervin, 1964). Grammars were conceptualized as abstract rule systems representing an idealization that did not necessarily match linguistic performance within the context of natural communicative interaction. Unlike behaviorism, that attempted to describe language as the acquisition of behaviors, generative theories attempted to describe language as linguistic products and, therefore, were critially concerned with definitions of language.

Chomsky's (1957; 1965) influential theory of transformational grammar proposed that sentences are generated from abstract syntactic deep structures that contain formal constituents arranged hierarchically, like subject and object noun phrases. Transformational rules, operations that rearrange or delete deep structure constituents, change deep structures into surface structures, the lexical strings that comprise a sentence.

Child language research during the 1960's and the early 1970's reflected the theoretical prominence afforded syntax within the theory of transformational grammar. Researchers focused on characterizing the normal child's linguistic competence by describing the development of specific syntactic constituents, like the noun phrase (Brown & Bellugi, 1964) the development of transformations, like negation (Brown, 1968; Brown & Bellugi, 1964; Brown, Cazden & Bellugi-Klima, 1969; Klima & Bellugi-Klima, 1966) and by writing comprehensive child grammars (Braine, 1963; Brown, 1973; Miller and Ervin, 1964). Similarly, research in child language disorders attempted to chacterize the syntactic differences between the sentences produced by the specifically language impaired and the normal child (for example: Johnston & Schery, 1976; Lee, 1966; Leonard, 1972; Menyuk, 1964; Menyuk & Looney, 1972a; 1972b; Morehead & Ingram, 1973).

The paradigm shift from behaviorism to the generative theories had real consequences for intervention program planning. Since the generative theories highlighted definitions of language, they had considerable impact on goal-setting. Behavioral theories, less concerned with these definitional issues, were readily replaced as the major source of information for goal statements. Intervention goals no longer focused primarily on memorization of prototypical sentences— goals consistent with the behavioral views of language, but rather focused primarily upon increasing sentence lengths by teaching morphological and transformational rules — goals consistent with the generative syntactic theories (for example: Fygetakis & Gray, 1970; Gray & Fygetakis, 1968; Gray & Ryan, 1973; Hegde, 1980; Lee, Koenigsknecht, & Mulhern, 1975; Mulac & Tomlinson, 1977; Zwitman & Sonderman, 1979).

The early 1970's marked increasing dissatisfaction with a purely syntactic conceptualization of linguistic competence. Accordingly, generative theories were refocused to consider the child's knowledge of sentence meanings.

*Generative semantic theories,* prominent since the early 1970's, propose that an understanding of the relationship between language and cognition is critical to a description of linguistic competence. For example, many early emerging language categories appear to be semantic and to depend upon the acquisition of basic cognitive abilities (Bates, 1976; Nelson, 1974; Sinclair-de-Zwart, 1973; Slobin, 1973). Moreover, in order to explain the child's development of syntax, reference to the meanings underlying early utterances seems to be necessary (Bloom, 1970; Bowerman, 1973; Brown, 1973; Schlesinger, 1974; Slobin, 1973). Some researchers, therefore, have focused upon describing the emergence of early meaning relations in normal children's sentences (Antinucci and Parisi, 1973; Bloom, 1970; Bowerman, 1973; Brown, 1973; Greenfield and Smith, 1976).

Studies of child language disorders similarly questioned the nature of the specifically language impaired child's semantic knowledge (such as, Freedman & Carpenter, 1976; Leonard, Bolders, & Miller, 1976). With the modification of generative theories to highlight semantic rather than syntactic knowledge, intervention programs also reflected these shifts by assessing the child's semantic knowledge and by setting goal sequences that prioritized the child's acquisition of meanings (for example: Lahey & Bloom, 1977; MacDonald & Blott, 1974).

Researchers of the 1970's found that a characterization of semantic competence requires extensive reference to the verbal and nonverbal context associated with the language event. While some researchers have retained their primarily semantic orientation and viewed these contexts in which sentences are used essentially as interpretive support for sentence meanings, others have prioritized this contextual information. This latter view has become known as pragmatics.

*Pragmatics* has been interpreted in two distinct ways within the child language literature. The more popular view is a restricted interpretation of the theory. This interpretation narrowly defines pragmatics in terms of an additional set of language rules that the child acquires for using language structure in different conversational contexts. Descriptions of the range of communicative intentions coded by early utterances (Dore, 1975; Garvey, 1975; Greenfield & Smith, 1976;

Halliday, 1975) and of the normal child's sensitivity to major listener characteristics like age, sex, and status differences (Connor & Serbin, 1977; Maccoby & Jacklin, 1974; Shatz & Gelman, 1973) are notable examples of these lines of research.

Only a few studies have been published to date on these issues as they apply to child language disorders and their findings seem mixed. Although the ability of the specifically language impaired child to use language to communicate various intentions appears significantly deficient in comparison to that of the child with normally developing language (Brinton & Fujiki, 1982; Prinz, 1982; Shatz, Bernstein, & Shulman, 1980; Snyder, 1978), the specifically language impaired child does seem sensitive to the need to talk differently to different types of listeners (Fey, Leonard, & Wilcox, 1981).

If this more restricted interpretation of pragmatics is valid, then the impact of these perspectives on intervention will be circumscribed. A restricted interpretation would add one more level, use, to the present semantic and syntactic formulations of goal statements but would imply few other changes. Consistent with this restricted interpretation of pragmatic theory, recommendations for assessment presently include taxonomies for describing the child's use of language and for including use as a further specification of intervention goal statements (Blank & Franklin, 1980; Bloom and Lahey, 1978; Launer & Lahey, 1981; Miller, 1978).

In contrast to this restricted interpretation of pragmatics, a second, more expansive, interpretation is also possible. Description of the ways in which normally developing children link consecutive utterances within discourse to maintain coherency and to clarify messages (Bloom, Lightbown, & Hood, 1978; Bloom, Rocissano, & Hood, 1976; Gallagher, 1977; 1981; Garvey, 1977; Keenan, 1974; Keenan & Klein, 1975) seems to be a line of research that more clearly considers the integrated nature of structural and conversational rules. Again, research applying these analyses to the study of child language disorders has been limited (Gallagher & Darnton, 1978; VanKleek & Frankel, 1981). While additional data confirming these findings remain forthcoming, these studies indicate that the specifically language impaired child has considerable difficulty integrating structural and conversational knowledge. Integrative problems of this type are suggestive of basic pragmatic deficits within this disorder group. If this more expansive interpretation of pragmatic theory is valid, then the impact of these perspectives on intervention will be pervasive.

## The Impact of Theory Changes on Procedures

Although intervention program planning has consistently derived goal statements from the prominent language theory of the era, it is not clear that the selection of remedial procedures has developed in a parallel manner. Theories that focus upon variables affecting language acquisition influence the selection of intervention procedures in major ways. Reciprocally, theoretical orientations that de-emphasize the language developmental process have fewer consequences for intervention procedures.

*Behaviorism,* with its focus upon the process of language acquisition, has had a profound and durable impact upon intervention procedures. Behaviorism conceives of the child learning language as relatively passive. Within the behavioral view of language acquisition, the child's individual capacities are overlooked while the environmental manipulation of antecedent and consequent events is underscored. Speaking and listening presumably reflect habit patterns and learning, a time and response strength relationship. Language is viewed as an operant, a response controlled by subsequent events, which can be programmed for intervention in terms of stimulus events, imitative responses, progressive approximations, stimulus fading, type and schedule of reinforcement, and generalization of responses across situations. Extensive description of the principles underlying *operant conditioning,* the procedural orientation associated with behaviorism, is available in the literature (Brookshire, 1967; Costello, 1977; Deterline, 1962; Holland, 1960; Holland & Matthews, 1963; Holland & Skinner, 1961; Johnston & Harris, 1968; Risley, Hart, & Doke, 1972; Skinner, 1954; 1957; 1968; Sloan, Johnston, & Harris, 1968; Sloan & MacAulay, 1968).

Based upon these behavioral assumptions and principles, many intervention programs reflect highly elaborate procedural technologies and are remarkably similar across levels of language goals and types of language problems. Since behaviorism discounts individual differences, the same operant technologies theoretically can be applied to dissimilar client populations. Consequently, a wealth of language teaching programs based upon operant conditioning have been developed for children whose language problems are associated with quite diverse etiologies, for example, children with specific language impairments (Fygetakis & Gray, 1970; Gray & Fygetakis, 1968; Gray & Ryan, 1973), retarded, and autistic children (Bricker & Bricker, 1974; Guess, Sailor, & Baer, 1974; Kent, 1974). Operant conditioning is a particularly prevalent procedural framework for programs designed to teach language to the mentally retarded, however, a discussion of these many programs is beyond the scope of the present paper.

A pattern common to these many programs is one of theoretical mismatch between goals and procedures. Over time a few intervention programs have specifically updated their goal statements while still relying upon operant conditioning as the procedural framework. A notable example is the Miller and Yoder program developed for mentally retarded individuals. They modified the original sequence of syntactic goals (Miller & Yoder, 1972) to one that prioritized semantic functions as the basis for goal statements (Miller & Yoder, 1974) but maintained operant conditioning throughout.

It is not clear whether theoretical changes suggest similar implications for intervention programs designed for mentally retarded and for other types of language disorders. The basic cognitive deficits of the mentally retarded child may place additional constraints on intervention planning beyond those considered for the child with a specific language impairment. Recently, Friedman & Friedman (1980) compared the individual performances of expressively language delayed children and found that a less structured procedural approach (Interactive Language Development Teaching; Lee, Koenigsknecht, & Mulhern, 1975) optimized syntactic language gains for children with relatively high pre-training scores on measures of intelligence, syntax, and visual-motor integration while a more structured programmed approach (syntactic goals and operant procedures) optimized syntax gains for low-scoring children. Perhaps operant conditioning combined with structural and conversational goals remains the most tenable procedural framework available for low functioning broadly impaired individuals such as the mentally retarded.

In general, the persistent manner in which intervention programs have reflected goals based upon linguistic and psycholinguistic information but procedures based upon operant conditioning can be traced, at least in part, to the fundamentally different purposes that motivated formulation of the original theories. Since behaviorism, as a psychological theory, emphasized *how* children learn language, the theoretical purposes were consistent with the procedural selection requirements of intervention. Not surprisingly, the resulting technology has had considerable impact upon choices for intervention procedures. In contrast to generative orientations, operant conditioning provides the clinician with step-by-step procedural sequences for intervention lesson planning.

Since generative syntactic theories emphasized *what* constituted language, these descriptions predictably had less impact upon the selection of remedial procedures. In particular, the nativist theories of the generative syntactic era (Lenneberg, 1967; McNeill, 1966) proposed that the ability to acquire language seems biologically determined and that children appear innately endowed with both knowledge of certain linguistic structures and cognitive processing abilities that relate specifically to language. Unfortunately, this perspective has little procedurally to offer the clinician faced with a child who, by definition, has failed to demonstrate this natural capacity to acquire language. Many intervention programs of the generative syntactic era, therefore, continued to reflect procedural selections derived from the past theoretical paradigm of behaviorism.

Although the linguistic innateness position of the nativist theories was tempered with the movement away from generative syntactic theories toward semantic descriptions of linguistic competence, again the procedural applications of these perspectives remain limited. *Mentalism,* the procedural orientation associated with generative semantics, proposes that the cognitive processing abilities possessed by children serve a primary role in language development (Bloom, 1970; Brown, 1973; Slobin, 1973) rather than the secondary role suggested by the nativists. Accordingly, children learn language as a result of cognition. This viewpoint is psycholinguistic in nature, rather than purely linguistic. It emphasizes the individual capacities of the child and conceives of the child as an active learner who creates a language system out of information gained by acting upon the environment. The translation of this orientation into intervention program planning deemphasizes the role of the clinician as an active participant in the language acquisition process. Within a mentalistic orientation, clinicians are viewed as facilitators of language growth rather than as teachers of language (Bloom & Lahey, 1978; Muma, 1978). Bloom & Lahey (1978) propose that the clinician's task as a facilitator is circumscribed, affecting only two dimensions of intervention, as follows: 1) The clinician can reduce any factors that seem to be maintaining the child's problem; and 2) the clinician can manipulate relevant language experiences to facilitate the child's induction of structural and conversational rules. Unfortunately, therefore, mentalism provides little specific direction to the clinician, and, as noted by Muma (1978), has not been widely accepted as the procedural basis of language intervention for children with specific language impairments.

Instead, most intervention programs continue to combine goals and procedures across paradigms. Staats (1974), from his orientation as a behaviorist, has proposed that this "rapprochement" is advantageous. Recognizing the difficulties inherent in trying to blend contrasting theoretical assumptions, however, Staats suggests that only a neutral form of rapprochement may be possible and primarily in the area of clinical applications. Muma (1975a) questions the feasibility of this rapprochement, basing his arguments upon irreconcilable philosophical differences. Furthermore, he underscores the cognitivist arguments against maintaining operant conditioning as a procedural framework for intervention and argues that natural contexts may be most revealing of potential intervention strategies while stimulus-response routines may distort critical relationships.

Overall, the implications of this debate deserve more attention. Intervention cannot continue to combine goals and procedures across paradigms. A theoretical mismatch between goals and procedures is problematic since goal-setting and goal-attainment are interlocking systems. Within a theoretical mismatch of this type, intervention lessons are internally inconsistent. The clinician must cope with this inconsistency by uncomfortably vascillating back and forth between paradigms. The clinician might alternate for example, between initial imitative vocabulary practice, to spontaneous play, to imitative sentence elicitations, to spontaneous play, all within a lesson focusing upon wh-question transformations. Since, unfortunately, neither mentalism nor behaviorism alone satisfies both the goal-setting and procedural selection requirements for intervention, and "rapprochement" is theoretically inconsistent, then new approaches to intervention need to be considered.

In summary, the paradigm shift from behaviorism to generative syntactic and subsequently generative semantic perspectives has had more impact upon the description of potential goals for intervention than upon the designation of appropriate remedial procedures. Behaviorism focused upon the relationship between the environment and the child. The resulting technology, formalized as operant conditioning, has had pervasive and continuous impact upon the selection of procedures for goal-attainment. Although goal statements have incorporated new linguistic and psycholinguistic information about the child's developing language system, intervention procedures have changed little beyond refining these operant techniques since the 1950's.

Mentalism represents an alternative procedural framework to operant conditioning. It is an example of the type of theoretical perspective needed for planning intervention in that it addresses definitional aspects of language important for goal-setting as well as factors contributing to the process of language acquisition important for procedural selections. Despite its attractiveness conceptually, mentalism has failed to achieve widespread translation into practice. This seems due in part to the passive role assigned the clinician within this type of approach. The more expansive interpretations of pragmatics also consider language not only in a definitional sense but also in terms of acquisition and, therefore, may offer an alternative means of resolving this practical dilemma.

## Implications of Pragmatic Theory for Procedures

A restricted interpretation of pragmatics implies few procedural consequences for intervention planning beyond perhaps modifying constructs established as part of operant conditioning or mentalistic approaches to language intervention. Other authors have expressed this concern as a need to up-date procedural constructs such as stimulus, reinforcement, and responding behaviors into more conversational forms (DeJoy, Rooney, & DeFeo, 1979; Longhurst & Reichle, 1975; Miller, 1978; Muma, 1975-b; 1978; Rees, 1978; Seibert & Oller, 1981).

A more expansive interpretation of pragmatics suggests fundamentally different approaches to the planning of intervention procedures. Pragmatic implications would not be circumscribed to influence only the goal-setting aspects of intervention but would also affect procedures. Communicative goals and effects would be preserved and considered the first, pervasive, and most basic step in intervention planning and not some final set of generalization skills. To be pragmatic, intervention must set goals more comprehensively, considering both the conversational nature and the structural representation of interactive sequences. Furthermore, since language is no longer viewed as an operant nor as totally under the child's developmental control, the intervention procedures that underlie goal-attainment need to be reconceptualized to fit the broader pragmatic perspectives better and the efficacy of these new procedures needs to be established experimentally.

An important issue in reconceptualizing intervention involves the selection of an appropriate analytical framework. A strategy other than modifying past theoretical constructs seems necessary. Intervention planning itself suggests a set of fundamental decision-making parameters. Muma (1978) identifies five basic dimensions for the clinician to consider in planning intervention as a whole. Three relate most critically to goal-setting and include:

Content—the formulation of the goal statement
Pacing—the timing for introducing new goals, and
Sequencing—the ordering of the goals.

The final two, context and reinforcement, although broadly inclusive, are procedurally based and suggest that basic dimensions can also be specified for the selection of the intervention procedures that underlie goal-attainment.

Clinicians planning daily intervention sessions repeatedly address the following questions in selecting procedures: who will interact with the child, what will this person do and say, and what will the child be expected to do and say? As a starting point for exploring a reconceptualization of language intervention procedures, in the following discussion each of these aspects of procedural selection will be examined in terms of the assumptions derived as legacies from previous theoretical orientations, the potentially alternative pragmatic implications, and some directions for the future.

1. *Intervention Agents* Who are the instruments of change in the child's intervention program? Intervention programs that stress highly prescribed interactions between the intervention agent and the child seem to rely upon the clinician as the primary person involved in changing the child's communication behaviors. Since operant conditioning approaches view language learning as prescribed response behavior, the clinician typically is the primary intervention agent. Additional intervention agents are few and only assist in implementing the clinician's plan (for example, an aide or parent might administer a pre-planned program in a practice session with a child.) These secondary intervention agents are trained in operant conditioning techniques before becoming involved in the child's intervention program. Consistency across intervention agents is stressed and no attempt is made to utilize the unique features of these interactants. For example an aide and a parent naturally represent an unfamiliar adult and an adult who shares considerable information with the child, respectively.

In contrast, since mentalism downplays environmental factors and focuses upon the child's individual capacities to induce rules, interactions between the child and the intervention agent are not highly prescribed. Many intervention agents, therefore, are possible and probably desirable. The greater the number of intervention agents involved, the greater the likelihood that the child will experience the appropriately frequent and salient contexts for induction of the language rule. Various intervention agents, including parents, teachers, peers, and siblings have the potential to meet these language stimulation requirements (Muma, 1978).

The literature on normal development indicates that the child's interaction with different partners accords a central role to adults who increase the child's potential for communicative success. The normal child typically progresses from mother-child interactions, to parentally-mediated child interactions with other adults and peers, to peer interactions that represent same status alignments (Corsaro, 1981). Children may experience more communicative success initially with adults because of the adult's controlling interactive style (frequent clarification requests, tags, and directive questions), that seems to represent an adaptation to the limitations of the child's primitive communicative system (Corsaro, 1977).

In normal development, peer social skills do not seem to evolve through maturation alone, nor through immediate generalization of skills developed with adults (Mueller and Brenner, 1977). It appears that children need opportunities to participate in social interaction with peers to become competent communicators in these contexts. Fey, Leonard, & Wilcox (1981) found that the specifically language impaired child makes some but not all of the predicted structural adjustments that the normal child makes in interacting with different partners, suggesting that some language-impaired children may need special help in these areas.

Pragmatics proposes that language is contextually variable and that the child's speaker behaviors vary as a function of major characteristics of the listener. Communicative competence, therefore, implies knowledge of how to converse with different partners and raises the question of the clinician's viability as the primary intervention agent. Obviously, if the clinician represents an atypical conversational partner within the child's life, then the usefulness of the child's learning to converse with this person seems limited. Since, however, the clinician's special expertise allows the child increased experience with communicative success, the clinician must be centrally involved, particularly early in the program, to equip the child with the communicative building blocks that underlie learning to express meanings in conventional ways. Perhaps the specifically language-impaired child would benefit from intervention opportunities that progress from interaction with the clinician, who highlights the relevant variables for adult and peer interaction, to interactions with adults and peers mediated by the clinician along target dimensions, to interaction with adults and peers alone. These different conversational partners no longer serve merely as agents of carry-over but provide the child with opportunities to learn how to interact with different conversational partners. Although other intervention agents are involved, the clinician does not relinquish responsibility for managing these interactions.

Particularly at this point in the development of our field, when so much information on intervention remains forthcoming, the assumption underlying operant conditioning that the clinician is the critical intervention agent should be preserved. Since pragmatics underscores both environmental factors and the individual capacities of the child, intervention no longer reflects a single focus and seems very complex. Planning and implementing intervention sequences now more than ever depend upon the well-trained clinician's knowledge of normal and abnormal patterns and on his/her skill in observing, analyzing, and modifying interactive patterns as they unfold.

2. *Clinician Behavior* What will the clinician or other intervention agent say and do during the intervention sequence? The answer to this question depends upon the active or passive nature of the role assigned the intervention agent.

Operant conditioning assigns a critical role to the clinician. The clinician is primarily responsible for planning and presenting stimulus and reinforcement events. The clinician functions as a "teacher" and, as Muma (1978) notes, the consequent interaction between the clinician and child seems a "jug and mug" relationship in which the clinician actively pours language into the waiting child. The operant concern for stimulus events is one that focuses upon the clarity of antecedent prompts. If the prompt is clearly and unambiguously presented, then the potential for an immediate and correct imitation is enhanced. Since consequent events are the bases for shaping and for increasing response strengths, then in prescribing clinician behavior, reinforcement also warrants considerable attention. The operant concern for reinforcement is one that focuses upon timing and type of reinforcement. As a whole, the clinician, therefore, assumes both an active and a highly prescribed role when interacting with the child within operant conditioning approaches.

In mentalism, the clinician functions as a "facilitator," highlighting salient language subcomponents and their inter-relationships and increasing the frequency with which the child has opportunities for experiencing these language events. Bloom and Lahey (1978) have noted that the clinician can increase the saliency of these relationships through both linguistic (manipulating sentence complexity and prosodic features) and nonlinguistic means (picture, object, or action-based demonstrations). When another intervention agent is involved in implementing these procedures, the clinician monitors the child's progress, analyzes responses, and modifies activities. Within this perspective, the clinician seems more critically involved in assessment than in implementing intervention procedures.

Some authors have argued that a basic issue in planning pragmatic approaches to language intervention involves preserving "natural" interactions (Bloom & Lahey, 1978; Muma, 1978; Seibert and Oller, 1981) and thereby indicate either explicitly or implicitly that unfortunately the clinician's role as an adult authority is naturally and inevitably prescribed and, therefore, circumscribed. These arguments really seem less critically related to who interacts with the child rather than how. Holland (1975) has observed that language intervention represents a "communication microcosm." Skilled clinicians can transcend roles as adult authorities and, to a large extent, create the opportunities for learning, which the language impaired child needs. The client thereby learns about naturally occurring conversational demands and rules for conversing within a context specially designed to assist the individual learning needs. Although the child's experiences within intervention should not be unnatural since they then may be counterproductive, it would be an unfortunate misinterpretation of the above authors' arguments to have to preserve naturalness for the clinician, also.

The arguments for "natural" communicative sequences also might be interpreted as contraindicating pragmatic language interventions within traditional therapy settings. Once more these concerns seem more critically related to how intervention is conducted than where. A concern with the background physical setting seems more consistent with the behavioristic assumption that distractions may interfere with the establishment of appropriate stimulus-response connections. For many years intervention has been conducted in starkly unattractive rooms devoid of physical stimuli unrelated to the intervention sequence. The clinician frequently has exclusive access to toy and picture prompts, keeping them hidden from the child's view until required as part of the stimulus event.

In contrast, interesting settings with potential to peak a child's curiosity seem the appropriate environment for mentalistic approaches to intervention. Again, however, since the assumption is that the child needs to induce the critical relationships between cognitive and linguistic variables, interferences (potentially decreasing the saliency of these relationships), must be avoided. Mentalistic approaches either enhance the saliency of a small set of stimuli within the traditional therapy room or, since different stimuli may be attractive and potentially an interference to different children, remove the child from the therapy room and attempt interventions in the child's home or school. Presumably in the latter settings, distractions remain present but are at least real and something with which the child cognitively needs to learn to cope. Unfortunately, the clinician's intrusion into the child's daily routines also seems unnatural. Furthermore, the clinician may be unable to increase the frequency with which the child experiences specific language events within these environments and a real strength in intervention, repeated opportunities for learning, are jeopardized. It seems simplistic to assume that there is anything inherently good or bad about conducting intervention in a speech clinic or speech classroom. These specialized learning situations allow intensive, individualized interventions and should not be abandoned prematurely for untested and perhaps less efficient settings. Instead, ways to mirror natural communicative experiences better without giving up the positive aspects of special learning situations need to be explored.

Since pragmatics proposes that both the child and critical aspects of the child's environment are potent forces in shaping language development, a melding of the operant conditioning perspective on the clinician and the mentalistic view of the child seems most appropriate for planning pragmatic approaches to intervention. In this regard, the clinician would direct all aspects of the child's intervention experiences but would do so in ways perceived as natural learning opportunities by the child.

Clinician behavior would be directive, dynamic, but perceived as naturally interactive if planned in terms of conversational roles. At any point in an intervention sequence, the clinician may be a "speaker" or a "listener" relative to the child. Although in this sense, the evolution of the sequence would be determined jointly by both clinician and child participants, the clinician would be able to plan and problem solve as the sequence unfolds. In contrast to the "teacher" and "facilitator" roles of the other major paradigms, within pragmatic approaches the clinician should function as a "trouble-shooter" for the child — locating and eliminating the source of trouble in any communicaton flow and thereby maximizing the child's communicative potential.

The planning of clinician behavior seemingly involves consideration of both the simultaneous nature of the different roles assumed by clinician and child and the sequential organization of these roles. For example, during a specific intervention sequence the child may be the speaker while the clinician assumes a listener role, planning how best to be either the next speaker by securing the turn from the child or to remain the listener by passing up opportunities to become the next speaker. Craig and Gallagher (1982) have described a number of potential conversational roles relative to turn exchanges that individuals assume within small groups and dyads. These roles may be useful as a model for planning intervention sequences, particularly for guiding clinician behavior. They include the following roles:

Speaker (the one who produces the language event)

Listener-Next-Speaker (the one who becomes the Speaker in the subsequent language event)

Listener-Non-Next Speaker (the one who remains a listener in the subsequent language event) for multi-party interactions when there is a non-simultaneous change in speaker turn

Speaker and Listener-Next Speaker (see definition above) for non-simultaneous turn exchanges within dyads

Speaker and Listener-Non-Next Speaker (defined as above) for non-simultaneous no speaker turn exchanges (Craig and Gallagher, 1982); Speaker, Simultaneous Speaker, and Listener-Non Speaker for simultaneous language events (Gallagher and Craig, 1982).

One way to begin incorporating information derived from the study of the normal child's conversational rules into intervention procedures, therefore, would be to plan clinician behavior in terms of the obligations and options associated with these speaker and listener conversational roles. In this sense, clinician behavior can be conceptualized pragmatically as a "role-bracketing dynamic." The clinician close-brackets a previous child turn by meeting the constraints established by that message and then establishes a new set of constraints or open-brackets a message to which the child must relate subsequently. Assuming that conversational options include discourse-opening, discourse-closing, and discourse-maintaining behaviors, then the intervention sequence can be dynamic, theoretically infininte in length, and communicatively rich and varied. An intervention approach of this type would alter the behavioristic assumption that an intervention sequence is a static, three-step, stimulus-response-reinforcement event and thereby would imply that the need to up-date these constructs is moot. This conceptualization of the clinician as a trouble-shooter who brackets the child's behavior in dynamic ways suggests interesting approaches for applying available pragmatic language information and indicates some directions for future research on intervention procedures.

3. *Child Behaviors* What is the child expected to do and say during the intervention sequence? Activities are the joint actions and events in which the child and clinician engage during a specific intervention sequence. Current practice typically distinguishes between activities and tasks. Activities represent a middle-ground or combined effort on the parts of both clinician and child while tasks seem more specifically related to child behavior. Although both tasks and activities relate to what the child is doing during an intervention sequence, the two can be planned fairly independently and differ along a number of continuums, as follows:

1) Activities are the actions and events in which the task is presented while tasks are the work-load or degree of effort expected on the part of the child.

2) Activities are overtly perceived, discussed, and remembered, while tasks are covertly perceived.

3) Activities are planned as specific actions or events while tasks are planned along general parameters (for example, observing, comprehending, producing, imitating, etc.).

Tasks and activities are essentially the same within operant conditioning approaches to language intervention. The child's activity/task is planned in terms of the ratio of clinician-client utterances, the feasibility of adequately controlling reinforcement, and the ease of calculating task criterion levels. The activities that seem to fit these requirements best are imitative picture naming unit-ten drills. Unfortunately, these activities so lack animation that elaborate reinforcement systems are frequently necessary to keep a specifically language impaired child on task, and considerable pre-program training is needed to establish a response set on the part of young children. Activities developed for operant conditioning approaches additionally seem physically circumscribed. Any stimulus not part of the immediate activity is carefully eliminated as a potential distraction or as an interfering variable within the stimulus-response connection.

In contrast, mentalism prioritizes activity planning. Within these approaches, the task for the child is induction of the appropriate rule. Since rule induction is a covert cognitive accomplishment, tasks and activities are viewed as indirectly related. The primary requirements for mentalistic activities are that the activities provide a variety of learning experiences for the child, that these experiences appear natural, and that they have the potential to recur. Play meets all of these requirements and is broadly adopted as the framework for planning intervention activities within mentalism. Furthermore, play maintains the indirectness between the task and the child's perception of the event in natural ways that do not distort critical relationships between linguistic and non-linguistic stimuli.

Play continues to offer an appropriate framework for planning activities within pragmatic approaches to intervention but for fundamentally different reasons. Play is the preferred basis for activities within pragmatic approaches because it provides natural contexts for communication between the child and the intervention agent. Communicative interactions are not the focus of play sequences within mentalistic approaches. Instead, the child's role is asymmetrically intense. The clinician presents and modifies events, but the child's exploratory responses predominate throughout any intervention sequence and the resulting child turn is unnaturally extended. A pragmatic focus on discourse as the procedural plan for intervention sequences alternatively implies more symmetry between clinician and child behaviors than is apparent within other intervention approaches. The child's behaviors as well as the clinician's can be planned in terms of conversational roles.

This new communicative orientation for play may jeopardize attempts to maintain an indirect relationship between tasks and activities within intervention. However, while generative tasks may have been difficult to explicate for children ("you can produce a noun phrase now by elaborating your present rule to optionally include an article or a possessive pronoun but not both at the same time, in front of the class of modifiers that you know") and, therefore, best presented indirectly, many aspects of the communicative framework currently proposed as the vehicle for structural growth seem amenable to more direct explanation. For example, recently within our clinical program, one three-year-old boy with normally developing language said to a child client with a specific language impairment who was having difficulty verbally taking turns within the interaction: "No-No. I'm gonna speak to you and then you speak back."

It may be possible to approach the teaching and learning of conversational rules in ways quite different from those implied by past theories. Although the conversational rules that underlie linguistically based social conventions may be induced from repeated experience with the relevant communicative events, it may be more efficient to state conversational principles for the child in explicit terms. Explicit verbal coaching, for example, has been found to produce immediate and long-term changes in the social interaction patterns of children with non-language interactive problems. Oden & Asher (1977) report considerable success in changing the social interaction patterns of school-aged "socially isolated" children using explicity stated instructions. Perhaps some of the communicative difficulties experienced by the specifically language impaired child can be resolved with innovative approaches to remediation of this type. These issues need to be addressed experimentally.

In planning the child's conversational role, it seems important to consider the basic pragmatic proposal that communication is the result of an interaction between the child's structural and conversational knowledge. Both sources of communicative constraint, therefore, should be recognized in placing demands upon the child. Shatz (1978) offers a useful framework for considering the communicative constraints that children experience. She argues, from the perspective of humans as limited-capacity information processors, that communication products can be viewed as a constant and that variable displays of linguistic ability result from the child's distribution of communicative resources while maintaining that constant. If considerable demand is placed on the child's cognitive resources, for example when the child is describing unfamiliar objects, the quality of the conversational interaction may be reduced in order to accomplish the overall task. Similarly, within intervention, if the clinician engages the child in socially complex interactions, the child's structural skills may appear depressed as a consequence of maintaining the communication constant in this more demanding context.

Since pragmatics prioritizes one type of cognition—social knowledge, the clinician planning pragmatic intervention approaches needs to consider the various cognitive-social and linguistic demands placed on the child and the child's pragmatic language resources for meeting these demands and should then modify expectations for the child's performance accordingly so that the child continues to experience communicative success. An example of how this perspective has been applied procedurally within our own clinic is as follows. A four-and-one-half-year-old-boy with a specific language impairment enrolled in our Developmental Language Programs has language comprehension scores within normal limits but severely delayed expressive scores. His ability to express himself seems quite different when he assumes a speaker-initiator role than when he becomes speaker-respondent. His utterances appear structurally more complex within speaker-initiating roles (requesting and commenting), seem stereotypic following requests, and are replaced by only nonverbal attention following comments. This verbal gradient became an important procedural component in planning intervention for this child. Within speaker-initiator utterances only structural goals were emphasized, but within speaker-respondent roles he was expected to provide new information to his stereotypic responses to requests and asked to acknowledge comments in a verbal mode stereotypically. This approach proved very valuable with this child, and although at present represents only a clinical anecdote, suggests that both conversational and structural components of messages must be considered in planning task hierarchies.

Clearly not enough information is available presently to delineate guidelines for planning activities and tasks. Research is needed on the ways in which pragmatic, social, and general cognitive demands interact to enhance or degrade learning, and the ways in which this information can be incorporated into planning the child's behavior within intervention.

## Summary

Intervention planning requires consideration of both goal-setting and procedural issues. Historically, goal-setting has reflected each of the prominent theories of child language acquisition but procedural selections have less clearly accommodated past theoretical shifts. The increasing prominence of pragmatic language theories has influenced goal-setting once more and has implications for procedural selections. Procedural implications seem to depend upon how expansively pragmatic theories are interpreted. The present paper discusses these issues and, based upon a more expansive interpretation of pragmatic theory, suggests implications for planning some basic procedural aspects of intervention.

## References

Antinucci, F.,& Parisi, D. Early language acquisition:A model and some data. In C. Ferguson & D. Slobin (Eds.),*Studies of child language development*. New York: Holt, Rinehart, and Winston, 1973.

Bates, E. Pragmatics and sociolinguistics in child language. In D. Morehead & A. Morehead (Eds.), *Language deficiency in children: Selected readings*. Baltimore: University Park Press, 1976.

Blank, M., & Franklin, E. Dialogue with preschoolers: A cognitively-based system of assessment. *Applied Psycholinguistics, 1980, 1,* 127-150.

Bloom, L. *Language development: Form and function in emerging grammars.* Cambridge: MIT Press, 1970.

Bloom, L. & Lahey, M. *Language development and language disorders.* New York: John Wiley and Sons, 1978.

Bloom, L., Lightbown, P., & Hood, L. Pronominal-nominal variation in child language. In L. Bloom (Ed.), *Readings in language development*. New York: John Wiley & Sons, 1978.

Bloom, L., Rocissano, L., & Hood, L. Adult-child discourse: Developmental interaction between information processing and linguistic knowledge. *Cognitive Psychology,* 1976, *8,* 521-552.

Bowerman, M. Structural relationships in children's utterances: Syntactic or semantic? In T. Moore (Ed.), *Cognitive development and the acquisition of language.* New York: Academic Press, 1973.

Braine, M.D.S. The ontogeny of English phrase structure: The first phase. *Language,* 1963, *39,* 1-13.

Bricker, W. A., & Bricker, D.D. A program of language training for the severely handicapped child. *Exceptional Children,* 1970, *37,* 101-111.

Bricker, W., & Bricker, D. An early language training strategy. In R. Schiefelbusch & L. Lloyd (Eds.), *Language perspectives — Acquisition, retardation, and intervention.* Baltimore: University Park Press, 1974.

Brinton, B., & Fujiki, M. A comparison of request-response sequences in the discourse of normal and language-disordered children. *Journal of Speech and Hearing Disorders,* 1982, *47,* 57-62.

Brookshire, R. Speech pathology and the experimental analyses of behavior. *Journal of Speech and Hearing Disorders,* 1967, *32,* 215-227.

Brown, R. The development of wh-questions in child speech. *Journal of Verbal Learning and Verbal Behavior,* 1968, *7,* 279-290.

Brown, R. *A first language.* Cambridge: Harvard University Press, 1973.

Brown, R., & Bellugi, U. Three processes in the child's acquisition of syntax. *Language and Learning: Harvard Educational Review,* 1964, *34,* 133-151.

Brown, R., Cazden, C., & Bellugi-Klima, U. The child's grammar from I to III. In J. Hill (Ed.), *Minnesota symposium on child development* (Vol. 2). Minneapolis: University of Minnesota Press, 1969.

Brown, R., & Fraser, C. The acquisition of syntax. In U. Bellugi & R. Brown, *The acquisition of language.* Monographs of the Society from Research in Child Development (Serial No. 92), 1964.

Bruner, J. The ontogenesis of speech acts. *Journal of Child Language,* 1975, *2,* 1-19.

Chomsky, N. *Syntactic structures.* The Hague: Mouton, 1957.

Chomsky, N. *Aspects of the theory of syntax.* Cambridge: MIT Press, 1965.

Chomsky, N., & Miller, G.A. Introduction to the formal analysis of natural languages. In R.D. Luce, R.R. Bush, & E. Galanter (Eds.), *Handbook of mathematical psychology* (Vol. II). New York: Wiley, 1963.

Connor, J.M., & Serbin, L.A. Behaviorally based masculine and feminine-activity preferences scales for preschoolers: Correlates with other classroom behaviors and cognitive tests. *Child Development,* 1977, *48,* 1411-1416.

Corsaro, W. The clarification request as a feature of adult interactive style with young children. *Language in society,* 1977, *6,* 183-207.

Corsaro, W.A. The development of social cognition in preschool children: Implications for language learning. *Topics in Language Disorders,* 1981. *1* (2), 77-95.

Costello, J. Programmed instruction. *Journal of Speech and Hearing Disorders,* 1977, *42,* 3-28.

Craig, H., & Gallagher, T. Gaze and proximity as turn regulators within three-party and two-party child conversations. *Journal of Speech and Hearing Research,* 1982, *25* (1), 32-42.

Darley, F.L., & Moll, K. Reliability of language measures of size of sample. *Journal of Speech and Hearing Research,* 1960, *3,* 166-173.

Deterline, W.A. *An introduction to programmed instruction.* Englewood Cliffs, NJ: Prentice Hall, 1962.

DeJoy, D., Rooney, T., & Defeo, A. The Catch 22's of Language Therapy. Paper presented at the Annual Convention of the American Speech-Language-Hearing Association, Atlanta, 1979.

Dore, J. Holophrases, speech acts and language universals. *Journal of Child Language,* 1975, *2,* 21-40.

Dunn, L.M. *Peabody picture vocabulary test.* Circle Pines, MN: American Guidance Service, 1959.

Ervin-Tripp, S. & Mitchell-Kernan, C. Introduction. In S. Ervin-Tripp & C. Mitchell-Kernan (Eds.), *Child discourse.* New York: Academic Press, 1977.

Fey, M., Leonard, L., & Wilcox, K. Speech style modifications of language-impaired children. *Journal of Speech and Hearing Disorders,* 1981, *46,* 91-96.

Freedman, P., & Carpenter, R. Semantic relations used by normal and language-impaired children at Stage I. *Journal of Speech and Hearing Research,* 1976, *19,* 784-795.

Friedman, P., & Friedman, K. Accounting for individual differences when comparing the effectiveness of remedial language teaching methods. *Applied Psycholinguistics,* 1980, *2,* 151-170.

Fygetakis, L., & Gray, B. Programmed conditioning of linguistic competence. *Behavior Research & Therapy,* 1970, *8,* 153-163.

Gallagher, T. Revision behaviors in the speech of normal children developing language. *Journal of Speech and Hearing Research,* 1977, *20,* 303-318.

Gallagher, T.M. Contingent query sentences within adult-child discourse. *Journal of Child Language,* 1981, *8,* 51-62.

Gallagher, T., & Craig, H. An investigation of overlap in children's speech. *Journal of Psycholinguistic Research,* 1982, *11* (1), 63-75.

Gallagher, T., & Darnton, B. Conversational aspects of the speech of language-disordered children: Revision behaviors. *Journal of Speech and Hearing Research,* 1978, *21,* 118-35.

Garvey, C. Requests and responses in children's speech. *Journal of Child Language,* 1975, *2,* 41-63.

Garvey, C. The contingent query: A dependent act in conversation. In M. Lewis & L.A. Rosenblum (Eds.), *Interaction, conversation, and the development of language.* New York: John Wiley and Sons, 1977.

Gray, B., & Fygetakis, L. Mediated language acquisition for dysphasic children. *Behavioral Research and Therapy,* 1968, *6,* 263-280.

Gray, B., & Ryan, B.P. *A language program for the nonlanguage child.* Champaign, IL: Research Press, 1973.

Greenfield, P.M., & Smith, J. *The structure of communication in early language development.* New York: Academic Press, 1976.

Guess, D., Sailor, W., & Baer, D. To teach language to retarded children. In R.L. Schiefelbusch & L. Lloyd (Eds.), *Language perspectives — Acquisition, retardation, and intervention.* Baltimore: University Park Press, 1974.

Guess, D., Sailor W., & Baer, D. Children with limited language. In R. Schiefelbusch (Ed.), *Language intervention strategies.* Baltimore: University Park Press, 1978.

Halliday, M.A.K. *Learning how to mean: Explorations in the development of language.* London: Edward Arnold, 1975.

Hegde, M. An experimental-clinical analysis of grammatical and behavioral distinctions between verbal auxiliary and copula. *Journal of Speech and Hearing Research,* 1980, *23,* 864-877.

Holland, A. Language therapy for children: Some thoughts on context and content. *Journal of Speech and Hearing Disorders,* 1975, *40,* 514-523.

Holland, A.L., & Matthews, J. Application of teaching machine concepts to speech pathology and audiology. *Asha,* 1963, *5,* 474-482.

Holland, J.G. Teaching machines: An application of principles from the laboratory. In A.A. Lumsdaine & R. Glaser (Eds.), *Teaching machines and programmed learning.* Washington, D.C.: National Educational Association, 1960.

Holland, J.G., & Skinner, B.F. *The analysis of behavior.* New York: McGraw-Hill, 1961.

Johnson, W., Darley, F.L., & Spriestersbach, D. *Diagnostic methods in speech correction.* New York: Harper & Row, 1952.

Johnston, J., & Schery, T. The use of grammatical morphemes by children with communication disorders. In D. Morehead & A. Morehead (Eds.), *Normal and deficient child language.* Baltimore: University Park Press, 1976.

Johnston, M., & Harris, F. Observation and recording of verbal behavior in remedial speech work. In H. Sloane & B. MacAulay (Eds.), *Operant procedures in remedial speech and language training.* Boston: Houghton Mifflin Co., 1968.

Keenan, E.O. Conversational competence in children. *Journal of Child Language,* 1974, *1,* 163-183.

Keenan, E.O., & Klein, E. Coherency in children's discourse. *Journal of Psycholinguistic Research,* 1975, *4,* 365-380.

Kent, L. A language acquisition program for the retarded. In J. McLean, D. Yoder, & R. Schiefelbusch (Eds.), *Language intervention with the retarded.* Baltimore: University Park Press, 1972.

Kent, L. *Language acquisition program for the severely retarded.* Champaign, IL: Research Press, 1974.

Klima, E., & Bellugi-Klima, U. Syntactic regularities in the speech of children. In J. Lyons & R. Wales (Eds.), *Psycholinguistic papers.* Edinburgh: Edinburgh University Press, 1966.

Lahey, M., & Bloom, L. Planning a first lexicon: Which words to teach first. *Journal of Speech and Hearing Disorders,* 1977, *42,* 340-350.

Launer, P.B., & Lahey, M. Passages: From the fifties to the eighties in language assessment. *Topics in Language Disorders,* 1981, *1*(3), 11-29.

Lee, L. Developmental sentence types: a method for comparing normal and deviant syntactic development. *Journal of Speech and Hearing Disorders,* 1966, *31,* 311-330.

Lee, L., Koenigsknecht, R., & Mulhern, S. *Interactive language development teaching.* Evanston, IL: Northwestern University Press, 1975.

Lenneberg, E. *Biological foundations of language.* New York: John Wiley & Sons, 1967.

Leonard, L. What is deviant language? *Journal of Speech and Hearing Disorders,* 1972, *37,* 427-46.

Leonard, L., Bolders, J., & Miller, J. An examination of the semantic relations reflected in the language usage of normal and language disordered children. *Journal of Speech and Hearing Research.* 1976, *19,* 371-392.

Longhurst, T. M., & Reichle, J. E. The applied communication game: a comment on Muma's 'Communication game: dump and play'. *Journal of Speech and Hearing Disorders,* 1975, *40*(3), 315-319.

Lovaas, O. I., Berberich, J. P., Perloff, B. F., & Schaeffer, B. Acquisition of imitative speech by schizophrenic children. *Science,* 1966, *151,* 705-707.

Maccoby, E., & Jacklin, C. *The psychology of sex differences.* Stanford: Stanford University Press, 1974.

MacDonald, J., & Blott, J. Environmental language intervention: The rationale for a diagnostic and training strategy through rules, context and generalization. *Journal of Speech and Hearing Disorders,* 1974, *39,* 244-257.

MacNamara, J. Cognitive basis of language learning in infants. *Psychological Review,* 1972, *79,* 1-13.

McCarthy, D. Language development in children. In P. Mussen (Ed.), *Carmichael's manual of child psychology.* New York: John Wiley & Sons, 1954.

McNeill, D. Developmental psycholinguistics. In F. Smith & G. Miller (Eds.), *The genesis of language: A psycholinguistic approach.* Cambridge: MIT Press, 1966.

Menyuk, P. Comparison of grammar of children with functionally deviant and normal speech. *Journal of Speech and Hearing Research,* 1964, 7, 109-121.

Menyuk, P., & Looney, P. Relationships among components of the grammar in language disorder. *Journal of Speech and Language Research,* 1972a, *15,* 395-406.

Menyuk, P., & Looney, P. A problem of language disorder: length vs. structure. *Journal of Speech and Hearing Research,* 1972b, *15,* 264-279.

Miller, G. Four Philosophical problems of psycholinguistics. *Philosophy of Science,* 1970 *37,* 182.

Miller J., & Yoder, D. A syntax teaching program. In J. McLean, D.E. Yoder, & R. Schiefelbusch (Eds.), *Language intervention with the retarded: Developing strategies.* Baltimore: University Park Press, 1972.

Miller, J., & Yoder, D. An ontogenetic language teaching strategy for retarded children. In R. Schiefelbusch & L. Lloyd (Eds.), *Language perspectives — Acquisition, retardation, and intervention.* Baltimore: Univeristy Park Press. 1974.

Miller, W., & Ervin, S. The development of grammar in child language. In U. Bellugi-Klima & R. Brown (Eds.), *Monographs of the Society for Research in Child Development,* 1964, *29,* 9-34.

Miller, L. Pragmatics and early childhood language disorders. *Journal of Speech and Hearing Disorders,* 1978, *43,* 419-436.

Morehead, D., & Ingram, D. The development of base syntax in normal and linguistically deviant children. *Journal of Speech and Hearing Research,* 1973, *16,* 330-352.

Morris, C. *Signs, language and behavior.* Englewood Cliffs, NJ: Prentice-Hall, 1946.

Mueller, E., & Brenner, J. The origins of social skills and interaction among playgroup toddlers. *Child Development,* 1977, *48,* 854-861.

Mulac, A., & Tomlinson, C. Generalization of an operant remediation program for syntax with language-delayed children. *Journal of Communication Disorders,* 1977, *10,* 231-244.

Muma, J. Review of Schiefelbusch, R., and Lloyd, L., *Language perspectives: Acquisition, retardation, and intervention. Asha,* 1975a, 18, 371-373.

Muma, J. The communication game: Dump and play. *Journal of Speech and Hearing Disorders,* 1975b, *40*(3), 296-309.

Muma, J. *Language handbook - concepts, assessment, intervention.* Englewood Cliffs, NJ: Prentice-Hall, Inc., 1978.

Nelson, K. Concept, word, and sentence: interrelations in acquisition and development. *Psychological Review,* 1974, *81,* 267-285.

Oden, S., & Asher, S. Coaching children in social skills for friendship making. *Child Development,* 1977, *48,* 495-506.

Prinz, P. An investigation of the comprehension and production of requests in normal and language-disordered children. *Journal of Communication Disorders,* 1982, *15,* 75-93.

Rees, N. Pragmatics of language: Applications to normal and disordered language development. In. R. L. Schiefelbusch (Ed.), *Bases of language intervention.* Baltimore: University Park Press, 1978.

Risley, T.R., Hart, B.M., & Doke, L. Operant language development: The outline of a therapeutic technology. In. R.L. Schiefelbusch (Ed.), *Language of the mentally retarded.* Baltimore: University Park Press, 1972.

Schlesinger, I. Relational concepts underlying language. In R. L. Schiefelbusch & L. L. Lloyd (Eds.), *Language perspectives — Acquisition, retardation, and intervention.* Baltimore: University Park Press, 1974.

Searle, J. *Speech acts.* Cambridge: Harvard University Press, 1969.

Seibert, J. M., & Oller, D. K. Linguistic pragmatics and language intervention strategies. *Journal of Autism and Developmental Disorders,* 1981, *11,* 75-88.

Shatz, M. The relationship between cognitive processes and the development of communication skills. In B. Keasey (Ed.), *Nebraska symposium on motivation, 1977.* Lincoln: University of Nebraska Press, 1978.

Shatz, M., Bernstein, D., & Shulman, M. The responses of language disordered children to indirect directives in varying contexts. *Applied Psycholinguistics,* 1980, *1,* 295-306.

Shatz, M., & Gelman, R. The development of communication skills: modifications in the speech of young children as a function of listener. *Monographs of the Society for Research in Child Development,* 1973, *38.*

Sinclair-de-Zwart, H. Language acquisition and cognitive development. In T. Moore (Ed.), *Cognitive development and the acquisition of language.* New York: Academic Press, 1973.

Skinner, B. F. The science of learning and the art of teaching. *Harvard Educational Review,* 1954, *24,* 86-97.

Skinner, B. F. *Verbal behavior.* New York: Appleton-Century-Crofts, 1957.

Skinner, B. F. *The technology of teaching.* New York: Appleton-Century-Crofts, 1968.

Sloane, H. N., Johnston, M. K., & Harris, F. R. Remedial procedures for teaching verbal behavior to speech deficient or defective young children. In H. N. Sloan & B. MacAulay (Eds.), *Operant procedures in remedial speech and language training.* Houghton Mifflin Co., Boston, 1968.

Sloan, H., & MacAulay, B. Teaching and the environmental control of verbal behavior. In H. Sloane & B. MacAulay (Eds.), *Operant procedures in remedial speech and language training.* Boston: Houghton Mifflin Co., 1968.

Slobin, D. Cognitive prerequisites for the acquisition of grammar. In C.A. Ferguson & D.I. Slobin (Eds.), *Studies of child language development.* New York: Holt, Rinehart, and Winston, 1973.

Snyder, L. Communicative and cognitive abilities and disabilities in the sensorimotor period. *Merrill-Palmer Quarterly,* 1978, *24,* 161-180.

Staats, A. Behaviorism and cognitive theory in the study of language: A neopsycholinguistics. In R. Schiefelbusch & L. Lloyd (Eds.), *Language perspectives — Acquisition, retardation, and intervention.* Baltimore: University Park Press, 1974.

Stark, R., & Tallal, P. Selection of children with specific language deficits. *Journal of Speech and Hearing Disorders,* 1981, 46, 114-122.

Stern, D., Jaffe, J., Beebe, B., & Bennett, S. Vocalizing in unison and in alternation: Two modes of communication within the mother-infant dyad. In D. Aronson & R. Rieber (Eds.), *Developmental psycholinguistics and communication disorders.* Annals of the New York Academy of Sciences, 1975, 263.

Templin, M. Certain language skills in children. *Institute of Child Welfare Monograph Series,* No. 26, Minneapolis: University of Minnesota Press, 1957.

VanKleek, A., & Frankel T. Discourse devices used by language disordered children: A preliminary investigation. *Journal of Speech and Hearing Disorders,* 1981, *46,* 250-257.

Waryas, C., & Stremel-Campbell, K. Grammatical training for the language-delayed child. In R. Schiefelbusch (Ed.) *Language intervention strategies.* Baltimore: University Park Press, 1978.

Zwitman, D., & Sonderman, J. A syntax program designed to present base linguistic structures to language-disordered children. *Journal of Communication Disorders,* 1979, *12,* 323-337.

# 6

# ANSWERS TO WH-QUESTIONS: RESEARCH AND APPLICATION

*Martha M. Parnell*
*Southwest Missouri State University*

*James D. Amerman*
*University of Missouri, Columbia*

## Introduction

*T*he emergence of behavior prerequisite to the exchange of information through discourse can be observed even in a child's first months of life. Strategies for informational exchange at first are primarily nonverbal, with verbal discourse behaviors appearing subsequently. Much of the young child's experience with informational exchange occurs in question-answer situations. The verbal stimulation experienced by children is heavily laden with questions (Broen, 1972; Ervin - Tripp, 1971; Leach, 1972; Nelson, 1973), with *wh*-question forms accounting for a substantial percentage.

The status of knowledge concerning the development of children's *wh*-question comprehension limits our capability to judge their competence in this area. Although there have been numerous investigations of children's ability to ask *wh*-questions, relatively few researchers have attempted to describe the emergence of skills for interpreting and responding to them (Brown, 1968; Brown, Cazden and Bellugi-Klima, 1969; Cairns and Hsu, 1978; Dore, 1977; Ervin-Tripp, 1971; Hooper, 1971; Rodgon, 1979; Toler and Bankson, 1976; Tyack and Ingram, 1977). Attention to *wh*-question response has been limited, indirect, or incidental in several of these studies.

The lack of information concerning this area of linguistic development is surprising in view of evidence (Brown, 1968; Hood, 1977; Soderburg, 1974) that children learn to formulate particular forms of *wh*-questions only after they have learned to respond to questions of the same form (Bloom and Lahey, 1978). The first section will review investigations which have contributed data on this topic.

## Review of the Literature

The question-answering behaviors of a small group of children aged approximately two years were observed for a year and a half by Ervin-Tripp (1970). She later interviewed 24 children at monthly intervals, sampling an age range of 2;6 to 4;2 years. The children were asked similar *wh*-questions each time concerning the same picture book. Each session included three questions from each of the following types: *why, who*-subject, *who*-object, *how, where*-from, and *when*. Responses were described in terms of "category agreement" and "verb agreement." A child's response had "category agreement" if it was appropriate in terms of 'grammatical category' and provided the type of information solicited by a particular *wh*-word. The author observed that when a child failed to categorize a particular question form correctly, "he frequently replied as though the question were of a form he had in his repertoire" (p.106). Despite substantial intersubject variability and a limited set of questions representing each type, Ervin-Tripp offered a tentative hierarchy of difficulty. Strategies for answering *what* questions appeared to be mastered earliest, followed by those for answering *where, what do, whose, who, why, where*-from, *how* and *when*, respectively. Four strategies which appeared to explain a high percentage of children's answers were:

1. If you recognize the word, give a correct reply.
2. If there is a transitive verb, respond with the object of that verb.
3. If you are over three, and there is an animate subject and an intransitive verb, give a casual explanation.
4. For the remaining intrasitives, give a locative or direction if it is missing (p. 96-97).

Toler and Bankson (1976) examined the relationship between types of interrogative forms used by adults and children's ability to answer those forms correctly with reference to the children's ages. Three subjects aged 3;6 to 4;0 participated in an informal interaction with their mothers as well as in an examiner-administered 90-item probe task utilizing pictorial stimuli. The average percentage of the mothers' questions which were *wh*-forms was 64.4%; a further 1.4% were *yes/no* questions in which a *who*-clause was embedded. The *wh*-interrogative nominal segment was the most frequently used form (54%).

Responses were scored according to Leach's interrogation model (1972), which specifies form variations of acceptable answers as well as the particular constraints posed by each question type (e.g. *wh*-interrogative-locate time segment question: a) form variations - when or what time? b) response constraints - *wh*-response, locating time). There was no question category for which all the children demonstrated a similar percentage of appropriate responses during both the mother-child interaction and the interrogative probes. In general the children gave their best performances in response to the interrogative probes. A high percentage of the mothers' questions were forms which the children demonstrated ability to answer adequately during the probe sessions. Averages of the percentages of correct responses by the three subjects yielded the following order (easiest to most difficult) for the *wh*-questions on the next page.

1) *Wh*-interrogative - nominal segment (questions beginning with *who, which, what, what one, which one, who else, what other)*
2) *Where* interrogative - locate space (beginning with *where*)
3) *Wh*-interrogative verbal segment (beginning with *what* + do)
4) *Wh*-interrogative - adjectival segment (beginning with *what kind of, what sort of, how many, how much, how old, how tall, how far)*
5) *Wh*-interrogative - locate time (beginning with *when* or *what time*)
6) *Wh*-interrogative - no segment (beginning with *why* or *how*)
7) Interrogative-adverbial segment (beginning with *how often, how well, how easy).*

One hundred children participated in a question comprehension study by Tyack and Ingram (1977). Ten boys and 10 girls were included in each of the following age groups: 3;0 to 3;5, 3;6 to 3;11, 4;0 to 4;5, 4;6 to 4;11, 5;0 to 5;5 years. Photographs of six staged scenes showing children, adults, and common objects were presented to the subjects. The scenes were designed to minimize or eliminate the context as a cue for *wh*-word selection in the formulation of responses. Vocabulary was controlled, and two syntactic frames were chosen for the questions to permit control of syntactic complexity, particularly with reference to verb construction:

1. *Wh*-word + is + the + boy/girl + verb + ing?

2. $\dfrac{What}{Who}$ + is + verb + ing + the + boy/girl?

Verb types were scrutinized closely, in consideration of Ervin-Tripp's (1970) observation that transitive and intransitive verbs had a differential effect on children's response patterns. Three transitive verbs were selected from the first thousand words in the *Thorndike and Lorge Book of 30,000 Words* (Thorndike and Lorge, 1944) for use in the stimulus sentences. The *wh*-forms examined in this study were: *where, why, when, who, what.* The authors note that "questions were constructed with such rigid control that some of them may have influenced our data, though the children did not react to the questions as if they considered them unusual" (p. 217). Responses were scored according to the criteria described below:

*Who* questions required an animate noun response, either verbal or pointing;

*What* questions required an inanimate noun response, either verbal or pointing;

*Where* questions required a location, usually a locative *there* or a prepositional phrase;

*Why* required a cause, usually explicitly introduced by *because* or implicitly in the logic of the response;

*How* questions required a response indicating manner-gestures were acceptable if accompanied by a statement such as "like this";

*When* questions required a response indicating time (p. 218).

The percentage of 'correct' responses increased as a function of subject age. The particular question word, verb, and syntactic frame also influenced accuracy.

Ranking of the question categories by percentages of correct answers (highest %
to lowest) are:

1. *Where* - intransitive
2. *Why* - intransitive, *why* - transitive, *who* - subject
3. *Where* - transitive
4. *What* - object, *who* - object, *when* - intransitive, *when* - transitive
5. *How* - transitive, *how* - intransitive, *what* - subject

Tyack and Ingram's (1977) interpretation emphasized the importance of the
"semantics of the verb and its position in the sentence" and led them to postulate
that the strategies suggested by Ervin-Tripp should be modified as follows:

A. If you have acquired the particular question word, give an appropriate
   subject (same as Ervin-Tripp).
B. If you have not acquired the question word, respond on the basis of the
   semantic features of the verb.
C. Process a verb that ends a sentence as intransitive (p. 222-223).

Children's strategies for answering *who, when, why,* and *how* questions were
the focus of an investigation by Cairns and Hsu (1978). The subjects were 50
children aged 3;0 to 5;6 years, with an approximately equal number of males and
females in each of five six-month age groupings. The children viewed five
videotaped segments and subsequently were asked six questions, including one
from each of the *wh*-types:

1. *Who*-subject, e.g. "Who hugged the boy?"
2. *Who*-object using progressive aspect, e.g. "Who was Daddy feeding?"
3. *Who*-object with *do,* e.g. "Who did the boy feed?"
4. *Why* e.g. "Why did the dog eat the sandwich?"
5. *How,* e.g. "How did the girl feed the dog?"

Responses to the *who* question variations were scored as correct, incorrect, or
'no response.' The *who*-subject questions and the *who*-object questions with *do*
elicited performance levels superior to those elicited by *who*-object using the progressive aspect. Previous studies (Ervin-Tripp, 1970; Tyack and Ingram, 1977)
included *who*-subject questions but only progressive forms of *who*-object questions. These reports concluded that *who*-object questions were more difficult
than *who*-subject questions. Cairns and Hsu's (1978) data, based on sampling an
additional variation of *who*-object forms, does not substantiate the increased difficulty of *who*-object questions in general. Instead they propose that the superior
performance observed in children's responses to *who*-subject and *who*-object
with *do* constructions relative to *who*-object with progressive aspect stems from
the identity of the questioned grammatical relation being available to the listener
earlier in the former two questions than in the latter form.

A multidimensional scoring system was applied to facilitate further description
of *why, when* and *how* responses:

Type 1. A totally uncomprehending response, either "I don't know" or
        complete failure to respond.
Type 2. A response indicating some understanding of the question type
        but inability to formulate more than a minimal response (e.g.,
        now, because).

Type 3. A response indicating understanding of the questioned material but inability to formulate a completely correct answer. The answers were almost right, but slightly incorrect either syntactically or semantically.

Type 4. A completely correct, contextually accurate, adult quality response (p. 480).

For all age groups, *who*-object using *do* support and *who*-subject questions were easiest, followed by *who*-object using progressive aspect and *why* questions; *when* and *how* items were the most difficult. The ordering of question forms by difficulty is in accord with that of Tyack and Ingram (1977) except for *why,* which may result from the more stringent scoring critieria for *why* responses applied by Cairns and Hsu.

A significant age effect was found to differentiate among all age groups, with the exception of the 4;0 to 4;5 versus the 4;5 to 5;0 year groups. Analysis also revealed that the rate at which a question form is mastered is significantly related to the difficulty of that form.

The four investigations described above (Cairns and Hsu, 1978; Ervin-Tripp, 1970; Toler and Bankson, 1976; Tyack and Ingram, 1977) all emphasized the relative complexity of the *wh*-forms and their response demands in what appears to have been an "examination" type of dyadic communicative interaction. The examiner who presented the questions already knew the answers, and presumably, the situational context suggested to the child that these questions were "test" questions. The pragmatic function or illocutionary intent of the *wh*-questions was relatively fixed, not an independent variable. Therefore, the response patterns reported from such investigations should be interpreted with this constraint in mind, namely, that they represent response capabilities or strategies for dealing with *wh*-questions with one type of pragmatic function asked by an adult in one type of situational context. In reality, questions are asked both by adults and children for a variety of pragmatic functions.

Dore's (1977) approach to the study of what makes a child's answer to a question "appropriate" was based on observations of responses to both yes/no and *wh*-questions which occurred in a wide variety of interactions between children and their nursery school teachers and classmates. Systematic description and comparison of specific *wh*-forms and their responses was not undertaken. However, the spontaneous nature of the interactions permitted an interesting analysis of children's strategies for coping with some pragmatically determined question demands, which could not be determined by the form or literal meaning of the question alone.

Videotaped samples were obtained of the interactions of four boys and three girls over a period of seven months. Dore's analysis was based on samples obtained during the last four months of the study; at the beginning of that period the children ranged in age from 2;10 to 3;3 years. Responses to questions were divided into three major groups:

1. Canonical responses - "the most expected, predictable, and grammatically matched form, given only the form of the question" (p.149).

2. Noncanonical responses - "provided relevant information but not standard or highly predictable" (on the basis of form alone) (p. 149).
3. No answers (deliberately unanswered or otherwise).

Approximately 47% of the subjects' responses were 'canonical' or in 'categorical agreement' (Ervin-Tripp, 1970). Several factors may have contributed to this surprisingly low incidence:

1. Equivocal questions which could be interpreted as requests for action with no requirements for verbalization (e.g. *Why* don't you sit down until you're finished?).
2. Unintelligible responses which may have been canonical.
3. Instances of 'no response.'

Observation of the children's behavior and tallying the number of unanswered questions supported the assumption that "If the first decision an addressee must make after grammatically processing a question is whether or not to answer, then no answer seems to be a viable alternative for children, and one which does not appear to violate a social obligation" (p. 153). Further analysis of responses to the *wh*-questions suggested the strategies described below. According to Dore, the child will provide canonical information in his response to *wh*-questions if he:

1. Comprehends the proposition underlying the question.
2. Believes the proposition is true or accurate.
3. Recognizes the addresser's expectation in asking the question.
4. Believes the addresser wants the requested information.
5. Believes the addresser does not know the requested information or, in the case of examination questions, the addressee wants to display his knowledge.
6. Is able to (knows the answer).
7. Is willing, that is, has no more pressing desire  (p. 155).

"If any one of these conditions fails to apply, the child will respond noncanonically or will not answer" (p. 155). "When the child replies with a canonical response we can assume that he fully comprehended both the propositional meaning and the pragmatic intention of the question" (p. 153).

Hooper (1971) examined the influence of what he termed "communicative demand" and also introduced a "context" variable in a study of children's responses to questions. His "communicative demand" situations included:

1. Yes/no questions, e.g. "Is this a spoon?"
2. Labeling-use questions, e.g. "What do you do with a spoon?"
3. Explanatory questions, e.g. "Why do we eat with a spoon?"
4. Open-ended question, e.g. "How do you eat with a spoon?"

The three 'context' conditions were distinguished by the degree to which subjects could depend on having an object available as a possible aid for formulating responses. In the "context-present" condition, an object was in the subject's view as the question was asked concerning the object. For the second condition (context absent), the examiner removed the object before asking the question, and in the third, context interference condition, the examiner held an object in the subject's view while asking a question about a different object. The adequacy of the response from the standpoint of the communicative demand of the question was judged according to the *form* and *function*. Form judgments were based on the number and kind of lexical items (proper nouns, articles, etc.) and the kinds of grammatical units (dependent clauses, prepositional phrases, etc.) employed in the response. Function referred to the purpose for which units of grammar were used, e.g. making reference to an object, explaining the relationship among objects, etc.

Twenty-four 3 and 4-year-olds participated in the experiment by responding to 24 stimulus questions. The 4-year-olds performed significantly better than the 3-year-olds in terms of functionally adequate answers, but a statistically significant difference for grammatical (form) correctness was not evidenced between the age goups. Open-ended and explanatory questions produced more errors than did questions requiring labelling or yes/no answers. The authors observed trends indicating that one communicative demand situation may be more challenging than another grammatically, yet less difficult in terms of function requirements. Differences among the context conditions were non-significant, but a pattern was observed for the fewest errors to occur with the object present, more with the object removed, and the greatest number of errors to occur when the interfering object was presented.

Until recently Hooper's investigation was somewhat unique in its focus on a factor which has received scant attention from researchers in language science, i.e. variation in the type and degree of availability of referential sources which accompany verbal questions. Leach (1972) points out that "accompanying the gross syntactic correlates, there are referential features which may place additional constraints upon responses" (p.36). The type of informational source and its degree of availability to the child fall within the domain of 'referential features.' Leach emphasizes the importance of categorizing the referential features of questions because "there are suggestions in language-acquisition literature (Brown and Bellugi, 1964) that adults apparently shift from immediate referential sources with young children to more abstract or nonimmediate referential sources with older children" (p. 36).

An investigation by Parnell, Patterson & Harding (1980) and Parnell, Amerman, Patterson & Harding (1982) represented an attempt to supplement existing knowledge of children's *wh*-question comprehension in several areas. Specifically, the study provided for: 1) sampling of nine *wh*-forms, 2) upward extension of the age range of the experimental population from that of previous investigations, which typically sampled a range of two and three years with a ceiling of 5;6 to include observation of children of early elementary as well as preschool ages, and 3) examination of the possible effects of three basic variations in the type and availability of referential sources which accompanied the verbal questions. The experimental population consisted of 40 linguistically normal subjects, 10 in each of the following age groups: 3;0 to 3;11, 4;0 to 4;11, 5;0 to 5;11, 6;0 to 6;11 years. Each age group included five male and five female children.

The 81 stimulus items represented nine *wh*-question forms: *what* + be, *what* + do, *where* + be, *which* + be, *who* + be, *whose* + be, *why, when,* and *what* happened? Each question form was represented nine times. Three of the nine questions for each question form referred to an action, person, or object stimulus immediately available to the subject visually, e.g. "What's that?" (Stimulus Type I). Three additional questions concerned a picture stimulus in the subject's view, e.g. "What's he doing?" (Stimulus Type II). Three final questions had no immediate visual referential source, e.g. "When do you brush you teeth?" (Stimulus Type III).

*Wh*-question items were focused directly on the child, his family, his teachers, his friends, and his daily activities whenever possible. Attempts were made to include referential vocabulary, topics, and situations which were within the child's personal experience. The length and complexity of question items, as well as the length and complexity of minimally acceptable responses, were controlled across *wh*-forms and stimulus types.

Each response was judged according to two criteria. Responses which provided the distinctive kind or category of information required by the particular question form were designated as *functionally appropriate* answers. Responses were also judged according to the *functional accuracy* of the informational content. *Functionally accurate* responses provided factual, acceptable, logical, believable information. Only responses which were judged *functionally appropriate* could receive a + for *functional accuracy*. Lack of phonological, morphological, or syntactic completeness was not penalized. Examples of scoring are shown below:

| Question | Stimulus | Response | Functional Appropriateness | Functional Accuracy |
|----------|----------|----------|----------------------------|---------------------|
| *Why* are the leaves falling off the trees? | Type II (picture) | Because the wind blowed them | + | + |
| *Why* are the leaves falling off the trees? | Type II | Because it's spring | + | − |
| Why are the leaves falling off the trees? | Type II | On the ground | − | − |

The questioning in this experiment was clearly established as an "examination" situation; responses were expected. Additionally, no items necessitated the type of pragmatic interpretation required by some of the questions in Dore's (1977) less structured experiment which could be interpreted as needing no verbal response, e.g. "Why don't you sit down until you're finished?"

Statistical analyses revealed main effects for subject age, stimulus type, and *wh*-question form, as well as a significant interaction for stimulus type and *wh*-question form. Both the *functional appropriateness* and the *functional accuracy* of the answers reflected the significant influence of subject age, *wh*-question form, and stimulus type. As expected, chronological age in this normally developing child population (aged 3;0 to 6;11 years) was significantly related to the ability to provide 1) the category of information requested by specific *wh*-forms i.e. *functionally appropriate* answers, and 2) accurate, factual, believable, and logical information, i.e. *functionally accurate* answers. Stimulus Type III (no immediate referential source) questions were significantly more difficult for all age groups than questions of Type I or II. The main effect for type of *wh*-question was also significant for the *functionally appropriate* and *functionally accurate* scoring procedures. The easiest question form based on the *functionally appropriate* scoring criteria was *where* (98.6% correct responses). The *what happened* question was the most difficult (87.3%) format. The *why, when* and *what happened* question forms were significantly more difficult for subjects to respond to with *a functionally accurate* answer than were the remaining six question forms. Children demonstrated *appropriateness* of response to a substantially greater degree than *accuracy* of response. This *appropriateness/accuracy* discrepancy was particularly marked for the younger children (3- and 4-year olds). Children who had demonstrated ability to give acceptable responses in terms of both *functional appropriateness* and *functional accuracy* to the simpler *wh*-forms of Stimulus Type I or II format frequently were observed to give answers that were inadequate in one *(accuracy)* or both *(appropriateness* and *accuracy)* scoring dimensions when faced with more difficult *wh*-forms and/or *wh*-forms presented in a Type III format.

The types of *functional appropriateness* errors made by the subjects, in which one *wh*-question form was answered as if it were another *wh*-question form, can be summarized by the following trends:

| *Wh-Question Form* | *Wh-Response Confusion* |
|---|---|
| What + do? (Stimulus Type II) | Where, how |
| Where? (Stimulus Types II and III) | What + do |
| Which? (Stimulus Type III) | What + be |
| Who? (Stimulus Types I and III) | What + be |
| Whose? (Stimulus Types II and III) | What + be, who, what kind |
| Why? (Stimulus Types I, II and III) | Where, what + be, when |
| When? (Stimulus Types I and III) | What + be, what happened, where |
| What happened? (Stimulus Type III) | What + be, when |

As in previous studies, most errors were answers which would have been *functionally appropriate* responses to *wh*-question forms for which comprehension had occurred at an earlier age. As expected, Stimulus Type III question items elicited the majority of *wh*-question confusion errors.

We also observed various additional 'qualitative' differences among children's responses to questions of particular *wh*-forms and stimulus types *within* the categories of *functional appropriateness* and *functional accuracy*. Some of these tendencies were evident only in certain subject age groupings; others were typical of the 3 to 7-year-old experimental population as a whole. Many of the response dimensions which came to light hinted at developmental aspects of *wh*-question response strategies which may be of value ultimately for clinical consideration, but which would require analysis beyond the present *functional appropriateness/accuracy* model. Naturally, comparative data from both linguistically normal and disordered populations will be needed to explore these trends and to assess their significance.

*When, why,* and *what happened* questions are particularly interesting in this respect. These three question forms proved most difficult for children and appeared especially sensitive to developmental changes. Several characteristic patterns of logic, reasoning, egocentricity, and social and personal values implicit in the responses differentiated the age groups and emphasized the association between cognitive and linguistic development. A system for further qualitative description of responses, particularly within the domain of *functional accuracy,* would be a significant addition to a diagnostic model.

For *what happened* questions in particular, adaptation of measures similar to those reported by Yorkston and Beukelman (1980) appear promising. Because the "functional accuracy" criterion was most noticeably insufficiently sensitive to obvious age-related differences in answers to Type II *what happened* questions, the Yorkston and Beukelman (1980) measures for analysis of the language of aphasic patients were adapted for application to our data (Parnell et al., 1980; 1982). Although our analysis was limited by the brevity of most responses and the simplicity of the picture stimuli, our preliminary findings suggest that within the 3-7 year age range, the total number of informational units or "content units" and the communicative efficiency, measured as syllables/unit time and content units/unit time, may be expected to increase with advances in age and linguistic maturity. More in-depth evaluation of the efficacy of these measures, using more suitable pictorial or verbal stimuli, may provide clarification of the potential clinical usefulness of Yorkston and Beukelman's procedures for assessment of normal and disordered child language.

We also observed several instances of perceptible and measurable variation in the response latencies (reaction times) of individual children for particular question forms. Direct analysis of a link between response latency and the *appropriateness* or *accuracy* with which question items were answered in our experiment could not be pursued because of the potentially confounding effects of nonidentical structure, sentence length, and type of required response. However, the patterns we observed were most closely associated with the questions which yielded the lowest performance levels, e.g. *when, why* and *what happened.* This suggests an area worthy of further investigation; reaction time or response latency might indicate marginal processing difficulties not signaled by overt errors.

## Summary of Literature Review

Collectively, previous investigations have demonstrated that the response constraints associated with certain *wh*-question forms are comprehended more readily than those associated with other forms. With advances in age and linguistic maturity, normal children apply increasingly effective strategies to formulate responses likely to be judged adequate by adult listeners. Additionally, Parnell et al. (1980, 1982) indicate that recognition and delivery of the general category of information required by a *wh*-form may substantially predate the ability to respond with fact, logic, credibility, etc. Their data also suggests that children in the

3 to 7 year age range are notably less successful in determining the *kind* of information as well as less able to provide the *specific* information desired by the originator of the question when the question refers to objects, events, or persons not represented in the immediate setting. With increasing age it becomes easier for a child to provide both appropriate and accurate information in response to *wh*-questions of different forms and in association with varied types of referential sources. Most previous studies also suggest the existence and potential significance of multiple additional factors which might interact with the various *wh*-forms to affect the overall processing difficulty associated with a specific question. These variables are not only based in syntactic form, but reflect semantic, pragmatic, and sociolinguistic considerations as well.

# A Model for Further Study of Assessment and Intervention in the Area of WH-Question Comprehension

The literature shows that many factors need to be considered in determining the degree of difficulty a specific *wh*-question poses for the respondent, in assessing the respondent's ability to answer, and in evaluating the nature of the response from the viewpoint of whether and to what degree it satisfies the listener. The various investigations summarized above have each addressed, described, or controlled a few of these factors. When the findings are synthesized, it becomes clear that the results must be interpreted in light of the fact that no one study has taken into account all of these factors.

Generating productive models for the study of normal communication development and for effective clinical assessment and intervention for communicatively disordered children requires awareness of all the factors, including those relevant to the questioner, the respondent, and the communicative situation. The failure to take into account all of the critical cues or behaviors will obscure interpretation of the strategies used by normally developing or disordered children in question-answer exchanges and may lead to invalid assumptions in assessment and inadequate teaching procedures.

An accurate diagnostic clinical index which is applicable to intervention will require continued endeavors to:

1. Identify the roles of and interrelationships among the various cues, references, and contexts associated with *wh*-forms, specifying the capacity of these factors to determine, confirm, or alter *wh*-question processing strategies during the course of linguistic maturation.

2. Describe responses to *wh*-questions in terms of their relation to relevant constraints of the question, their impact on the originator of the question (and/or on other listeners in the communicative situation), and their effect on the subsequent communicative behaviors in the interaction.

# Context and Design of WH-Question Stimuli

Variables which appear to be significant determinants of the nature and adequacy of children's responses to *wh*-questions include the following:
1. Pragmatic function of the question.
2. Immediacy of referential source (which includes consideration of the "abstractness" or semantic complexity of the question topic, which is difficult at times to separate completely from the simple visual availability of the referent.
3. *Wh*-question form (and certain syntactic features closely tied to the *wh*-form).

In the study of communication development in general and in assessment and intervention with language disordered children, the strategies a child uses to interpret and respond to *wh*-questions can be examined more completely and precisely if the variables listed above are acknowledged and manipulated systematically and their impact described both separately and as interaction cues.

## Pragmatic Function of Wh-Questions

Most of the investigations discussed here of children's responses to *wh*-questions were conducted within the framework of an examiner-child dyad with the examiner asking the questions, which dealt with pictures, video-tapes, or common and personalized conversational topics. In all cases the examiner intended the questions to be answered by the child, and the perlocutionary effect of the questions varied minimally. Most children probably assumed that the examiner already knew the answers and was "testing" them (their willingness to answer depended on their interest in displaying their knowledge) or that the examiner was genuinely seeking information (the response was dependent on the child wishing to "help out" the examiner). In situations such as these, the child is not called upon to process *form* independently of *function,* as he/she may be required to do frequently during less structured spontaneous communicative interchanges.

These investigations tested only one or two basic pragmatic functions. An investigation which explored all possible pragmatic functions, while representing all *wh*-forms and controlling the immediacy of referential sources and the question length and complexity, etc., would be a monumental task. It probably would result in the early demise of all participants and undoubtedly would include a high percentage of bizarre and bewildering question items. The "traditional" experimental tasks represent attempts to deal with a variety of *wh*-forms systematically in a realistic amount of time, while exerting a modicum of control over the experimental variables of question length, topic, and syntactic complexity. In accord with standard research protocol, the situation, or "experimental setting," usually is controlled, which represents the greatest restriction on the extent to which a variety of pragmatic functions can be introduced into the sample. The "examination type" or "information seeking" pragmatic functions certainly are more amenable to manipulation by investigators. If only one type of pragmatic function can be observed realistically within the time or situational constraints of an investigation, the "examination-type" question function may be the most relevant or critical, because it accounts for a high, if not the highest, proportion of adults' questions to children and children's questions to other children.

The disadvantage of the "examination" type or "information-seeking" situations is clear. The child's sensitivity to communicative demands associated with varying attributes of person, setting, topic, and task are obscured. This important pragmatic interpretive ability cannot be tapped. The likelihood of a child answering *wh*-questions to the examiner's satisfaction in a structured situation and yet failing to provide effective responses to those *wh*-question forms when they require alternative pragmatic interpretation has not been well documented in rigidly controlled studies, but it is cited frequently in the language and learning disabilities literature. A thorough assessment of children's language abilities should sample each *wh*-form of interest separately according to the pragmatic function served, e.g. the informational function, the directive function, the conversational function (these can be divided further into subcategories. See Dore, 1977; Searle, 1969; Shatz, 1979). Certain *wh*-forms appear to be used more often than others for specific pragmatic functions (Dore, 1977; James and Seebach, 1982; Shatz, 1979) and sampling procedures may reflect this, de-emphasizing the use of atypical form/function pairing.

With careful preparation, even in a clinic environment, a skilled examiner may be able to direct activities and conversation so that some variety of pragmatic functions encoded as *wh*-questions may be sampled. However, a more desirable way to sample a child's response to *wh*-questions with varying pragmatic functions would be to enlist parents and teachers who interact spontaneously with the child on a day-to-day basis. They could tape selected interchanges or keep a log of the child's answers to *wh*-questions which they deemed unacceptable or which required assistance or revision by the speaker. The parent or teacher might log or tape question-answer interactions during a specified activity or time of day. The materials could then be submitted to the language specialist for analysis. The assistance of a family member, teacher, or care-taker in sampling has several benefits over the examiner-child interaction. The perlocutionary effect of questions is affected not only by situational or contextual variables and by the nonverbal communicative behavior of the participants, it also may be subject to the influence of speaker-listener familiarity. That is, a child may need to have some experience with a speaker in a variety of circumstances in order to view that speaker's utterances as having a variety of pragmatic functions. For example, the child who knows his/her clinician primarily as a very directive person who engages rarely in social amenities or in spontaneous conversation with him or her may view that clinician's attempt to use *wh*-questions for a conversational function, in indirect request, etc., in terms of the functions that are more "typical" of that speaker. Errors that occur in circumstances like this may penalize a child unduly, underestimating his/her communicative skill in most other interactions.

Until recently, the study of children's responses to *wh*-questions emphasized the role of the adult examiner as the interrogator. Results reported by James and Seebach (1982) suggest that when a child asks questions spontaneously, he/she may not ask them for the same reasons and in the same proportions for each pragmatic function as has been reported for adult interrogators. An interesting question for future research is how a child might adjust (or fail to adjust) his/her interpretation of questions to accomodate the age/illocutionary intent relationship when communicating with partners of varying ages and linguistic levels.

## Immediacy of Referential Sources — A Contextual Consideration

Maturation is associated with improved ability to cognize and encode linguistically events which are removed in time or place. Parnell et al. (1980, 1982) discovered that children in the 3 - 7-year age range are less successful in determining the kind of information as well as less able to provide the specific information desired by the originator of a question when that question refers to objects, events, or persons not represented in the immediate setting. In this situation both the *functional appropriateness* and the *functional accuracy* of responses decreased for children who demonstrated these capabilities when the same *wh*-question form referred to entities which were present in the immediate environment or to pictures. This effect is particularly striking when we consider that all of the Type III questions (nonimmediate referential source) constructed for that experiment dealt specifically with the child and his/her own activities. It appears likely that the "displacement" effect of Type III stimuli constitutes a relatively minor challenge compared to the processing demands involved in questions dealing with less personalized and less thoroughly familiar topics, e.g. grocery shopping, the zoo, the weather, as well as the more abstract and semantically complex curriculum related topics which are more numerous at each successive grade level, e.g. current events, sports, nutrition, history, literature, the life sciences.

The level of cognitive and linguistic competence needed to decode and respond to specific *wh*-forms in daily conversation is a complex issue. We are aware that the effect of non-immediate referential sources as stimuli in that experiment represents the influence of many factors which may be inherent in interrogation situations dealing with less tangible topics. However, the progressively more difficult situations which a child must manage competently to achieve academic, vocational, and social success involve entities removed in time and place. Normally-developing children *do* master the *wh*-questions which occur under widely diverse conditions and constraints. We need to define the complete sequence of skills which lead a child to develop the sophisticated strategies required for efficient information exchange under these circumstances. If we can accomplish this, we should be able to refine our descriptive capabilities and expand the scope of our clinical indices in the area of child language.

Although the questions in the Parnell et al. study were confined to very basic levels of abstraction, further research should investigate the possibility that more semantically complex, less personalized questions would be equally or even more sensitive to the advances in processing strategies which accompany maturity, or to the deficits that may occur. Information regarding the importance of immediate versus nonimmediate referential sources as determiners of linguistic processing load also suggests that manipulation of questioning and cueing formats from immediate (Type I, II) to nonimmediate (Type III) might assist the child to extend his/her control of functional question-answering strategies to meet the demands posed by the variation of speakers, listeners, referents, topics, and intents which characterize common conversational questioning situations.

## Relative Difficulty of Wh-Question Form

A review of investigations of *wh*-question comprehension reveals the need for caution in proposing developmental hierarchies of *wh*-question form difficulty or developmental stages for linguistic processing strategies. These schedules, hierarchies, or orderings, when based on limited numbers and types of questions, may be misleading unless one keeps in mind the limitations of the experimental results from which such proposals are derived. We suggest that variations in the syntactic structures of questions as well as in the type of visual stimuli associated with the *wh*-forms are primarily responsible for the "migration" of some question forms along an ease-difficulty continuum which is apparent when we compare available studies. Although the influence of those variables should be controlled in future investigations, a clinically useful index of *wh*-question difficulty should reflect the wide variety of syntactic structures, topics, and stimulus constraints with which *wh*-questioning proceeds in everyday situations.

Thus far, our data suggest that for efficient preliminary assessment or screening, attention should be directed first to the question forms and stimulus types which have proved most difficult for linguistically normal children, that is, *how, when, why,* and *what happened* question forms, particularly those of   Type III design. Successful responses to these most difficult question forms would indicate less likelihood that the remaining *wh*-forms presented in I, II, or III formats would be beyond a child's ability. Difficulty in dealing with the more difficult items, conversely, would indicate a need for further probing with other *wh*-forms using Type I and II formats. However, linguistically deficient children do not always develop in a way which is identical to but slower than normals; they may have particular difficulties with certain questions due to specific cognitive, perceptual, conceptual, or linguistic disabilities. Therefore, thorough evaluation of *wh*-question comprehension should incorporate an array of items systematically representing many *wh*-forms and variations in stimulus types.

Care should be taken in preparing specific question items for assessment or teaching activities; we should recall the evidence submitted by Ervin-Tripp (1970), and Tyack and Ingram (1977) which demonstrates that not all questions of a particular *wh*-form can be considered equivalent in difficulty nor can they be expected necessarily to evoke equivalent response strategies. Recognition and manipulation of synactic variations within one *wh*-category (e.g., use of transitive as well as intransitive verbs with *why* questions) should reveal the expertise with which a child may handle the *wh*-form in general, as well as in specific structural environments.

# Classification/Scoring of Responses

From a theoretical standpoint, a child's response to a *wh*-question may fail to conform to the communicative and linguistic expectations of the questioning party in a variety of respects:

1. Pragmatic error. The child misunderstands the communicative intent or pragmatic function of the question, e.g. he/she believes no response is necessary and either ignores questions or changes the topic. For example, he/she responds to teacher's remark, "What do we do if our hands are dirty?" with a verbal answer "Wash our hands" but takes no action to clean up his/her dirty hands.

2. Functional appropriateness error (similar to category agreement). The child provides the wrong kind of information, although he/she is not mistaken about the pragmatic function of the question. For example, in response to "When do you go out to play?" the child replies, "in the playground" or "yep."

3. Functional accuracy error. The child provides the general kind of information requested, but the response is deficient in accuracy, fact, logic, or credibility. For example: "When do you brush your teeth?" "Oh, about five years ago" or "When I gots a pink toothbrush." Alternatively, in response to "Who's picking you up after school?" "Big Bird."

4. Structural accuracy error. The child fails to conform to accepted standards for morphologic and syntactic structure. For example: "Whose shoes are these?" (Examiner points to child's shoes) "Them me shoes."

## Pragmatic Considerations in Response Classification

Pragmatic errors in responses to questions may be judged on the basis of the relevance of the reply to the situation and to the pragmatic function of the question. Awareness of context is very important for question interpretation. As Dore (1977) remarked, "The context is often crucial in determining an illocutionary act. Contextual features, in fact, often override the literal meaning of a proposition" (p. 144). Replies which are pragmatically relevant are not necessarily correct in terms of functional appropriateness, functional accuracy, or grammaticality (structural accuracy). However, pragmatically incorrect responses would preclude judgments of adequacy in terms of functional appropriateness or functional accuracy.

Frequently, it may be impossible to discern whether a response would be more aptly classified as a pragmatic error or as an error involving functional inappropriateness, e.g. a child who gives "I know" or "I don't know" or no response. Routine or frequent use of such strategies might suggest pragmatic dysfunction, whereas selective use might indicate pragmatically appropriate delaying strategies, confessions of ignorance, or evasions, some of which might be followed by functionally appropriate verbal or nonverbal responses.

Scoring responses according to pragmatic correctness in a variety of situational interactions which incorporate *wh*-forms and stimulus types as widely varied as possible should clarify to what extent the *wh*-question form and form variations themselves are causing a child difficulty and to what extent determining the pragmatics of the situation is the root of the problem. Precise description of the communicative interaction also will facilitate many decisions about response adequacy in areas besides pragmatic interpretation, e.g. it can facilitate judgments of functional appropriateness. For example, without knowledge of the context and the situational and communicative intents involved in each child's language-learning interactions, it may be difficult, if not impossible, in many instances to judge whether replies like "when it's raining" to questions like "when do we wear a raincoat?" indicate that:

1. The child has interpreted a *when* question as a *why* question incorrectly and is giving a causal reply *or*

2. The child has interpreted the *when* question correctly and is giving an answer which for him or her reflects a temporal, but *not* a causal relationship *or*

3. The child has interpreted the *when* question correctly and is giving an answer which reflects a temporal as well as a causal relationship.

### Scoring According to Functional Appropriateness and Functional Accuracy

The application of scoring criteria for functional appropriateness ensures that we observe children's sensitivity to the general kind of information required by a particular *wh*-question form and that we see the pattern of question form confusions which might occur. Both issues clearly have clinical relevance. However, such scoring protocols alone may lack adequate descriptive power and may be unable to provide sufficient direction for the design of intervention programs dealing with deficiencies in *wh*-question comprehension and response formulation.

The research of Brown, Cazden, and Bellugi-Klima (1969), Brown and Hanlon (1970), and Wood (1981) suggests that adult listeners place a higher premium on the truth, factualness, credibility, and logic of children's answers than on their structural merits. Errors in "functional accuracy" are likely to influence seriously an adult's impression of a childs' maturity and competence as a conversational partner, regardless of the functional appropriateness of the response. Functional accuracy should be examined as a distinct entity.

Both "functional appropriateness" and "functional accuracy" were reported (Parnell et al. 1980, 1982) to be sensitive to subject age, stimulus type, *wh*-question form, and certain interactions among those variables. Monitoring the interaction between functional appropriateness and functional accuracy in association with chronological age permits us to infer changes in children's response strategies beyond the age-related gains in ability to determine the category of information demanded by the various *wh*-forms. The increasing complexity of verbal informational exchange requires examining the proficiency with which a child consolidates and applies to linguistic tasks a fund of general information reflecting his/her cognitive development and experience with the world around him or her. The somewhat "purer" but in some respects superficial scrutiny of "categorical agreement" or "functional appropriateness" alone does not ensure that all relevant aspects of children's question-answering competence will be tapped.

Generally, we see that the recognition and delivery of the general category of information required by a *wh*-form may substantially predate the ability to respond in terms of functional accuracy. These abilities began to converge in our subjects, but the process was not completed. *When, why,* and *what happened* questions illustrated particularly the tendency for younger children's answers, even when functionally appropriate, to remain deficient in accuracy, fact, logic, credibility, etc. The results of our investigation support separate scores for the appropriateness," and for "functional accuracy," which reflects a later developing cognitive-linguistic skill and which appears to be a potentially stricter criterion.

The pattern with which normal children progress from giving functionally inappropriate and thus also functionally inaccurate answers, to giving appropriate but not necessarily accurate responses, to providing finally answers which are acceptable in both respects can be interpreted as support for a teaching method which first demands only that a response indicate ability to distinguish the informational category constraints of a particular *wh*-question form (that the response be functionally appropriate). Only later should the response be required to be not functionally appropriate but also complete, truthful, logical, and in other words "accurate."

## Structural Aspects of the Response

Most of the previous investigations of *wh*-question comprehension focused upon whether (or the degree to which) children's responses met criteria similar to Ervin-Tripp's (1970) "categorical agreement" or to Parnell's "functional appropriateness" (Parnell et al. 1980, 1982). An additional or concurrent emphasis on morphological and syntactic aspects also has appeared in several reports.

We have at our disposal a multitude of commercially prepared and experimental inventories which we can utilize to examine a child's receptive and expressive control óf morphology and syntax. To dwell on the maturity of structure in children's responses to questions ignores the heart of the question-answer contingency in favor of a relatively trivial aspect. Structurally accurate responses are not necessarily adequate with respect to pragmatics, functional appropriateness, or accuracy. We must go beyond the concern with structure to determine whether the child understands the purpose of the question, the semantics of the proposition, his/her own role as the recipient of the question, and whether she/he is willing to fulfill the respondent role and has the general fund of information to draw upon in order to produce a factual, true, logical answer which is likely to satisfy the person who asked the question, or which at the very least does not result in an irretrievable breakdown of the communicative flow.

# Limitation of Commercially Available Instruments, Use of Multiple Trials and Response Consistency Measures

Results of evaluations of children's strengths or weaknesses in *wh*-question comprehension and response should have strong implications, not only for speech-language pathologists but also for educators involved with the general academic program. These analyses could be used to advantage by classroom teachers who wish to adapt their general verbal "language of instruction" and curriculum materials carefully to the comprehension level of particular classes, groups, or individual children. At present, commerically available tests of child language development incorporate *wh*-questions minimally, providing limited variation in communicative context (pragmatic functions, referential source, etc.) and restricted numbers of *wh*-forms and trials for each form, and they offer no opportunities for in-depth analysis of individual strategies. Most available commercial instruments for language assessment are also limited by lack of multiple opportunities for the child to display his/her knowledge of a particular aspect of language. Consistent with most observations of developing abilities, the subjects in our study (Parnell et al. 1980, 1982) did not always answer, nor did they consistently fail to answer, all *three* items representing a particular question form or stimulus type according to the two scoring criteria. We found it useful to view informally the degrees of consistency of the responses as predictors of whether the necessary strategies were unobservable, emerging, or reasonably stable. We encourage clinicians to provide multiple opportunities or trials whenever feasible, particularly since as yet specific question items have not been assessed critically for their relative diagnostic value.

For the time being, speech-language pathologists and other language-learning specialists will need to devise their own assessment tools, with prior review and consideration of available research in the area of *wh*-question comprehension and response, in order to obtain a thorough inventory of a child's competence in understanding and answering questions that is applicable to learning in a variety of functional contexts. In designing *wh*-question evaluation or teaching tasks, the clinician should consider seriously the limitations of normative group data for predicting the strategies or instructional needs of any individual child. The response data of most *wh*-question - related studies reveal substantial variation among subjects in overall performance and in the particular linguistic strategies employed. The clinician's evaluative model, selection of question items, and scoring procedures need to be weighed and modified to answer the needs of each individual child and designed to gain the most revealing and representative glimpses of the child's question-answering strategies as they are employed in the contexts of his/her daily experiences in language learning, social growth, and development as a communicatively competent individual.

## Research Needs and Considerations

At present, we do not have sufficient knowledge of the questioning demands children experience from adults or other children. We are particularly uninformed about their conversations with persons other than their mothers and about the questions addressed to children in a school or clinic setting. An index which specifies the relative frequency with which children are faced with a particular *wh*-question form and which takes into account variation in communicative setting, pragmatic function, and the proportion of immediate and nonimmediate referential sources would be extremely valuable. The literature suggests that adults adapt their interrogation by *wh*-forms fairly closely to the children's ability to respond. However, we need more specific data concerning the interaction of pragmatic function, *wh*-form, and referential source in questions posed to children of varying ages and developmental levels as a guideline for designing models for assessment and intervention.

Similarly, we lack precise understanding of the ways in which adults and children actually judge the adequacy of the responses they receive from the conversational partners to whom they have addressed a *wh*-question. The scoring models proposed by the researchers reviewed earlier remain models in need of confirmation. Investigation of the criteria which parents, peers, and teachers apparently employ in judging the acceptability of answers and of the ways in which their overall impression of the child's linguistic ability and social competence may be related to these criteria appears to be a logical next step. Further information about the actual questioning demands experienced by children (both normal and language-disordered) and about the consequences of particular response strategies for listener judgment and for the communicative encounter itself, along with developmental data about *wh*-question mastery would help us to devise sensitive, predictive diagnostic measures and to prioritize the goals of intervention.

Obviously there is much that we do not know about normally developing children's patterns of interpretation and response to *wh*-questions and about the role of the communication context in fostering this aspect of communication development. However, the scarcity of data revealing the strategies and limitations of language-disordered children is equally striking. It is imperative that the information that *is* available at present be used to guide efforts to discover in what ways a language-disordered child may fail to learn effective question-answering strategies and by what means those strategies may be shaped toward greater communicative efficiency.

# References

Bloom, L., & Lahey, M. *Language development and language disorders* New York: John Wiley & Sons, 1978.

Broen, P.A. The verbal environment of the language-learning child: *ASHA monograph* 17, Washington D.C.: American Speech and Hearing Association, 1972.

Brown, R.W. The development of Wh questions in child speech. *Journal of Verbal Learning and Verbal Behavior,* 1968, *7,* 279-290.

Brown, R.W., & Bellugi, U. Three processes in the child's acquisition of syntax. *Harvard Educational Review,* 1964, *34,* 133-151.

Brown, R.W., Cazden, C., & Bellugi-Klima R. The child's grammar from I to III. In J.P. Hill (Ed.), *Minnesota symposia on child psychology.* Minneapolis: University of Minnesota Press, 1969.

Brown, R.W., & Hanlon, C. Derivational complexity and order of acquisition in child speech. In J.R. Hayes (Ed.), *Cognition and the development of language.* New York: John Wiley & Sons, 1970.

Cairns, H.S., & Hsu, J.R. Who, why, when and how: A development study. *Journal of Child Language,* 1978, *5,* 478-488.

Dore, J. Oh Them Sheriff: A pragmatic analysis of children's responses to questions. In S. Ervin-Tripp and C. Mitchell-Kernan, (Eds.), *Child discourse.* New York: Academic Press, Inc., 1977.

Ervin-Tripp, S. Discourse agreement: How children answer questions. In J.R. Hayes (Ed.), *Cognition and the development of language.* New York: John Wiley & Sons, 1970.

Ervin-Tripp, S. An overview of theories of grammatical development. In D. Slobin (Ed.), *The ontogenesis of grammar.* New York: Academic Press, 1971.

Hood, L. A longitudinal study of the development of the expression of causal relations in complex sentences. Unpublished doctoral dissertation, Columbia University, 1977.

Hooper, R. Communicative development and children's responses to questions. *Speech Monographs,* 1971, *38,* 2-9.

James, S.L., & Seebach, M.A. The pragmatic function of children's questions. *Journal of Speech and Hearing Research,* 1982, *25,* 2-11.

Leach, E. Interrogation: A model and some implications. *Journal of Speech and Hearing Disorders,* 1972, *37,* 33-46.

Nelson, K. Structure and strategy in learning to talk. *Monographs of the Society for Research in Child Development,* 1973, Serial 149, *38.* 1—2.

Parnell, M.M., Patterson, S., & Harding, M.A. Understanding of Certain Wh-Question Forms by Young Children. Paper presented at ASHA convention, Detroit, MI, 1980.

Parnell, M.M., & Amerman, J.D., Patterson. S., & Harding, M. Answers to *Wh-*Questions: A Developmental Study. Unpublished Manuscript, (1982).

Rodgon, M.M. Knowing what to say and wanting to say it: Some communicative and structural aspects of single-word response to questions. *Journal of Child Language,* 1979, *6,* 81-90.

Searle, J. *Speech Acts.* London: Cambridge University Press, 1969.

Shatz, M. How to do things by asking: Form-function pairing in mother's questions and their relation to children's responses. *Child Development,* 1979, *50,* 1093-1099.

Soderburg, R. The fruitful dialogue, the child's acquisition of his first language; Implications for education at all ages. *Project child language syntax,* Reprint No. 2, Stockholm University, Institution for Nordiska Sprak, 1974.

Thorndike E., & Lorge, I. *The teachers word book of 30,000 words.* New York: Teacher's College Press, Columbia University, 1944.

Toler, S.A., & Bankson, N.W. Utilization of an interrogative model to evaluate mother's use and childrens comprehension of question forms. *Journal of Speech and Hearing Disorders,* 1976, *41,* 301-314.

Tyack, D., & Ingram, D. Childrens' production and comprehension of questions. *Journal of Child Language,* 1977, *4,* 211-224.

Wood, B.S. *Children and communication: Verbal and nonverbal language development.* Englewood Cliff, N.J.: Prentice-Hall, Inc., 1981.

Yorkston, K.M., & Beukelman, D.R. An analysis of connected speech samples of aphasic and normal speakers. *Journal of Speech and Hearing Disorders,* 1980, *45,* 27-36.

# 7

# LANGUAGE DEVELOPMENT AND READING*

## Paula Menyuk
Boston University

## Introduction

*I*n a paper concerning the use of language to control and plan motor behaviors Wozniak (1972) presents the following paradox: How can we tell ourselves something we don't already know? In this statement Wozniak is presenting the dilemma of researchers who attempt to explore the relation between "cognition" and "language." Although, in general (there are exceptions), the child doesn't talk about things he/she doesn't know about, it is clear that talking about what one knows about, either to oneself or aloud, modifies what is known. It has become evident to researchers in this area that simple-minded notions about dependency relations between non-linguistic cognitive development and linguistic cognitive development do not provide adequate explanations of development in either domain or developments that depend on interaction of the two domains. (Menyuk, 1980).

"How can one read what one does not know in oral language?" would be stating a paradox similar to the one cited above concerning the relation between cognition and language. Researchers who are concerned with the relation between oral and written language development have become increasingly uncomfortable with the simplistic notion that written language processing is wholly dependent on oral language knowledge. The reading researcher is interested in obtaining a detailed description of the relations between oral and written language development just as the developmental researcher is interested in determining, in detail, the relations between the non-linguistic and linguistic domains of development.

In this paper, I will present some notions about possible relations between developments in the two domains of oral and written language. I will do this by first discussing the findings of studies of oral language development that seem

*Paper prepared for "Understanding Reading Comprehension," James Flood (Ed), International Reading Assoc.

germane to the issue. Some hypotheses concerning the relation between the two domains of development and some data directly assessing the proposed relation will then be reviewed. Finally, some conclusions will be drawn about possible relations. These will, of necessity, be highly tentative conclusions since detailed explorations of relations between the domains of development are still in their infancy stage.

## Oral Language Development

The latest (over the past ten years) studies of oral language development have seriously challenged the notion that the child knows most of what she/he has to learn about the structure and use of oral language by the age of five to six years. Before that time it was thought that "almost" adult competence in, at least, phonological and syntactic knowledge was achieved by that age (Mc Neill, 1970). More recent studies indicate that developmental changes in knowledge of syntactic and morpho-phonological rules continue to occur after age five and, indeed, throughout the school years. Therefore, it is not the case that the child on entrance to school "has" a fully mature grammar of the language which might then be available for processing all types of written material presented. There are areas of structural knowledge which remain to be acquired.

Despite the above statements, the normally developing child does know a great deal about the language on entrance to school and has been communicating effectively with others in his/her environment for a number of years. This substantial knowledge exists in all aspects of language: pragmatics, semantics, syntax, and morpho-phonology (Menyuk, 1977). Further, and importantly, this competence in communication has been achieved by all normally developing children *in their native language* regardless of socio-economic status (Ervin-Tripp, 1971). Emphasis has been placed on the term "in their native language" since varying degrees of competence are to be expected in use of a second language.

The questions that arise, then are: what do most children know about language at age five and what are they yet to learn over the school years and what differences in language knowledge exist among normally developing children that may affect acquisition of written language? The remainder of this section will attempt to deal with these questions.

It was stated above that normally developing children at age five have acquired substantial knowledge of all aspects of language. What children appear to know in each of these aspects will be discussed separately since, it will be argued, each aspect of oral language knowledge plays a differing role in the acquisition of written language knowledge.

The pragmatic rules of a language are concerned with how to convey the purpose of the utterance; that is, to assert, command, request, question, negate, etc. These purposes have been termed "speech acts" (Clark and Clark, 1977). Another aspect of pragmatic competence is knowledge of how to engage in conversation. This latter requires the ability to keep track of what is being said and has been said in the conversation as well as physical parameters that are crucial to clarity of communication. Cultural rules of how to say what to whom under what circumstances (for example, rules of politeness) must also be learned.

Pragmatic competence, then, involves both knowledge of structural rules and rules of use of language that require both on-going memorial abilities (keeping track in conversation) and, in some instances, retrieval from memory of past exchanges. In addition, particular cultural rules for exchange must be kept in mind and these require both situational and addressee appraisal for appropriate communication. A great deal of what makes for pragmatic competence depends on inferencing abilities (for example, interpretation of paralinguistic cues of intonation, stress and gesture and keeping in mind referents or deducing referents from situational cues) rather than merely understanding the utterances produced.

Although the child at age five communicates very efffectively with members of his/her own linguistic community and know how to generate the speech acts listed above there are any number of communicative situations the child has yet to learn about (for example, how to converse with a teacher), a number of domains of discourse that the child has relative unfamiliarity with (for example, formal mathematical and scientific notions) and a number of speech acts that the child has yet to engage in (for example, commissives or argumentation based on causal, conditional or hypothetical physical conditions). Development of these abilities will continue over the school years. Development of these abilities is highly dependent on further experience. The domains of discourse in the home and classroom and the written materials children are exposed to are the experiences which will broaden pragmatic competence. Domains of discourse are also a critical source for acquisition of word knowledge.

Semantic and syntactic knowledge is knowledge of word meanings in the context of varying structures. For example, comprehension of the sentence "The boy kissed the girl." requires knowledge of the meaning of each morpheme in the sentence (boy, kiss, ed, girl) and the relation between morphemes (the modifies boy and girl; the boy is the actor and the girl the object; ed modifies kiss).

By the time the child enters school he/she has acquired a vocabulary of some two to three thousand words and is using these words in structurally complete utterances. The child's acquisition of word knowledge is derived initially from physical contextual information and then from the linguistic contexts in which words are used. An unfamiliar word such as "avocado" might be partially identified in a context such as "He likes avocadoes in his salad." The two areas of development, semantic and syntactic, are mutually interdependent. In addition to the child having acquired a sizable lexicon by the time he/she enters school he/she is also able to understand a number of structurally different types of utterances which allows further interpretation of old lexical items and interpretation of new lexical items. These new lexical items allow, in turn, acquisition of knowledge of still other syntactic structures. It should be stressed that comprehension of the meaning of utterances is dependent on both lexical and syntactic knowledge.

The further developments of word knowledge that occur after entering school are, obviously, an increase in the size of the available lexicon and, less obviously, changes in the meaning of the words in the lexicon. This developmental change takes place in two ways. One way is an increased hierarchical organization of words which provides connections between words. For example, red, white, blue, etc. are organized into the category of color and have the same privileges of occurrence in sentences; man, woman, boy, girl, etc. are humans; plants, animals, humans are living things; run and jump are action verbs; believe, think, know are stative verbs. A second direction in which word knowledge grows is the understanding that words can have more than one meaning and play different roles in sentences.

Knowledge of the syntactic possibilities in the language also grows. Knowledge of types of structures such as double function relative clauses ("The cat that the dog chased ran into the bushes."), complement ("Joe promised Bill that he would go.") are acquired over the school years and beyond. Further, just as in semantic development, not only is further knowledge acquired but the depth of knowledge changes as well. The child becomes aware of structural paraphrase possibilities in the language (there is more than one way to say the same thing) and, therefore, connections between structures. The child, also, becomes aware of ambiguities (there is more than one meaning that a sentence can have). Again, these developments continue over the school years and beyond.

By the time the child enters school he/she is able to discriminate between all the phonological segments in the language that are crucial for word identification and can accurately generate most of these segments with the possible exception of strident clusters (/str/, /spr/, etc.). In addition the child is able to apply plural and tense markers appropriately, although she/he may still be having some difficulty with strong nouns ("feet") and, more frequently, strong verbs ("brought"). Despite this clear ability to accurately perceive and produce phonological distinctions in the language, many children are unable to segment words into phonological components at this age. Others have difficulty in rhyming words ("cat," "hat," "bat") or generating words that have the same initial sounds ("bat," "ball," "boat"). These abilities develop over the early school years and, as with other areas of development, are probably enhanced by engaging in the reading acquisition process. Thus, although children tend to group words on the basis of their surface structure (phonology) rather than meaning at four years of age (in the series "cap," "can," "hat," "cap," and "can" are grouped and not "cap" and "hat") and to provide "clang" responses to unknown words on a word association task, there does not appear to be a conscious awareness of phonological segments as belonging to a category among all children on entrance to school.

A further development that takes place over the school years in the morphophonological aspect of language is acquisition of knowledge of 1) rules of stress to create different syntactic categories (**permit, permit**) and to create nominal compounds (**bird**house) and 2) rules of phonological change to create different syntactic categories ("sane - sanity", "discuss - discussion"). These phonological developments are like developments in other aspects of language. Some of these developments require acquisition of new knowledge (derivational rules for complex words such as "indisputable") and other developments require reorganization of old knowledge; observation of similarities in sets of categories (segmental and syllabic "paraphrases"). Unlike category developments in other aspects of language many of the segmental and syllabic categorizations the child must make are unrelated to meaning. The categories /b/ or /t/, /ub/ or /ut/ carry no meaning.

The above findings indicate that, although the child at age five or six appears to be a highly competent speaker-listener of the language, further developments occur in all aspects of language over the school years. Many of these developments, as we shall argue, seem particularly important for the reading acquisition process. Figure 7-1 presents a summary of these further developments in each aspect of language. In all aspects of language new categories of language knowledge are acquired and this knowledge is applied in new contextual and linguistic domains. For example, pragmatic discourse knowledge is applied to an increasing number of differing situations, lexical knowledge is used in an increasing number of areas of inquiry, semantax knowledge is applied in increasingly different and abstract contexts, phonological knowledge is applied over increasingly longer and more complex words. In three aspects of language (lexicon, semantax and phonology) relations between or paraphrase of categories is observed. In two (lexicon and semantax) multiple meanings are acquired.

**FIGURE 7-1**
**Summary of development in each aspect of language over the school years**

## Aspects of Language

| Pragmatics | Lexicon | Semantax | Phonology |
|---|---|---|---|
| New categories | New categories | New categories | New categories |
| New domain application | New domain application | New domain application | New domain application |
| | Relations between categories | Relations between categories | Relations between categories |
| | Multiple meanings | Multiple meanings | |

The above data address the first questions posed: what do children know about language on entrance to school and what are they yet to learn? The second question (what differences in language knowledge are there among normally developing children which may affect reading acquisition?) is a more difficult question to answer since it is not entirely clear exactly what children have to know about language to acquire reading. There are, however, some obvious differences in language knowledge which affect the reading acquisition process. Clearly, different children develop at different rates. Theoretically, then, different children aged five or six years, will bring to the reading acquisition process different sets of knowledge about the varying aspects of language. As we will argue below, these differences in language knowledge might certainly affect what material can be read and understood but it is not clear that such differences should affect the reading acquisiton process per se when the material to be read is very simple structurally and lexically.

Another source of difference which might seriously affect the acquisition process itself are differences in the content and organization of a child's language knowledge. It has been argued that the orthography is indifferent to dialectal or native language variation (Menyuk, 1976). All readers are required to translate the orthography into their lexical-phonological representations to access word meaning. However, if a "double" translation is required (that is, from orthography to a second language and then to the native language) then the task may not only be more difficult but also depend on the accessibility of such translations to the reader (Chu-Chang, 1979). The ease with which these latter children engage in the acquisition process may, therefore, be very dependent on the degree of familiarity these children have with the lexicon of the second language. The organization and content of their knowledge of other aspects of language will affect how they continue to read.

# Possible Relations to Reading

It was stated above that the amount of knowledge about language as indicated in spontaneous language production does not appear to be the factor that crucially distinguishes between good, average and poor readers who do not have a obvious difficulty in oral language. Weak, although significant, correlations have been found between such measures as vocabulary and sentence length and reading performance at grades one and two (Bougere, 1969). It is, of course, during the early years of school (grades one through three) that reading materials are carefully controlled and do not seriously challenge the language knowledge acquired by most children at ages five through seven or eight. As discussed below, this does not continue to be the case throughout the school years. It was also stated that speakers of another native language might have difficulty in acquiring reading because of, possibly, being confronted with a double translation task.

The statements above are meant to suggest that the relation between oral language knowledge and reading differs depending on the nature of the reading task and over time. They are further meant to suggest that oral language knowledge differences between good, average and poor readers may vary and that particular differences will affect the reading behavior of the individual child initially and over time.

What will be argued throughout this section is that different aspects of oral language knowledge and state of knowledge of these aspects are required in the processing of written material over time. It will also be argued that with time or maturation these relations undergo a change. That is, it will be suggested that Vygotsky (1978) was partially correct when he stated, " . . . written language consists of a system of signs that designate the sounds and words of spoken language, which in turn are signs for real entities and relations. Gradually this intermediate link, spoken language, disappears and written language is converted into a system of signs that directly symbolize the entities and relations between them " (p. 106). Vygotsky's statement implied that at the beginning of the reading acquisition process reference is always made to a linguistic representation of an orthographic category (letter, word, sentence). This requires bringing to conscious awareness these linguistic representations. But, as the process becomes mature it no longer requires bringing to conscious awareness these linguistic representations. The process becomes automatic. My first statement implies, however, that if the orthography represents linguistic entities and relations that are not easily accessible to the reader and then the process does require bringing these entities and relations to conscious awareness. Therefore, orthographic representations of well learned structures will be read automatically, representations of less well learned structures will require conscious awareness of their oral language representations and representations of structures that have not yet been acquired will be incorrectly read because of approximations made to the text based on structures that are available (Menyuk, in press).

The three categories of reading tasks to be considered in this discussion are: acquisition, comprehending and comprehension. The first and initial task, acquisition, has been viewed in two ways; as a decoding or word attack task or as a procedure to discover how language is represented in orthography. There is a vast array of data collected by Goodman (1976) supporting the fact that children during the earliest and later stages of reading make guesses about the words they read based on the linguistic context of what they are reading and extra-linguistic knowledge. There is an equally impressive array of data which indicates that the first step in accessing the lexicon in reading is via translation of the orthography of the word into the phonological representation of that word. These latter data also suggest that the process of translating the orthography into a phonological representation requires bringing to conscious awareness this phonological representation by relating the letters of the words to sound segments and reconstituting them (Liberman, Liberman, Mattingly and Schankweiler, 1978). These researchers find, for example, that there is a significant correlation between the ability of young children to count the number of segments in CVC (consonant - vowel - consonant) words and reading achievement during the early grades.

It is not clear that these two positions are mutually exclusive even at the beginning stages of reading except when words are presented in isolation. Then accessing must be through phonological representation. But when the child is reading a sentence the sentential context in conjunction with minimal orthographic-phonological cues may elicit guesses that are correct in terms of semantic field (for example "toy" for "train") or partially correct phonologically but incorrect semantically (for example "fort" for "fortune"). These examples are taken from Goodman's article. These so-called miscues may be corrected by reference to phonological representations of orthography or by reference to both phonology and semantics.

Since it seems to be the case that being taught to read helps to develop awareness of phonological segments and that, in fact, illiterate adults have difficulty in segmenting words (Liberman, et al., 1978), it may be the case that semantic representations may interact with phonological representations to store in memory relations between orthographic representations, phonological representations and meanings during the beginning of the reading process. When this does occur for a particular word then the reading of the word becomes automatic and no longer requires bringing to conscious awareness either the phonological or semantic representation of that word. A parallel processing procedure would be required initially in which both phonological and semantic representations must be brought to conscious awareness.

At the beginning stages of reading a word, or in the process of reading acquisition, therefore, phonological segments and semantic features must be brought to conscious awareness. If the child has yet to achieve the ability of phonological segmentation and reference to orthography, then learning to read will be a difficult process. Similarly, if the child is able to relate orthography and phonology but has no semantic representation for the product or has difficulty in accessing this representation, there would be equal difficulty in reading. There are two populations in whom this latter difficulty is observed; children with so-called word retrieval problems (Wolf, in press) and children required to read a language with which they have little familiarity. Gleitman and Gleitman (1979) note that the difficulty in word segmentation and reconstruction continues to distinguish successful from unsuccessful readers through twelfth grade. They suggest that poor readers have acquired a logography; a set of memorized words, and that, therefore, as the list of words to be read rapidly exceeds this finite list the reader who is unable to apply word attack skills will flounder. It might be the case, however, that word attack skills, alone, are not the only requirement in comprehending written sentences. Further knowledge of other aspects of the language are required when the materials to be read are sentences and not simply words.

Listening to and comprehending sentences clearly requires not only phonological accessing but, also, lexical, syntactic and pragmatic knowledge. For example, the listener when attempting to understand a double function relative clause such as "The horse that raced past the barn fell," needs to have knowledge of the syntactic possibilities of the language, the meaning of words, a strategy for determining clause boundaries (Bever, 1970) and the ability to keep in mind the whole sentence in order to comprehend it. One would assume that reading and comprehending sentences also calls upon each and every one of these aspects of linguistic knowledge and not simply translation of orthography into phonology. One can also assume that the child's knowledge of all these aspects of language changes with maturation.

At the beginning stages of reading acquisition the materials that children are required to read are usually simple sentences that are well within their level of syntactic and lexical knowledge. Additionally, the subject matter is usually within the child's experience. The beginning reader reads about topics and relations that he/she is familiar with and which, usually, meet his/her pragmatic expectations.

Some examples, again taken from Goodman (1976), make the point clear. For the beginning reader the following is provided:

Jimmy said, "Come here, Sue, look at my toy train. See it go."

For the older reader the following passage was read:

"So education it was! I opened the dictionary and picked out a word that sounded good."

The relative lexical and syntactic complexity of the two passages is evident. Further, in the first passage how Jimmy is talking to Sue and what he is talking about seems reasonable if not an exact representation of what might be said. The assumption being made is that it is "easier" for the beginning reader to read language that is composed of linguistic categories and relations that the young child can easily process. Thus, at the beginning stages of reading the principal requirement is translation of word orthography into phonological and semantic representations. However, after this task has been achieved (it is clearly not a minimal one for some beginning readers) the reference to lexical entries and sentence relations in the material are probably automatic since the words are well known and are in sentence structures that are well learned. Comprehending written sentences of these simple forms becomes an automatic process and does not require bringing to conscious awareness the relations beings expressed.

Some children who learn how to read the materials presented to them in the first through third grade encounter difficulty in the fourth grade. This difficulty has been attributed to the sudden requirement to read materials that are no longer carefully controlled for vocabulary and structure. It is probable that the problem lies not in the nature of the reading material but, rather, in the reader since a large number of children do not find this change in the structure of material a source of difficulty. The problem may lie in the fact that while the child is learning more about the structure of language (and as we have indicated previously, the child learns a great deal more about language over the school years than he/she knew before) he/she is, simultaneously, being confronted with more complex written material. This material is more complex in all structural aspects of language (lexicon, syntax and morpho-phonology) and is also less familiar in terms of topic.

A possible source of difficulty for some readers might then be in comprehending sentences that contain structures that are relatively unfamiliar. What appears to be universal in the reading process is that the process initially requires the ability to bring to conscious awareness the structural categories and relations in language and that with time the process becomes automatic. But automaticity requires easy availability of the structures being read. If these categories and relations are not easily accessible to the reader (be they morpho-phonological, lexical or syntactic) the reader encounters difficulty in comprehending the sentences read.

Reading a passage or story requires still other linguistic skills. These latter skills are needed in comprehension of the content and interpretation of connected sentences. The ability to integrate information across sentences and retain (remember) crucial information is required. The task is somewhat similar to listening to and comprehending a story or oral lecture. In this latter task verbatim recall of sentences becomes impossible and listeners attempt to select, integrate and organize linguistic information across sentences (Clark and Clark, 1977).The reader also must select, integrate and organize linguistic information. Varying descriptions of these abilities have been used. For example, some researchers have described organizational ability as employment of a story grammar (Stein and Glenn, 1979) when the context *is* a story. Other researchers have described selection and integration of materials as inferencing abilities (Frederickson, 1976).

In summary, the processes employed by the reader depend on the structure of the material to be read. Reading of words engages different aspects of language knowledge from that of reading of sentences which, in turn, engages different aspects from that of reading of passages. The different types of knowledge required in reading are presented in Figure 7-2.

**FIGURE 7-2**
**Levels of language required depending on reading task**

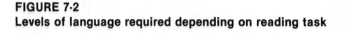

Phonological decoding

Word retrieval
    ⟶ Word level

Phrase analysis

Sentence analysis
    ⟶ Sentence level

Integrate information

    across sentences

    (ex: pronominalization)

    across passages
    ⟶ Passage level

    (ex: inference)

Memorial processes

The highest level of processing (passage) requires some processing at other levels. The processing is parallel and, therefore, requires some information from all levels simultaneously but just as in oral language processing, does not require complete information from all levels.

Further, the linguistic knowledge of the reader changes with development as does the material he/she is required to read. As the child's linguistic knowledge increases and as his/her linguistic processing abilities mature, the complexity of the materials to be read increases. In many instances these two developments are congruous but in some instances they are not. Still further, a reciprocal arrangement appears to exist between having linguistic knowledge available, bringing it to conscious awareness, and reading. That is, the process of reading requires the intuitive language user to initially bring to conscious awareness the categories and relations in language. Learning how to read and reading, therefore, provides new insights into the structure of language to the language user. However, and importantly, if the reader does not have oral language knowledge of certain categories and relations available they obviously cannot be brought to conscious awareness for the reading task. The most obvious level at which awareness is required is the morpho-phonological and lexical level. Indeed, it has been suggested that difficulty at this level alone can account for most of the difficulty of poor readers from childhood to adulthood (Gleitman and Gleitman, 1979). It has been suggested here that availability of categories and relations in all aspects of language contribute to comprehending and comprehension of written material.

The above statements are hypothetical. There is very little evidence available to support the above position. There is a wealth of direct evidence concerning the importance of phonological awareness in acquisition of reading. There is, however, also a wealth of evidence, based on miscues in reading, to support the notion that other aspects of language are actively used in the reading process. In the next section some additional evidence will be presented to support the notion that awareness of structural relations in sentences plays a role in the reading process.

## Some Preliminary Data

There have been two studies which have, in differing ways, examined the relation between syntactic development and reading. Bowey (1980) found upon examining the abilities of third, fourth and fifth grade readers to read differently structured sentences aloud, that significantly more errors occurred with complex sentences as compared to simple sentences. For example, children had more difficulty with passive and relative clause sentences than they did with active and question sentences. Goldsmith (1977) found that children aged 9 to 11 years had greater difficulty in comprehending orally and in written form relative clause sentences as compared to conjoined sentences. The dyslexic children in this population had more difficulty with relative clause sentences than did the non-dyslexic children but both groups of children had increasing difficulty with more complex types of relative clause sentences than with simpler types. For example, the children found sentences such as "The boy who kissed the girl ran away" easier to understand than sentences such as "The cat that the dog chased ran into the house."

These data indicate that relative unfamiliarity with structures leads to greater difficulty in reading them aloud and greater difficulty in comprehending these sentences in either oral or written form. It seems reasonable to suggest that the further syntactic developments that occur over the school years in oral language development can account for the differences found in reading performance with different structures. These further developments are either more delayed in a dyslexic population (i.e. the more complex structures are simply not available at the same age) or the processing skills required for comprehending these more complex structures are not available to the dyslexic children. In either case, and with both normal and dyslexic readers, there seems to be a relation between syntactic oral language knowledge and reading performance.

Oppenheim (1981) examined the oral linguistic processing skills of average kindergarten children and their later reading performance. Two aspects of language processing were examined; phonological and syntactic. She found that the ability to segment words *and* the ability to comprehend sentences with embedded structures was significantly predictive of later reading performance. The two liguistic processing behaviors appeared to be related in that those children with better segmenting abilities were also those children who were better able to comprehend sentences with embedded structures. These latter findings may indicate that some of the processing abilities required at the word and sentence level are the same and that these same processing skills are required in reading as well as listening.

Two studies have examined the morpho-phonological processing of complex derived words. Myerson (1976) examined the ability of children aged eight to seventeen years to derive words from nonsense stems by the application of appropriate phonological rules (for example, "glanity" from "glane" using the model of "sane" - "sanity"). Myerson found that there were developmental changes in the ability of children over this age range to apply the appropriate rules and that some children, at age seventeen, could not apply all the rules required in the task. Myerson also found that there were significant differences between poor, average and good readers in their ability to apply these rules.

Loritz (1981) studied third and fifth grade children's ability to read aloud real and nonsense polysyllabic words. The question being examined was the possible relation between the ability to decode polysyllabic words by application of appropriate stress rules and reading and spelling abilities. Loritz found developmental differences between the grades in application of simple (left-right) versus more advanced (right-left) application of rules. Among the fifth graders, also, there were differences in application of rules. Age alone did not determine ability to apply appropriate rules. Acquisition of advanced rules was found to be significantly correlated with standardized measures of vocabulary, spelling and reading.

Just as syntactic knowledge increases over the school years so does morpho-phonological knowledge. The decoding or word attack skills required with polysyllabic words which have undergone derivational changes from base stems demand more than the ability to segment base words and relate them to phonological representation. Both of the above studies provide evidence that those children who have acquired more advanced knowledge or morpho-phonological rules are also the more advanced readers for their age and/or grade. Most of the studies discussed so far indicate that level of phonological and syntactic knowledge affects how written linguistic structures are processed. However, it was previously suggested that it is simply not how much one knows intuitively about the differing aspects of language which; predict reading performance but, rather, that the degree of knowledge of any particular structure, as indicated by being able to bring it to conscious awareness, predicts how well that category or relation will be read. What has been found, developmentally, is that children appear to intuitively comprehend and produce linguistic structures before they achieve the ability to judge whether a sentence is correct or incorrect and they achieve this latter ability before they are able to correct incorrect forms. It has also been found that the most sophisticated behaviors (judgment and correction) occur with differing structures as the child matures. Intuitive knowledge of varying structures precedes conscious knowledge of these structures. The most sophisticated form of knowledge of structures is being able to bring this knowledge to conscious awareness. However, this ability does not appear for all structures at a particular period of development. The ability to bring differing structures to conscious awareness depends on how well the child has learned particular structures. For example, at the time when a child can bring to conscious awareness tense and plural markers he/she may still be unable to bring to conscious awareness the relation expressed in center-embedded relative clauses (Menyuk, 1977). As indicated previously, reading aids in bringing structures to conscious awareness but the structures must be there for reading to aid in awareness.

All of the oral language tasks and, by definition, the reading tasks described above require bringing to conscious awareness knowledge of varying syntactic and morpho-phonological structures. However, none of the above studies explicitly examined meta-linguistic awareness of particular structures and the ability to read these same structures. A study undertaken by Flood and Menyuk (1979) indicated that ability to read structures might be dependent on awareness of structures. Developmental data from studies of oral language processing abilities had indicated that the ability to paraphrase occurs during the middle childhood years and that, further, the ability to paraphrase lexically occurs before the ability to paraphrase structurally. The same sequence of abilities appears when the task is one of detecting ambiguity but the ability to paraphrase precedes the ability to detect ambiguity in the lexical domain and the same sequence is observed in the structural domain. Using these data as a basis, Menyuk and Flood examined the ability of fourth grade average and above average readers to read and paraphrase lexically and structurally, to read and detect lexical and structural ambiguities and to paraphrase the two (or more) underlying meanings of ambiguous sentences. It was found that the ability to carry out the two types of tasks was significantly correlated with reading ability. It was also found that there were differences between the average and above average readers in terms of the complexity of the structures they could paraphrase and the options for paraphrase they selected. The above average readers could more easily deal with structural paraphrase and more frequently selected to paraphrase by structural rather than lexical means than did the average readers. The data indicated developmental differences between average and good readers in meta-linguistic awareness of the same structures.

To more directly test the hypothesis, rather than relying on the findings of other studies, a pilot study has been carried out to examine metalinguistic awareness of varying structures in oral language processing *and* written language processing (Menyuk and Flood, in preparation). This research was supported by the deed grant from Boston University. Fourth, 7th, 10th grade and adult good and poor readers were asked to judge and correct non-grammatical and anomalous sentences and to paraphrase sentences and detect ambiguities in sentences in both the oral and written mode. The preliminary findings, in comparing good and poor readers, indicate that poor readers perform more poorly than good readers at all age/grade levels in both modes of processing. In fact, adult poor readers do worse than 4th grade good readers. There are developmental changes which occur in both the modes of processing for all the aspects of meta-linguistic awareness assessed in good readers but much less marked developmental changes in the poor reading population. The order of difficulty of processing the varying structures is similar throughout the age range for both good and poor readers and across listening and reading tasks. The ability to paraphrase and to judge anomaly and non-grammaticality is consistently better than detection of ambiguity when the sentence is presented either orally or in written form, This is quite consistent with other developmental findings. The reading and listening behavior of good readers is quite similar but there is a tendency for poor readers to do somewhat better in detecting ambiguity in the listening mode and somewhat better with paraphrase in the reading mode. This makes sense if the assumption is correct that well-learned structures (i.e., those easily available) can be processed more easily in the written than in the oral mode because the former mode places less constraints on memory (Menyuk, in press).

These preliminary findings that varying aspects of meta-linguistic abilities continue to develop over the school years in good readers and that these abilities are related in listening to and reading sentences lend some support to the notion that oral language meta-knowledge is related to reading throughout the school years. However, these preliminary studies still leave many questions about the details of the relation over time and, importantly, about what differences exist between good, average and poor readers in meta-linguistic abilities.

The issue of application of language knowledge to the reading of passages has not yet been addressed. Although it may be the case that comprehending written sentences is a prerequisite to comprehension of passages, such comprehension clearly demands more and something different than the comprehending of sentences. It was previously stated that selection, integration, organization and recall are required in this task. There has been a great deal of research on children's early development of the ability to recall stories in terms of story grammer (Stein and Glenn, 1979), use of topical information to make inferences and references in stories (Brown, Smiley, Day, Townsend, and Lawton, 1977) and to infer, in general, from spoken language (Barclay and Reid, 1974). There has, however, not been a systematic examination of the developing child's ability to select, integrate, organize and recall the same material when presented orally and in written form. Until such comparisons take place we can simply point to some data which indicate that there is likely to be a relation between the two when recall constraints are similar in oral and written comprehension (i.e., when the written passage is not present for recall).

Two studies have been carried out with "special" populations that have some bearing on the issue. Wilson (1979) compared deaf and hearing children's ability to answer verbatim and inferential questions about short (4 sentences) stories presented through the air (orally and signed) and in written form. The children were reading at 2nd, 3rd, 4th and 5th grade levels. In this study the children's ability to comprehend the sentences containing various structures was pre-tested. The deaf children showed a significant developmental trend in the acquisition of linguistic inference abilities whereas no such trend was observed with hearing children; hearing children reading at 2nd grade level were able to answer inferential questions almost as well as those reading at higher levels. There were remarkable differences between the two groups in their ability to accurately answer inferential questions but not in their ability to answer literal questions. Very importantly, hearing subjects performed significantly better with spoken than with written presentation wheras the inverse occurred with the deaf children. These data indicate the very early ability of hearing children to draw inferences from heard stories. These abilities are then applied to written stories. This ability, as stated previously, is an important one in comprehension and recall of passages.

Another study provides some evidence concerning the importance of inferential abilities in comprehension and recall of spoken stories. In this study (Graybeal, 1981), the ability of language disordered and normally developing children to recall orally presented stories was examined. Sentence comprehending was also pre-tested. The principal difference between the groups was in the amount of information recalled. There was no difference between groups in the components of story grammar recalled or in the order in which they were recalled. It was also found that after two types of treatment conditions (one in which verbatim questions were asked and one in which inferential questions were asked) that the amount of information recalled by the language disordered children was markedly improved after inferential questions were asked but not after verbatim questions were asked. No such effect was observed with normally developing children. They were performing very well to begin with. Although the written language processing of these children was not assessed, the findings of this and the previous study described lend some support to the notion that inferential abilities are important in passage comprehension and recall for passage in either written or oral modes and that these abilities develop early and first in the domain of oral language processing and then are applied to the written language domain.

## Conclusions

The argument has been presented that oral language development has an important and continuing effect on written language development. It has also been argued that oral language development cannot be simply viewed as an increasing amount of intuitive knowledge acquired but, also, as a changing state of knowledge and developmental changes in how language is processed. If this argument has validity then one should be able to observe developmental changes in what is known intuitively about language, what is consciously known and in how oral language is processed. The interaction of these factors would predict what is comprehended and recalled in written language. There are also clear indications of a reverse effect; that is, the reading task per se changes the state of knowledge of oral language. Some examples of each of these arguments are presented below.

An obvious example of the effect of what is known about language on reading is lexical knowledge. If a lexical item is not in the vocabulary of a child then it cannot be comprehended in reading unless the context provides this information. A less obvious example would be the child's lack of comprehension of a syntactic structure as in "The boy who kissed the girl ran away." If the child does not understand this sentence orally, he/she will not comprehend it in written form. Something further, however, is required when reading the word or sentence. In the first instance the phonological representation of the word must be brought to conscious awareness; in the second instance the semantic/syntactic relations in the sentence must be brought to conscious awareness. How available (that is, how well learned) a structure is will affect how easily it is brought to conscious awareness. That is what is meant by state of knowledge of a structure. Thus, there are some structures that will be very well learned when the reading process begins (simple morpheme structure rules and certain semantic/syntactic structures in sentences) and others that will be less available and still others that remain to be acquired. Those that are very well learned will be processed automatically without the requirement of their being brought to conscious awareness.

How oral language is processed will have an effect on what is known about oral language. If, for example, oral language is processed by a surface-structure strategy with heavy reliance on contextual information for comprehension then the child will not be ready to understand sentences in which this strategy does not lead to correct interpretation (as in the example sentence above). How the child represents information about linguistic categories and relations in memory will have an effect on what the child knows about language. For example, if the child relies on imaginal representations rather than linguistic representations for storage and recall of lexical meanings, a behavior that is observed during the early years of life (Conrad, 1972) and continues to store imaginally syntactic-semantic relations in the early stages of acquisition of new structures (Kosslyn and Bower, 1974), then, linguistic representations will not be available and, therefore, cannot be brought to conscious awareness in the reading process. A shift from imaginal to linguistic representations has, in general, been observed at about 5 to 7 years.

But any particular child might yet be in the process of development of this shift during the early stages of reading acquistion.

The ability to draw inferences from the linguistic context and world knowledge appears to be crucial in the comprehension and recall of connected discourse. This ability is first exercised in the oral language domain and then applied to the written language domain. This seems to be a very early ability in the normally developing child but is somewhat delayed in children with developmental problems. However, again, there may be developmental differences among children in the age at which this processing strategy is available and is used plus differences in experiences which will affect the presence of or nature of the inferences that can be made.

Figure 7-3 is a graphic presentation of the notions expressed above. It suggests that as the child matures changes take place in the strategies used to process language, the set of linguistic rules the child has intuitive knowledge of, the set of rules the child is able to bring to conscious awareness if required to do so and the set of categories and relations which are automatically processed in reading.

**FIGURE 7-3**
**Developmental changes in processing strategies and state of knowledge of linguistic rules**

| Time 1 | Time 2 | Time 3 |
|---|---|---|
| Processing strategies Set 1 | Processing Strategies Set 2 | Processing Strategies Set 3 |
| Intuitive knowledge of Rules Set 1 | Intuitive knowledge of Rules Set 2 | Intuitive knowledge of Rules Set 3 |
| | Conscious knowledge of rules Set 1 | Conscious knowledge of rules Set 2 |
| | | Automatic processing of rules Set 1 in reading |

Particular linguistic experiences, particular social experiences, and possibly, biological capabilities can account for individual differences in the development of meta-awareness (conscious knowledge) of language categories and relations. These differences can account for individual differences in the development or rate of development of intuitive knowledge of categories and relations in the language as well as conscious knowledge of these categories and relations. Since conscious knowledge is dependent on intuitive knowledge then differing children will achieve differing sets of conscious knowledge and, as we have argued, this will affect what is comprehended in reading.

# References

Barclay, J.R., & Reid, M. Segmatic integration in children's recall of discourse. *Developmental Psychology,* 1974, *10,* 277-281.

Bever, T. The integrated study of language behavior. In J. Morton (Ed.), *Biological and social factors in psycholinguistics.* Urbana: University of Illinois Press, 1970, 158-209 (b).

Bougere, M. Selected factors in oral language related to first-grade reading achievement. *Reading Research Quarterly,* 1969, *5,* 31-58.

Bowey, J. Aspects of language processing in the oral reading of third, fourth and fifth grade children. Unpublished doctoral dissertation, University of Adelaide, Australila, 1980.

Brown, A., Smiley, S., Day, J., Townsend, M., & Lawton, S. Intrusion of a thematic idea in children's comprehension and retention of stories. *Child Development,* 1977, *48.* 1454-1466.

Chu-Chang, M. The dependency relation between oral language and reading in bi-lingual children. Unpublished doctoral dissertation, Boston University, School of Education, 1979.

Clark, H., & Clark. E. *Psychology and language.* New York: Harcourt, Brace and Janovich, 1977.

Conrad, R. The developmental role of vocalizing in short-term memory. *Journal of Verbal Learning and Verbal Behavior.* 1972, *11,* 521-533.

Ervin-Tripp, S. Social backgrounds and verbal skills. In R. Huxley and E. Ingram (Eds.), *Language acquisition: Models and methods.* London: Academic Press, 1971, 29-36.

Flood, J., & Menyuk, P. Detection of ambiguity and production of paraphase in written language. Final Report to National Institute of Education, November 1979.

Frederickson, C. Discourse comprehension and early reading. In L. Resnick and P. Weaver (Eds.), *Theory and practice of early reading.* Hillsdale, N.J.: L.E. Erlbaum Assoc., 1976.

Gleitman, H., & Gleitman. L. Language use and language judgment. In C. J. Fillmore, D. Kempler, and W. Wang (Eds.), *Individual differences in language ability and language behavior.* New York: Academic Press, 1979, 103-125.

Goldsmith, S. Reading disability: Some support for a psycholinguistics base. Paper presented at Boston University Conference on Language Development, Sept. 30-Oct. 1, 1977.

Goodman, K.S. Reading: A psycholinguistic guessing game. In H. Singer and R. Ruddell (Eds.), *Theoretical models and process of reading.* Newark, DE: International Reading Association, 1976.

Graybeal, C. Memory for stories in language impaired children. Unpublished doctoral dissertation, Boston University, Applied Pyscholinguistics Program, 1981.

Kosslyn, S., & Bower, G. The role of imagery in sentence memory. *Child Development,* 1974, *45,* 30-38.

Liberman, I.Y., Liberman, A.M., Mattingly, I.G., & Shankweiler, D. Paper presented at Cross-Language Conference on Orthography, Reading and Dyslexia, sponsored by NICHD and Fogarty International Center of NIH, Bethesda, MD, September 18, 1978.

Loritz, D. Children's knowledge of advanced phonics rules. Unpublished doctoral dissertation, Boston University. Applied Psycholinguistics Program, 1981.

McNeill, D. The development of Language. In P. H. Mussen, (Ed.), *Carmichaels manual of child psychology.* New York: John Wiley and Sons, Inc., 1970, 1061-1162.

Menyuk, P. Relations between acquisition of phonology and reading. In J. Guthrie (Ed.), *Aspects of reading.* Baltimore: The Johns-Hopkins University Press, 1976, 89-111.

Menyuk, P. *Language and maturation.* Cambridge: M.I.T. Press, 1977.

Menyuk, P. Non-linguistic and linguistic processing in normally developing and language disordered children. In N. Lass (Ed.), *Speech and language: Advances in basic research and practice,* Vol. 4, New York: Academic Press, 1980, 1-97.

Menyuk, P. Syntactic competence and reading. In J. Stark and S. Wurzel (Eds.), *Language, learning and reading disabilities: A new decade.* Cambridge: M.I.T. Press, in press.

Menyuk, P., & Flood, J. Meta-linguistic processes in oral and written language. In preparation.

Myerson, R. A study of children's knowledge of certain word formation rules and the relationship of this knowledge to various forms of reading achievement. Unpublished doctoral dissertation, Harvard University, Graduate School of Education, 1976.

Oppenheim, P. Selected relationships between linguistic processing skills and reading, Boston University, School of Education, Unpublished doctoral dissertation, 1981.

Stein, N.L., & Glenn, C.G. An analysis of story comprehension in elementary school children. In F.O. Freedle (Ed.), *New Directions in Discourse Processing. Advances in Discourse Process.* Norwood, N.J.: Ablex, Inc., 1979.

Vygotsky, L.S. *Mind in society & the development of higher psychological processes.* M. Cole, V. John-Steiner, S. Scribner and E. Souberman (Eds.) Cambridge: Harvard University Press, 1978.

Wilson, K. Inference and language processing in hearing and deaf children. Unpublished doctoral dissertation, Boston University, Applied Pscyholinguistics Program, 1979.

Wozniak, R. Verbal regulations of motor behavior. *Human Development,* 1972, *15,* 13-57.

# 8

# ISSUES IN USING AMER-IND CODE WITH RETARDED PERSONS

*Lyle L. Lloyd*
Purdue University

*Joanne Kelsch Daniloff*
University of Vermont

## Introduction

*T*he vast majority of mentally retarded individuals exhibit some form of communication dysfunction. In fact, functional speech is essentially absent for many of the most severely impaired. Justifiably, speech-language pathologists have redirected much of their clinical emphasis from speech and structured language toward the more general goal of effective communication. The development of various non-speech communication techniques has accompanied this shift (see Fristoe & Lloyd, 1979; Lloyd, 1976, 1980).

Because the techniques employed frequently incorporate speech, the use of non-speech communication intervention does not necessarily exclude the use of speech. Depending upon the characteristics of the patients involved, non-speech systems may provide (1) a temporary means of communication until effective speech develops; (2) a life-long means of communication (either as an alternative or an augmentation to speech); or (3) a means for facilitating the development of spoken communication.

Most non-speech communication intervention represents one of two approaches to symbol formation and/or symbol transmission: unaided and aided. The use of these terms is based on the classifications employed by Fristoe and Lloyd (1979) and subsequently incorporated in the ASHA (1981) position papers. Examples of unaided and aided symbols and systems are provided in Table 8-1. Extensive descriptions of many non-speech systems are available, including rationales for their selection and use; hence we will highlight only a few of them (see Fristoe & Lloyd, 1979; Lloyd, 1976; Silverman, 1980).

**TABLE 8-1**
**Communication Symbols and Systems***

| Unaided | Aided |
|---------|-------|
| Yes/no gestures | Objects |
| Pointing | Pictures |
| Mime | Basic rebus |
| Generally Understood Gestures | Picsyms |
| Amer-Ind | Pictogram Ideogram Communication(PIC) |
| Other gestures | Blissymbols |
| Esoteric signs | Expanded rebus |
| American Sign Language (ASL) or (Ameslan) | Other logographs |
| Manually Coded English (e.g., Paget-Gorman Sign System, Signed English, Signing Exact English) | Lana Lexigrams |
| Manual alphabet | Premack-Type Symbols |
| Gestural Morse Code | Printed words (Traditional Orthography or TO) |
| Eye blink codes | Writing (Traditional Orthography or TO) |
| Vocal codes | Modified Orthography (e.g., ITA) |
| Hand cued speech | Braille |
| Speech | Other Vibro-tactile codes |
| | Linear Printing (e.g., WRITE) |
| | Synthetic Speech (e.g., SAL, SPEEC) |

*These are "formal" or conventionalized symbols and systems; informal nonverbal or ritualized behaviors have not been included.

Graphic systems, including those using pictographic (e.g. photographs or drawings) and nonpictographic symbols (e.g. written words), exemplify aided approaches. Blissymbolics (Archer, 1977; Bliss, 1965) is a semantically based system that incorporates an ideograph and a representative English word. This particular system has been used successfully with severely physically and intellectually handicapped children (i.e. Harris-Vanderheiden, Brown, MacKenzie, Reinen, & Scheibel, 1975; McNaughton, 1976). The standard Rebus Glossary (Clark, Davies, & Woodcock, 1974) is a collection of individual pictographic symbols and combinations thereof, originally developed as a reading system. Lana Lexigrams and Premack's abstract symbols include graphic symbols that are being used experimentally with retarded persons (Parkel, White, & Warner, 1977; Premack & Premack, 1974).

The most commonly reported alternative system for the mentally retarded is the use of signs from American Sign Language (ASL), a bona fide language and an unaided system (Fristoe & Lloyd, 1978). There are numerous reports of the use of ASL with the mentally retarded (e.g. Carrier, 1976; Fristoe & Lloyd, 1979; Hobson & Duncan, 1979; Kopchick, Rombach, & Smilovitz, 1975; Peters, 1973; Richardson, 1975; Silverman, 1980; Stremel-Campbell, Cantrell and Halle, 1977). Various other unaided systems have been developed which insert ASL signs into standard English word orders. Examples of such systems include the Paget-Gorman Sign System (e.g. Paget, Gorman, & Paget, 1976), Seeing Essential English, SEE-1 (e.g. Anthony, 1974), Signing Exact English, SEE-2 (Gustason, Pfetzing, & Zawolkow, 1972), and Signed English (Bornstein, Hamilton, Saulnier, & Roy, 1975).

Gesture-based systems, which lack the restraints and abstract coding of languages, are also classified as unaided. They exhibit varying levels of abstraction.the simplest and earliest developing gestures, like pointing, and "demonstrative" gestures. "Descriptive" gestures imitate an object's movement or can include an outlined three-dimensional representation of an object. Symbolic gestures, the most abstract type, are like signs in that they are not directly associated with their referents. Demonstrative and descriptive gestures are especially useful with the retarded and are also relatively easy to teach (Fristoe & Lloyd, 1979). Pantomime, a gestural system that involves the use of the entire body, is also closely related to the ideas it represents. Although it is not standardized, it has been used with mentally retarded children of varying severity (e.g. Balick, Spiegel, & Green, 1976; Bricker, 1972; Levett, 1969, 1971; Topper, 1975; Vanderheiden and Harris-Vanderheiden, 1976).

# The Development of Amer-Ind Code

One uniform system that makes use of descriptive gestures is Amer-Ind Code. It was developed for use by speechless, adult patients who had undergone radical upper neck surgery, and it was based upon American Indian Hand Talk (Skelly, Schinsky, Smith, Donaldson, & Griffin, 1975). Amer-Ind Code was designed to be learned easily and not to require the signal receiver to have prior knowledge or training in order to comprehend much of it. Amer-Ind Code is not a language, insofar as no grammatical rules are required. Each Amer-Ind Code signal concretely represents a dominant characteristic of its referent. It is primarily a demonstrable, expressive system designed to communicate the functional daily needs of adult surgical patients with normal cognitive abilities.

American Indian Hand Talk, upon which Amer-Ind Code is based, originated in attempts to cross the language barriers between tribes. Little historical information was available about this communication form until non-Indian observers began recording descriptions late in the nineteenth century. Early archeological and linguistic reports included several of the signals (Clark, 1885; Mallery, 1881).

More modern accounts contain detailed pictures and descriptions aimed at preserving traditional Indian heritage (Amon, 1968; Cody, 1970).

In developing the Amer-Ind Code adaptation, some of the most culture specific signals were deleted along with those thought to be inappropriate for clinical use. New signals were created, and several historical signals were altered before the system was standardized (Skelly et al., 1975; Skelly, 1979, 1981).

Several reports have emphasized Amer-Ind Code's potential usefulness as a communication system for diverse adult populations, including individuals who have undergone cancer surgery, laryngectomy, or glossectomy and those manifesting oral apraxia, aphasia, and dysarthria (see Bonvillian & Friedman, 1978; Daniloff, Noll, Fristoe, & Lloyd, 1982; Holmes, 1975; Rao & Horner, 1978; Rao, Basili, Koller, Fullerton, Diener, & Burton, 1980; Skelly, 1979; Skelly et al., 1975; Skelly, Schinsky, Smith, & Fust, 1974). Several recent reports, which will be addressed later in detail, indicate the successful incorporation of Amer-Ind Code signals into communication programs for retarded individuals (Daniloff & Shafer, 1981; Duncan & Silverman, 1977, 1978; Freese & Frerker, 1979; Podleski, 1977; Topper, 1974).

Several areas of concern that bear upon the effective use of Amer-Ind Code with retarded individuals need to be addressed. These include the overall appropriateness of the Amer-Ind Code dictionary and its relationship to an initial core of concepts, the production requirements of Amer-Ind Code signals, and Amer-Ind Code's conceptual characteristics, i.e. its iconicity and transparency.

## Fundamental Issues in the Selection of an Initial Lexicon and the Amer-Ind Code Signal Repertoire

The selection of an initial *spoken* communicative lexicon should consider: (1) the course of language acquisition, (2) concepts functionally important to the individual, (3) initial goals that emphasize functional communication and not necessarily language, (4) the inclusion of objects that are present and actions that occur in the individual's immediate environment, (5) the relative ease with which a concept can be demonstrated in context, (6) concept usefulness, and (7) the categorization of items according to content (Holland, 1975; Lahey & Bloom, 1977). In addition, it is generally agreed that the selection of an initial expressive *sign* lexicon also should include the following considerations: (8) a concept should be present before a sign is taught and (9) the first signs taught should be either functional or easy to produce (e.g. Donellan-Walsh, Gossage, LaVigna, Schuler, & Traphagen, 1976).

Fristoe & Lloyd (1980) synthesized the available guidelines for teaching a spoken vocabulary and produced a suggested initial sign lexicon for individuals with severe communication disorders. They also provided a strong rationale for their selection of initial lexical items. Their sample vocabulary included approximately 80 signs meant for use with individuals who demonstrate essentially normal hearing sensitivity but are unable to acquire spoken communication (see Table 8-2).

Table 8-2 exemplifies the use of data from normal child language development. The balance of substantive and relational items should be noted. This increases the potential for the spontaneous combination of gestures. In addition, less specific lexical items offer the greatest potential for communication in a variety of settings. The items in Table 8-2 focus on concepts both important to and frequently occurring in the individual's life. The use of such a vocabulary is aimed at producing meaningful communication, rather than emphasizing syntactical development, morphological markers, or the suprasegmental complexities of language. The majority of the lexical items are functionally related to common daily activities. For successful acquisition, training likewise should be situational and concrete, i.e., signs should always be taught in context.

Since Amer-Ind Code was developed for adult surgical patients with normal cognitive abilities, it is not surprising that its signal repertoire does not conform entirely to the guidelines discussed in the previous section. For example, some of the vocabulary is not appropriate for children or young adults. Amer-Ind Code's proponents claim that its vocabulary is very "functional"; however, numerous signals (ARROGANT, JUSTICE, BRIBE, DEFY, OATH, DOMINATE, EAST, SURRENDER, and POMPOUS, to name a few) represent concepts which have little relevance for the retarded. Moreover, 18 of the items listed in Table 8-2 as appropriate initial lexical items for severely communication-impaired individuals do not appear in the Amer-Ind Code repertoire (APPLE, TOILET/POTTY, CANDY, COOKIE, DIRTY, DOG, FALL, HAT, HUG, MAKE, MILK, PANTS, PLAY, PUT, SHIRT, SOCK, SPOON, THIS/THAT). Seven additional items from the core require agglutinations in order to form standard Amer-Ind Code signals (BOY, FATHER, GIRL, MOTHER, SCHOOL, SHOE, TELEVISION). It is unreasonable to expect an inexperienced, retarded signaller to combine gestures into basic concepts. One previous study showed that only five of 21 severely profoundly retarded children were able to combine signals after 12 months of training (Daniloff and Shafer, 1981).

Another potential drawback of Amer-Ind Code is its lack of specificity. Each Amer-Ind Code signal represents one very broad concept with numerous related concepts subsumed under it, e.g. "heart" includes the concepts of emotion, feel, feeling, and love (Skelly, 1979). Proponents regard this as an asset, a characteristic that gives Amer-Ind Code a flexibility which true languages cannot provide. However, it may cause difficulties for some retarded individuals who operate on very concrete cognitive levels. For example, in Amer-Ind Code no distinction is possible among five of the core items, namely APPLE, CANDY, COOKIE, EAT, and SPOON. Likewise, the core items SOCK, SHOE, SHIRT, and PANTS are indistinguishable.

The inadequacy of the Amer-Ind Code repertoire for the needs of some of the populations currently being trained to use it has led to the incorporation of signals from other systems. Since the inclusion of non-standard, original, or esoteric signs or signals may be deleterious or confusing to the client or to other clinicians, only standardized signals should be substituted. Furthermore, it is essential for modifications to be recorded clearly in the client's communication records.

**TABLE 8-2**
**Sample Sign Lexicon with Amer-Ind Transparency Percentages***

| Sign | % | Sign | % |
|---|---|---|---|
| AFRAID | 77.5 | HELP | 87.5 |
| ALL GONE/USED UP/FINISHED | | HOT | 85.0 |
| ANGRY/MAD | 30.0 | HOUSE | |
| APPLE | | I | 60.0 |
| BABY | 77.5 | IN | |
| BAD | 75.0 | KISS | |
| BALL | 100.0 | LOOK/WATCH | 92.5 |
| BATHROOM/TOILET/POTTY | | MAKE | |
| BED/or SLEEP | | MAN | 2.5 |
| BIG | 35.0 | ME | |
| BIRD | 100.0 | MILK | |
| BOOK | 100.0 | MORE | |
| BOY | | MOTHER/MOMMY | |
| BREAK/BROKEN | 100.0 | MY | |
| BRING | | NAME SIGN | |
| CANDY | | NEGATIVE | |
| CAR | 100.0 | NOW | 5.0 |
| CAT | | ON | |
| CHAIR/SIT | 27.5 | OPEN | 55.0 |
| COAT | | PANTS | |
| COMB | 97.5 | PLAY | |
| COME | 100.0 | PUT | |

## TABLE 8-2 (Continued)

| Word | Value | Word | Value |
|---|---|---|---|
| COOKIE | | RUN | |
| CRY | 100.0 | SAD | |
| CUP | | SCHOOL | |
| DIRTY | | SHIRT | |
| DO | | SHOE | |
| DOG | | SOCK | |
| DOOR | 10.0 | SPOON | 15.0 |
| DOWN | 92.5 | STAND | |
| DRINK | 100.0 | STOP | 95.0 |
| EAT | 80.0 | TABLE | |
| FALL (verb) | | TELEVISION (T.V.) | |
| FATHER/DADDY | | THAT/THIS/THOSE | |
| GET | 2.5 | THROW | |
| GIRL | | UNDER | |
| GIVE | 90.0 | UP | 87.5 |
| GO | | WALK | 77.5 |
| GOOD | | WASH | 95.0 |
| HAPPY | | WATER | 87.5 |
| HAT | | WOMAN | 65.0 |
| HAVE/POSSESS | | YOU | |
| HEAVY | | | |

*Modified from Fristoe and Lloyd (1980).

The most obvious source of potential additional signals is the ASL signs, because they are standardized. Another alternative is to incorporate a differentiating alphabet signal with the more general Amer-Ind Code signal (i.e. "M" + DRINK for MILK). Since the ASL manual alphabet bears little resemblance to printed letters, we suggest Chen's (1968, 1971) Talking Hand. In this system, manual alphabet symbols resemble the printed letters they represent. An untrained receiver might be able to guess the meaning because he/she recognized the appearance of the letter. Obviously, alphabet letters have the disadvantage of being highly symbolic and arbitrary representations, and writing and reading are skills that severely communication-handicapped individuals rarely acquire. Still it is possible that a letter and signal combination may be less arbitrary than the ASL counterpart.

## Conceptual Characteristics of Amer-Ind Code Signals — Iconicity

Iconicity has been defined as any aspect of a sign which is defined by, suggests, or resembles its referent (Brown, 1977). That is, the formation of the sign (or signal) conveys potent cues to its meaning. This makes such signs or signals more transparent (or guessable) for the naive observer. Potential receivers need no special training to get the message. This increases the likelihood of effective communication with individuals in the signaller's environment, including parents, friends, and health care staff.

Amer-Ind Code signals demonstrate an advantage over ASL signs in this regard. Previous reports have indicated the abstract nature of most of the ASL lexicon. The degree of transparency (guessability), measured by the percentage of the total number of signs tested that exhibited obvious visual representaion of their referents, ranges from 10-30% (Hoemann, 1975; Kirschner, Algozzine, and Abbott, 1979; Klima and Bellugi, 1979; Lloyd and Fristoe, 1978, 1982;). Skelly and her colleagues have completed several projects to document the transmission of Amer-Ind Code signals to uninstructed receivers. Although there are discrepancies between the two reports that claim to describe the same projects, the outcomes are essentially the same. These reports claim that the corpus of Amer-Ind Code signals is 80-88% guessable for naive viewers. The most recent evidence suggests that Amer-Ind Code may be described more accurately as approximately 50% transparent to naive viewers (Daniloff, Lloyd, and Fristoe, in press; Kirschner, et al., 1979). Although this is much less than Skelly reports, it is still a significantly higher percentage than the 10-30% reported for ASL signs.

A rank ordering of the original Amer-Ind Code stimuli is available (Daniloff and Shafer, 1981) to help clinicians choose an initial vocabulary. Of the three types of Amer-Ind Code signals, the repetitive ones are more transparent than either the static or kinetic signals. Although this particular finding is not surprising, we must be cautious in general and remember that the available transparency values are based upon normal adult responses. Any conclusions we draw about the signals' iconicity are based upon what normal adults judge to be iconic. Data are not yet available that test retarded individuals' judgments of iconicity. However the signals which have received the highest transparency values based on the available data appear to be the easiest ones to teach (Daniloff, Lloyd, and Fristoe, in press; Fristoe and Lloyd, 1980). Kirschner, Algozzine, and Abbott (1979) have also demonstrated that Amer-Ind Code may be easier to learn and retained better than ASL signs. This seems to support the clinical hypothesis that iconic signals are the easiest ones to teach to individuals with severe communication impairment (Duncan and Silverman, 1977; Fristoe and Lloyd, 1980; Skelly, 1979).

## Production Requirements: Amer-Ind Code versus ASL

The production of ASL signs is dictated by four physical parameters: the place of sign production (the head, trunk, and hand), the handshape, the motion, and the orientation. The first three parameters were described by Stokoe (1960), and the fourth was added by Battison (1973). Although an indepth analysis is not yet available, some preliminary observations may be reported about the procduction of Amer-Ind Code signals with respect to these parameters. Daniloff and Vergara (1982) found that in general Amer-Ind Code signals conform to the parameters which have been outlined for ASL signs, but there are some important exceptions.

For example, Amer-Ind Code has 14 signals which are made outside the signing space defined for ASL (from the hips to the top of the head and from the signer's extreme left to extreme right, forming a 180° arc). However, about the same number of Amer-Ind Code signals as ASL signs are produced in the trunk region, which is the easiest region for sign or signal production.

One factor which makes Amer-Ind Code's production requirements simpler than ASL's is that fewer handshapes are involved in each signal (Daniloff and Vergara, 1982). Moreover, the majority of the handshapes used to form Amer-Ind Code signals are prehension patterns which appear in children under the age of 11 months: the neutral or flat hand, a pointed radial finger, the squeeze pattern, and lateral thumb opposition. This is in sharp contrast to the wide spectrum and varying complexity of handshapes employed to form ASL signs (Dennis, Reichle, Williams, and Vogelsberg, in press). There are, however, some notable exceptions, such as the complex shape of SIT. Daniloff and Vergara also found that Amer-Ind Code is more static, and the movements which are required are motorically less complicated. Also, while the distribution of palm and finger orientations does not differ significantly between ASL signs and Amer-Ind Code signals, fewer changes of palm orientation are required within each Amer-Ind Code signal.

Amer-Ind Code also has more signals that can be produced with one hand (Daniloff and Vergara, 1982). Of the 236 signals currently in the Amer-Ind Code repertoire, 131 normally are executed with one hand. The non-moving hand and arm hang loosely at the side of the body. This also makes Amer-Ind Code's production requirements simpler than ASL's. In ASL, the non-moving hand assumes one of six positions: a closed fist, a flat palm, a raised hand with fingers extended, the hand formed in a semi-circle, and the hand making a circle, with the finger tips meeting the thumb.

Amer-Ind Code is being used increasingly by individuals who do not have both hands available for signalling due to unilateral limb paralysis or paresis secondary to stroke. Thus the remaining 105 signals , normally produced with two hands, have been adapted for execution with one hand (Skelly, 1979). In most cases, the non-dominant hand does the signalling, because the left hemispheric brain injury that results in aphasia also frequently results in impairment to the motor coordination of the right side of the body. Five modifications have been introduced which allow 95% of the Amer-Ind Code repertoire to be produced with one hand. These are:

1) Two fingers on one hand substituted for the two hands normally used in the signal's production (applicable only to signals in which the movements of the two hands are symmetrical with each other).

2) Use of the impaired hand or substitution of a leg or nearby surface (applicable only to signals in which one hand is static and held in neutral position).

3) Substitution of sequential movement with one hand for movement normally produced simultaneously by both hands.

4) Use of an index finger to trace the signal either in the air in front of the signaller or in relation to the signaller's body.

5) Establishment of a flat base with the signalling hand, followed immediately by movement from that base (applicable to signals involving one static and neutral hand).

Eleven signals could not be adapted; thus entirely new signals or strings of signals (agglutinations) have been substituted. An example is WALK + IN for ENTER (Skelly, 1979). Skelly has claimed (1979, 1981 cf. Amerind Video Dictionary, 1975) that the one-handed versions can be guessed as easily as the two-handed. However, so far no data have been published to confirm this statement.

# Communication Programs That Utilize Amer-Ind Code with the Mentally Retarded

Amer-Ind Code communication programs for the retarded have included three 10-week trial programs and one 12-month program. One project (Podleski, 1977) initially involved 10 mentally retarded adults; seven were diagnosed as severely retarded and three manifested profound mental retardation. Early in this 10-week trial program, two of the profoundly retarded patients were dropped due to uncontrolled psychotic attacks or lack of eye contact. Training sessions were individual and all gestures represented very concrete referents. The average number of signals this group of eight patients was able to execute was 12.4. After an additional 10 weeks of training, the average number increased to 17.8. However, actual use of the signals was limited; none of the participants spontaneously initiated appropriate signals. In fact, the "usage" of signals by four participants was limited to facilitated imitations. At a later date, an additional six severely retarded adults were admitted to the same program. This group reportedly executed an average of 17.8 signals. Extreme care must be taken in interpreting these data since facilitated imitation by three of the six participants was categorized by the author as successful execution. These data simply do not indicate signal acquisition or functional usage. It is interesting that not a single participant described by Podleski (see Skelly, 1979, pp. 52-53) demonstrated spontaneous signal use.

Freese and Frerker (in Skelly, 1979) reported successful Amer-Ind Code communication by 21 severely and profoundly retarded mental hospital residents. One child, 11 teenagers, and 9 adults participated. Although the criterion for "signal acquisition" was not defined, the participants were said to have acquired an average of 25 signals after two 10-week training periods. There are no indications of pre-program communication levels in this report.

After 20 weeks of training, one participant was utilizing gesture to facilitate oral speech and another was utilizing gesture as an equivalent to propositional speech. Thirteen participants were utilizing self-initiated gestures and five were operating at levels involving imitation, facilitated productions, or presignal stimulation. None of the participants utilized gestures with staff other than the speech-language pathologists. In essence, no generalization was observed to occur. Deviant behaviors were reported to decrease noticeably.

Thirty-two moderately retarded children, with a mean age of 10.5 years, were included in the third 10-week trial Amer-Ind Code program (Duncan & Silverman, 1977). Mental ages ranged from two to five years, with pre-treatment speech intelligibility judged as ranging from 0% to 25%. The mean number of signals acquired was 48. Of the 32 participants, 27 utilized gestures spontaneously and 15 subjects increased their attempts to speak. In 13 cases maladaptive behaviors decreased.

Twenty-one school-aged, severely-profoundly retarded children were enrolled in a year-long Amer-Ind Code communication program (Daniloff & Shafer, 1981). Candidacy for this particular program was limited to those who had failed to make noticeable progress despite enrollment in some form of communication program for at least one year. The core vocabulary centered around actions and objects pertinent to the daily needs of the participants. Modifications of the Amer-Ind Scale of Progress were made that eventually produced a series of stages of acquisition relevant to the needs of the mentally retarded (see Table 8-3).

After three months of training, consisting of three or four 15-minute individual sessions per week, the average number of signals acquired was 5.5. A conservative criterion was utilized to define signal acquisition, in sharp contrast to the three previous reports. An acquired signal was defined as one that was self-initiated appropriately outside of the training room. Therefore, the rather large number of signals that were recognized or comprehended by the children, but not spontaneously produced, are not included in the data. Twelve months after the initiation of the program, the average number of signals acquired more than doubled, to 11.8. One participant moved away, and two failed to indicate progress after the initial 3-month period. However, in two cases, verbal output exceeded gesticulation. For three children, 2-signal agglutinations and some intelligible speech were evident. Twelve additional students manifested vocal accompaniment of gestures

**TABLE 8-3**
**Modified Amer-Ind Scale of Progress***

| Stage 1 | Stimulation for Minimal Response |
|---|---|
| Stage 2 | Signal Recognition |
| Stage 3 | Signal Execution |
| Stage 4 | Signal Retrieval |
| Stage 5 | Transition to Use |
| Stage 6 | Self-Initiated Signal Use |
| Stage 7 | Spontaneous Signal Use |
| Stage 8 | Signal Use as a Facilitator of Vocalization |
| Stage 9 | Spontaneous Agglutination |
| Stage 10 | Signal Use for Support of Verbalization |

*The complete copy of the Daniloff and Shafer (1981, pp. 260-263) modification of Skelly's (1979) Amer-Ind Scale of progress is provided in the Appendix.

over 50% of the time. Seven of these twelve were essentially *nonvocal* when the treatment program began. One child's vocal accompaniment increased, but was not quite evident 50% of the time.

## Clinical Implications

A key consideration in choosing an intervention strategy is whether the system is well suited to the patient population. The studies discussed in the previous section seem to indicate that many severely-profoundly retarded, as well as moderately mentally handicapped and various brain damaged populations, can be trained to use Amer-Ind Code. Those who operate at the most primitive level of Berger's Scale (Berger, 1972), with whom gross and specific gestures are the most appropriate strategy, can use this system. Whether many of the severely communication impaired individuals ever use speech effectively is a lesser concern. For some, the spontanous use of 10 gestures is an admirable long term goal. For individuals who are able to function at higher levels, Amer-Ind Code can facilitate vocalization as an adjunct to gesture and spontaneous verbalization in a small percentage of cases (Daniloff and Shafer, 1981).

The Amer-Ind Scale of Progress describes 10 levels of increasing competence in the use of Amer-Ind Code signals (Skelly, 1979). It is suggested that the scale be followed in teaching the signals, because it is believed that signal recognition, execution, and retrieval lead to self-initiation and propositional use. The highest levels include gestural facilitation of verbalization and, finally, verbalization with some gestural support.

Several modifications and deletions have been found to be necessary to adapt the scale for retarded individuals with severe communication impairment (Daniloff and Shafer, 1981, see Appendix). Successful signal acquisition has been observed in some of these individuals, despite the absence of "skills" normally trained in Levels I and II. Neither pointing responses, consistent head movements, nor sustained eye contact (all Level I skills) were trained in the population studied by Daniloff and Shafer. Signals were not recognized as associated with concrete objects or actions (Level II skills) until skills representative of Level IV (Signal retrieval) were acquired. Also, for those operating at Level III (signal execution), pictures, agglutinations, and mirror-work were avoided. Furthermore, the use of simultaneous speech and gestures (i.e. multimodality stimulus input) was deferred until acquired signals were ready for extension to use with other people and other environments (Level VI: transition to use). At Level VIII, vocal, not verbal accompaniment to gestures was expected 50% of the time. One child who achieved Level IX combined signals spontaneously. Those who attained Level X utilized gesture to facilitate comprehensible verbalization.

Gesture appears to facilitate adjunct speech and vocal behaviors in many individuals. References abound that cite observation of this facilitation in various brain-injured populations being taught to gesture (Bonvillian & Friedman, 1978; Chen, 1968; Daniloff & Shafer, 1981; Duncan & Silverman, 1977; Eagleson, Vaughn, & Knudson, 1970; Fitch, 1972; Koller, Schlanger, & Geffner, 1975; Peters, 1973; Rao & Horner, 1978; Schlanger & Schlanger, 1970; Stremel-Campbell, Cantrell, Halle, 1977; Skelly, 1979; Skelly et al., 1974, 1975). Some of these references include rather dramatic cases, where nonverbal clients began to speak or where nonvocal individuals began to vocalize.

Why this facilitation occurs in some patients is not known at this point. Perhaps more compelling is why it fails to occur in others. We are just beginning to sort out which clinical characteristics are likely to overlap with verbal and vocal facilitation through gesture. We know this much: no additional training besides the simultaneous preservation of gestural stimuli with speech is necessary to evoke it. Even though the reasons behind it are enigmatic, the fact that it does occur supports our use of gesture-based communication.

Moreover, the four reports discussed above detailing the impact of Amer-Ind Code on retarded people indicated observable decreases in the maladaptive behaviors of some of the participants. These alterations in behavior were often dramatic, affecting some of the most unmanageable individuals, and rapid, occuring within a few weeks. There is additional evidence that some behaviors remained extinguished for the duration of a year (Daniloff and Shafer, 1981). Apparently, many disruptive individuals can be controlled once they achieve some form of communication. Perhaps many aggressive behaviors diminish when a person successfully manipulates his environment in a more socially acceptable manner.

A summary of Amer-Ind Code's potential liabilities would include the questionable appropriateness of some of its vocabulary for retarded people, the use of one signal to represent more than one concept, the potentially inappropriate use of agglutinations, and the need to modify the scale of progress for use with populations other than the one for which Amer-Ind Code was developed originally. We feel that advantages of Amer-Ind Code far outweigh the disadvantages.

The comparative simplicity of its physical production requirements, the transparency and iconicity of its signals, and Amer-Ind Code's potential for decreasing maladaptive behaviors while facilitating vocalization and verbalization all indicate that it is an effective non-speech system.

# A Proposed Amer-Ind Code Vocabulary

A list of those signals which we believe would serve as an initial core vocabulary for use with the retarded is provided in Table 8-4. Amer-Ind Code signals dominate the list. Selection was based upon a number of factors, but the basic model was that put forth previously by Fristoe and Lloyd (1980). Further consideration included transparency values and general functionality. Items appear in alphabetical order; in no way is this meant to represent the order in which the signals should be taught. Asterisked signals are the ones we suggest be taught initially. Those items designated with a number 1 include signs from ASL. A number 2 indicates a slightly altered Amer-Ind Code signal substitution; the alternative gesture is described along with the signal. Four additional items, represented by standard agglutinations, follow the main list.

The ultimate selection of signals, including the agglutinations, is left up to the discretion of the clinician. Likewise, the order in which the signals are taught is a decision that the clinician must make. Certainly, the individual needs of each potential client precluded the presentation of anything, but suggested guidelines.

# Acknowledgment

Appreciation for their thoughtful comments in the development of this outline and the materials presented is extended to our following colleagues: George R. Karlan, Research Scientist on leave from the Department of Special Education at the University of Illinois, and Donald R. Rabush, Chairman and Associate Professor of Special Education at Western Maryland College, on sabbatical at Purdue when this manuscript was written. The development of this paper was partially supported by a grant from the Office of Special Education and Rehabilitation Services, United States Education Department (#G007901347). However, the contents do not necessarily represent the policy of that agency and you should not assume endorsement by the federal government.

**TABLE 8-4**
**A Proposed Amer-Ind Code Core Lexicon**

| | | |
|---|---|---|
| AFRAID | *EAT/FOOD | NOW |
| ALL-GONE² = GOODBYE | FALL¹ | ON |
| *APPLE¹ | FATHER = MAN + BABY | OPEN |
| *BABY | GET | PANTS¹ |
| BAD/NO | GIRL = LITTLE + WOMAN | PLAY¹ |
| *BALL/THROW | GIVE | PUT¹ |
| *BED/SLEEP | GO | RUN |
| BIG | GOOD/YES | SAD/CRY |
| BIRD | HAPPY/DANCE | SCHOOL² = SHELTER + BOOK |
| BOOK/READ | HAT¹ | SHIRT¹ |
| BOY = LITTLE + MAN | HAVE/POSSESS/MINE | SHOE² = WALK + point |
| BREAK | HEAVY | SOCK¹ |
| BRING | HELP | SPOON¹ |
| *CANDY² = TASTE | HOT | STAND |
| CAR | HOUSE/SHELTER | STOP |
| CHAIR/SIT | *HUG/KISS² = self-embrace | TABLE |
| COLD | HURT/PAIN | TELEVISION² = BOX + SEE |
| COME | IN | THIS/THAT¹ |
| COOKIE | LOOK/SEE | *TOILET/POTTY² = clutching the groin area; can be clarified with a wince |
| *CUP/DRINK | MAD | |
| DIRTY² = PIG | MAN | UP |
| DO | MAKE¹ | WASH |
| DOG¹ | *ME/I | WATER |
| DOOR | MILK¹ | WOMAN |
| DOWN | MOTHER = WOMAN + ME | YOU |
| DRESSING/CLOTHING¹ | *MORE¹ | |

*Suggested as initial items
¹Use ASL signs
²Modified from Amer-Ind

# References

*Amerind Video Dictionary* (VC 76 pt. 1 - Pt. 3). St Louis, MO: Veterans Administration Hospital, Learning Resources Center, 1975.

Amon, A. *Talking hands: Indian sign language.* Garden City, NY: Doubleday Press, 1968.

ASHA position statement on nonspeech communication. *ASHA,* 1981, *23,* 577-581.

Anthony, D. *The seeing essential English manual.* Greeley, CO: The University of Northern Colorado Bookstore, 1974.

Archer, L. A. Blissymbolics - A Non-verbal Communication System. *Journal Speech and Hearing Disorders,* 1977, *43,* 568-579.

Balick, S., Spiegel, D., & Green, G. Mime in language therapy and clinician training. *Archives of Physical Medicine and Rehabilitation,* 1976, *57.* 35-38.

Battison, R. Phonology in American sign language: 3-D and digitvision. A presentation at the California Linguistic Conference, Stanford, California, 1973.

Berger, S. A clinical program for developing multimodal language responses with atypical deaf children. In J. E. McLean, D. E. Yoder, & R. L. Schiefelbusch (Eds.), *Language intervention with the retarded: Developing strategies.* Baltimore: University Park Press, 1972, pp.212-235.

Bliss, C. *Semantography.* Sydney Australia: Semantography Publications, 1965.

Bonvillian, J. S., & Friedman, R. J. Language development in another mode: the acquisition of signs by a brain-damaged adult. *Sign Language Studies.* 1978, *19,* 111-120.

Bornstein, H. A., Hamilton, L. B., Saulnier, K. L., & Roy, H. L. *The signed English dictionary for preschool and elementary levels.* Washington, D.C.: Gallaudet College Press, 1975.

Bricker, D. D. Imitative sign training as a facilitator of word-object association with low functioning children. *American Journal of Mental Deficiency,* 1972, *76,* 509-516.

Brown, R. Why are signed languages easier to learn than spoken languages? Keynote address presented at the National Association of the Deaf Symposium, Chicago, June 1977.

Carrier, J. K., Jr. Application of nonspeech language system with the severely language handicapped. In. L. L. Lloyd (Ed.), *Communication assessment and intervention strategies.* Baltimore: University Park Press, 1976, pp. 523-545, Chapter 13.

Chen, L. Y. "Talking hand" for aphasic patients. *Geriatrics,* 1968, *23,* 145-148.

Chen, L. Y. Manual communication by combined alphabet and gestures. *Archives of Physical Medicine and Rehabilitation,* 1971, *52,* 381-384.

Clark, C.R., Davies, C.O., & Woodcock, R.W. *Standard rebus glossary.* Circle Pines, MN: American Guidance Service, 1974.

Clark, W. P. *Indian sign languages.* Philadelphia: L. R. Hammersley & Co., 1885.

Cody, I. E. *Indian talk: Hand signals of the American-Indians.* Healdsburg, CA: California Naturegraph Co., 1970.

Daniloff, J. K., Lloyd, L. L., & Fristoe, M. Amer-Ind transparency. *Journal of Speech and Hearing Disorders,* in press.

Daniloff, J. K., Noll, J. D., Fristoe, M., & Lloyd, L. L. Amer-Ind recognition in patients with aphasia. *Journal of Speech and Hearing Disorders,* 1982, *47,* 56-62.

Daniloff, J. K., & Shafer, A. A gestural communication program for severely-profoundly handicapped children. *Language, Speech, and Hearing Services in Schools,* 1981, *12,* 258-267.

Daniloff, J. K., & Vergara, D. Amer-Ind cherology. A paper presented at the annual convention of the American Association on Mental Deficiency, Boston, Massachusetts, June 3, 1982.

Dennis, R., Reichle, J., Williams, W., & Vogelsberg, R. T. Motoric factors influencing the selection of vocabulary for sign production programs. *Journal of the Association for the Severely Handicapped,* in press.

Donnellan-Walsh, A., Gossage, L. D., LaVigna, G. W., Schuler, A., & Traphagen, J. D. Issues in teaching communicative skills. In *Teaching makes a difference: A guide for developing classes for autistic and other severely handicapped children* (teachers' manual). Santa Barbara, CA: Santa Barbara County Schools, 1976.

Duncan, J. L., & Silverman, F. H. Impacts of learning American Indian sign language on mentally retarded children: A preliminary report. *Perceptual and Motor Skills,* 197, *44,* 1138.

Duncan, J. L., & Silverman, F. H. Impacts of learning Amerind sign language on mentally retarded children. In J. R. Anderews & M.S. Burns (Eds.), *Remediation of language disorders.* Evanston, IL: Institute for Continuing Professional Education, 1978.

Eagleson, H. M., Vaughn, G. R., & Knudson, A. B. Hand signals for dysphasia. *Archives of Physical Medicine and Rehabilitation,* 1970, *51,* 111-113.

Freese, J., & Frerker, V. Amer-Ind in mental retardation. In M. Skelly (Ed.), *Amer-Ind gestural code based on universal American Indian hand talk.* New York: Elsevier North Holland, Inc., 1979.

Fitch, J. L. Treatment of a case of cerebral palsy with hearing impairment. *Journal of Speech and Hearing Disorders,* 1972, *37,* 373-378.

Fristoe, M., & Lloyd, L. L. A survey of the use of non-speech communication systems with the severely communication impaired. *Mental Retardation,* 1978, *16,* 99-103.

Fristoe, M., & Lloyd, L. L. Nonspeech communication. In N. R. Ellis (Ed.), *Handbook of mental deficiency: Psychological theory and research* (2nd Ed.). New York: Lawrence Erlbaum Associates, 1979.

Fristoe, M., & Lloyd, L. L. Planning an initial expressive sign lexicon for persons with severe communication impairment. *Journal of Speech and Hearing Disorders,* 1980, *45,* 170-180.

Gustason, G., Pfetzing, D., & Zawolkow, E. *Signing Exact English.* Rossmoor, CA: Modern Signs Press, 1972.

Harris-Vanderheiden, D., Brown, W. P., Mackenzie, P., Reinen, S., & Scheibel, C. Symbol communication for the mentally handicapped. *Mental Retardation,* 1975, *13,* 34-37.

Hobson, D. A., & Duncan, P. Sign learning in profoundly retarded people, *Mental Retardation,* 1979, *17,* 1.

Hoemann, H. W. The transparency of meaning of sign language gesture. *Sign Language Studies,* 1975, *13,* 34-37.

Holland, A. Language therapy for children: Some thoughts on context and content. *Journal of Speech and Hearing Disorders,* 1975, *40,* 514-523.

Holmes, J. *Manual signing with an aphasia patient.* Abstract of a paper presented at the 13th Academy of Aphasia, Vancouver, British Columbia, 1975. (abstract).

Kirschner, A., Algozzine, B., & Abbott, T. B. Manual communication systems: A comparision and its implications. *Education and Training of the Mentally Retarded,* 1979, *14,* 5-10.

Klima, E. S., & Bellugi, U. *The signs of language.* Cambridge, MA: Harvard University Press, 1979.

Koller, J. J., Schlanger, P. H., & Geffner, D. S. Indentification of action words and activity pantomines by aphasics. *Asha,* 1975, *17,* 613.

Kopchick, G. A., Rombach, D. W., & Smilovitz, R. A total communication environment in an institution. *Mental Retardation,* 1975, *13,* 22-23.

Lahey, M., & Bloom, L. Planning a first lexicon: Which words to teach first. *Journal of Speech and Hearing Disorders,* 1977, *42,* 340-349.

Levett, L. M. A method of communication for non-speaking severely subnormal children. *British Journal of Disorders of Communication,* 1969, *4,* 64-66.

Levett, L. M. A method of communication for non-speaking severely subnormal children — trial results. *British Journal of Disorders of Communication,* 1971, *6,* 125-128.

Lloyd, L. L. (Ed.). *Communication assessment and intervention strategies.* Baltimore: University Park Press, 1976. (N.B. Chapters 1, 7, 11-15).

Lloyd, L. L. Non-speech communication: Discussant's comments. In B. Urban (Ed.), *Proceedings of the XVIIth World Congress of Logopedics and Phoniatrics* (Vol. II). Washington, D.C.: American Speech-Language and Hearing Association, 1980, pp. 43-48.

Lloyd, L. L., & Fristoe, M. Iconicity of signs: Evidence in vocabularies used with severely impaired individuals in contrast with American Sign Language in general. *Proceedings of the Eleventh Annual Gatlinburg Conference on Research in Mental Retardation,* March 8-10, 1978. (abstract)

Lloyd, L. L., & Fristoe, M. Transparency of manual signs used with individuals having severe communication impairment. Manuscript in preparation for publication, 1982.

Mallery, S. Sign language among North American Indians compared with that among other peoples and deaf mutes. In *First annual report of the bureau of ethnology to the secretary of the Smithsonian Institution 1879-1880.* Washington, D.C.: Government Printing Office, 1881, pp. 263-552.

McNaughton, S. Bliss symbols—Alternate symbol systems for the non-vocal pre-reading child. In G. C. Vanderheiden and K. Grilley (Eds.), *Non-vocal communication techniques and aids for the severely physically handicapped.* Baltimore: University Park Press, 1976.

Paget, R., Gorman, P., & Paget, G. *The Paget-Gorman sign system* (6th ed.). London: Association for Experiment in Deaf Education, Ltd., 1976. (Formerly known as *Systematic sign language.)*

Parkel, D. A., White, R. A., & Warner, H. Implications of the Yerkes technology for mentally retarded human subjects. In D. M. Rumbaugh (Ed.), *Language learning by a chimpanzee: The Lana project.* New York: Academic Press, 1977.

Peters, L. Sign language stimulus in vocabulary learning of a brain-injured child. *Sign Language Studies,* 1973, *3,* 116-118.

Podleski, J. *Amer-Ind with the mentally retarded.* A paper presented at the Amer-Ind Conference, St. Louis, Missouri, 1977.

Premack, D., & Premack, A. J. Teaching visual language to apes and language-deficient persons. In R. L. Schiefelbusch & L. L. Lloyd (Eds.), *Language perspectives — Acquisition, retardation, and intervention.* Baltimore: University Park Press, 1974.

Rao, P. R., & Horner, J. Gesture as a deblocking modality in a severe aphasic patient. In R. H. Brookshire (Ed.), *Clinican aphasiology conference proceedings.* Minneapolis: BRK Publishers, 1978.

Rao, P., Basili, A. G., Koller, J., Fullerton, B., Diener, S., & Burton, P. The use of Amer-Ind code by severe aphasic adults. In Burns and Andrews (Eds.), *Neuropathologies of speech and language diagnosis and treatment: Selected papers,* Institute for Continuing Education, Evanston, IL: 1980.

Richardson, T. Sign language for the SMR and PMR. *Mental Retardation,* 1975, *13,* 17.

Schlanger, P. H., & Schlanger, B. B. Adapting role-playing activities with aphasic patients. *Journal of Speech and Hearing Disorders,* 1970, *35,* 229-235.

Silverman, F. *Communication for the speechless.* Englewood Cliffs, NJ: Prentice-Hall, 1980.

Skelly, M. *Amer-Ind Gestural Code: A simplified communication system based on Universal Hand Talk.* New York: Elsevier North Holland, 1979.

Skelly, M., Schinsky, L, Smith, R. W., Donaldson, R. C., & Griffin, J. M. American Indian Sign: A gestural communicaiton system for the speechless. *Archives of Physical Medicine and Rehabilitation*, 1975, *56*, 156-160.

Skelly, M., Schinsky, L., Smith, R. W., & Fust, R. S. American Indian Sign (AMERIND) as a facilitator of verbalization for the oral verbal apraxic. *Journal of Speech and Hearing Disorders*, 1974, *34*, 445-456.

Skelly, M. *Amer-Ind code repertoire*, Video cassette, Auditec, St. Louis, 1981.

Stokoe, W. Sign language structure: An outline of the visual communication system of the American deaf. *Studies in Linguistics—Occasional Papers No.9*, 1960.

Stremel-Campbell, K., Cantrell, D., & Halle, J. Manual signing as a language system and as a speech initiator for the non-verbal severely handicapped student. In E. Sontag, J., Smith, & N. Certo (Eds.), *Educational programming for the severely and profoundly handicapped*. Reston, VA: The Council for Exceptional Children, Division on Mental Retardation, 1977, pp. 335-347.

Topper, S. T. *Gesture language for the severely and profoundly mentally retarded*. Denton, TX: Denton State School, 1974.

Topper, S. T. Gesture language for a non-verbal severely retarded male. *Mental Retardation*, 1975, *13*, 30-31.

Vanderheiden, G. C., & Harris-Vanderheiden, D. Communication techniques and aids for the nonverbal severely handicapped. In L. L. Lloyd (Ed.), *Communication assessment and intervention strategies*. Baltimore: University Park Press, 1976.

# Appendix

**Reprinted from: Daniloff, J. and Schafer, A. A gestural communication program for severly-profoundly handicapped children.** *Language, Speech, and Hearing Services in the Schools* **1981,** *12,* **258-267.**

The progression of acquisition of a gesture through execution and transmission was based upon the Amer-Ind Scale of Progress (Skelly, 1979). Although the scale developed by Skelly is chronological, serveral stages can co-occur and overlap. In this system, signal recognition, execution, and retrieval lead to self-initiated and spontaneous gestures.

The following is an outline of the program steps used to teach gestures. Using the Amer-Ind Scale of Progress, the authors made modifications of the scale which were specific to the needs of the severely and profoundly retarded.

*Stage 1: Stimulation for a minimal response.* A child at this level demonstrated intermittent eye contact in response to verbal or gestural stimuli. The Amer-Ind Scale suggests the conditioning of pointing responses and consistent head movements. Since most students had failed at previous attempts to program these responses, we did not attempt to do so.

*Stage 2: Signal recognition.* In accordance with the Amer-Ind Scale, this stage involved the association of a gesture with a concrete referent such as an object and a picture. However, since we were concerned about overloading and confusing the children with matrix selection to gestural stimuli, as suggested in the Amer-Ind Scale, we deferred signal recognition training until Stage 5.

*Stage 3: Signal execution.* At this level, motor programming progressed from an initial facilitated imitation to unaided replication. The clinician gestured while facing the child, then helped the child mimic the gesture. Once cooperation was established, aided imitation was performed in the presence of an actual object. In conditioning *eat,* for example, the child's hand was first passively brought to her face in a manner similar to the clinician's demonstration. Shortly thereafter, some of the child's lunch was presented, and the gesture was demonstrated by the clinician. After the movement had been facilitated in the child, she was immediately rewarded with the food.

We utilized only gesture at this stage of training, avoiding multimodality input like simultaneous speech with gestures. We also avoided mirror work, the use of pictures and agglutination (the combining of gestures), all contrary to what was outlined in the Amer-Ind Scale. Stimuli were all concrete and limited to actual objects or plastic models of them.

*Stage 4: Signal Retrieval.* The goal at this level was for the child to demonstrate unaided recall of the signal for several appropriate stimuli. In almost every case there was an obvious transition stage between Stages 3 and 4: the child demonstrated a signal to an appropriate stimulus *only* after the clinician reached towards and touched his arm. This behavior was readily extinguished and invariably led to unaided signalling.

We chose not to distinguish specifically between object and action stimuli at this level, as was suggested by the Amer-Ind Scale. We did, however, use at least five different concrete stimuli for each signal. For example, lunch, cookies, bread, pudding, candy and sandwich were all used to elicit *eat.*

*Stage 5: Transition to use.* The aim was to extend unaided use to other people and environments. Once Stage 4 was attained, the teachers, teacher aides, parents and health care staff were encouraged to stimulate retrieval in other environments. Several new features were introduced, including the initiation of simultaneous speech with the gestures. Concepts under Signal Recognition of the Amer-Ind Scale of Progress were initiated, including the addition of photographs, simple object and action pictures, and matrix selection to gestural stimuli. These served as alternative stimuli for the concrete objects previously used exclusively. Initially, we found it helpful if (a) the speech-language pathologist was near the new person demanding signal retrieval and (b) if retrieval had already been demonstrated with the speech-language pathologist in a particular location.

*Stage 6: Self-initiated signal use.* In at least half of the children, self-initiated use occurred with no obvious additional encouragement from the staff. These children appeared to recognize how readily they could manipulate their environment through gestures. Strategically designed situations were used with the other group of children, to *prompt their self-initiation.* When announcing lunchtime, for instance, a teacher might ask members of the class, "Who wants to eat?". Beginning with a child who would spontaneously respond, other children would observe and were prompted to comply by pointing to themselves. Prior to entering the lunchroom, students were encouraged to gesture *eat.* They were also encouraged to greet their teachers in the morning with a wave, and to gesture *goodbye, bus,* and *go* upon leaving.

Increasing responsibility was given to the students in initiating communication. Most teachers readily incorporated gestures into their daily lesson plans.

*Stage 7: Spontaneous signal use.* At this level, the children were self-directed and responded to varied people and circumstances in their environment. Obvious examples indicative of function at this stage included communicating the need to void or desire to drink without prompting. Rudimentary exchange of information between teachers and students took place. A student in the lunchroom might gesture *drink* or *more* when his or her glass was empty. In order to capitalize on the situation, the child might be presented three pictures with (e.g., glasses of milk, orange juice, or water) in order to choose the drink desired.

For the majority of the students in the program, this level was conceivably the highest stage attainable. Therefore, at this level, we shifted our concentration to increasing the gestural vocabulary. We did not emphasize the possibility that gesture might ever be used as an equivalent for propositional speech.

*Stage 8: Signal use as a facilitator of vocalization.* This stage differs dramatically from Level VIII of the Amer-Ind Scale of Progress. Children who had reached this stage demonstrated vocal accompaniment at least 50% of the time that they gestured. Often a dramatic increase in spontaneous vocalization, totally independent of gesture, was charted as well. No additional training was used to establish vocal behavior besides the simultaneous speech plus gestural presentation of stimuli. When the behavior was observed, it was richly rewarded. Since almost no vocal accompaniment was noted prior to the individual's entering Stage 3, we assume that simultaneous speech and gesturing on our parts mediated the appearance of this behavior.

*Stage 9: Spontaneous agglutination.* A child operating at this level suddenly began to combine two separate gestures to form expanded ideas, like *more + drink* and *me + potty.* Obviously, several different gestures needed to be acquired before this stage could be reached. In fact, all of the children who eventually began to combine gestures had acquired at least 10 signals at Stage 7 levels. Again, no specific training was used besides the obvious combinations presented by the speech-language pathologists and staff when addressing the students. Agglutinations were encouraged and rewarded whenever they appeared. Stage 9 varied from Level IX of the Amer-Ind Scale.

*Stage 10: Signal use for support of verbalization.* This stage varied considerably from Level X of the Amer-Ind Scale. By the time a child had reached Stage 10, significant communication growth had occurred. Adjunct vocal behavior was transformed into comprehendible verbalization. Gesture, in a sense, had served as a facilitator to speech. From a facilitatory role, gesture was deposed to a supportive role, and the use of spoken words superseded the gestural repertoire. Stage 10 was looked upon as a long-term goal for several of our less severely impaired children. We believe that even if this stage were attained, maintenance of the gestural repertoire still needed to be conducted. In any event, any use of spoken words was greatly encouraged.

Relative to previous reports, we established a very conservative criterion as a measure for acquisition: a signal was not considered to be acquired until it had reached Stage 7 levels, or until it was appropriately self-initiated. Only when a signal was demonstrated at this level was another introduced. However, if spontaneous use beyond the classroom was not evident within 2 days, the additional signal was temporarily dropped.

# 9

# SPEECH - LANGUAGE PATHOLOGY: EMERGING CLINICAL EXPERTISE IN LANGUAGE

## John R. Muma
Texas Tech University

## Introduction

*T*his is a new era in Speech-Language Pathology (SLP). It is a period in which SLP is emerging with significantly improved conceptualizations about language which have resulted in major theoretical and substantive advances in clinical assessment and intervention.

We have detailed some of these advancements elsewhere (Muma, 1981; Muma, Lubinski, and Pierce, 1982; Muma and Pierce, 1981). These other presentations were cast in the framework that the emerging competencies in SLP have resulted from a shift from a *data* game to an *evidence* game. The distinction between data and evidence is that evidence is *relevant* data. Speech-Language Pathologists have shifted from an orientation toward simplistic a priori 'canned' assessment-intervention activities which defined them as *technicians* to rather sophisticated descriptive procedures which define them as true *clinicians*.

The relatively new competencies can be appreciated by considering the rationale and theoretical bases which have precipitated major advances in assessment and in intervention.

## Clinical Assessment

The psycholinguistic literature over the past two decades has provided major new insights which have resulted in the reconsideration of the theoretical bases for assessment. In the past, it was sufficient to assert construct validity in a categorical sense, simply to assert that psycholinguistic abilities, vocabulary, or language was being tested (Geffner, 1981; Hammill and Bartel, 1978; Reid and Hresko, 1981; Wallace and Larsen, 1978) without laying down an adequate or even a relevant psycholinguistic perspective. This was done under the guise of face validity. It resulted in various assessment tests and procedures of dubious value, notably the Illinois Test of Psycholinguistic Abilities (Kirk, McCarthy, Kirk, 1968), the Peabody Picture Vocabulary Test (Dunn, 1965), the Developmental Sentence Scores (Lee, 1974), various speech discrimination tests (Goldman, Fristoe, Woodcock, 1970; Wepman, 1973), and developmental profiles. Unfortunately, these tests have been widely used across the country by speech-language pathologists and learning disability teachers. It is unfortunate because the assessment process has become vested in a psychometric model which merely yields *data* rather than *evidence* about an individual's psycholinguistic abilities. Some illustrations are given below which make the point.

## Assessment Rationale and Theoretical Perspectives

Psycholinguistic developments over the past two decades have resulted in some major shifts in assessment rationales and theoretical perspectives. These developments have raised questions about the *validity* of assessment in general (Messick, 1980) and language assessment in the clinical fields (Muma and Muma, 1979). Face validity as evidenced in many of the widely used assessment tests and procedures has been found to be simply inadequate. Construct validity is being addressed in new, more appropriate ways, i.e., relativity, conditionality, complexity, dynamism, and ecology as shown in Table 9-1.

**TABLE 9-1**
**Five major aspects of construct validity — manifestations and clinical implications.**

| Domains of Construct Validity | Manifestations | Clinical Implications |
|---|---|---|
| Relativity | Behavioral Patterns | Systems & Processes Approach |
| Conditionality | Contexts | Contexual Influences |
| Complexity | Intact Systems & Processes | Less Distortion |
| Dynamism | Continuous Change | Tracking |
| Ecology | Natural Behavior | Representative |

*Relativity* pertains to the fact that behaviors are interrelated and relative to each other (Kagan, 1967). The implication is that behavioral patterns *within* a system or process are needed as evidence about the underlying system or process.

This means that it is inadequate and inappropriate to infer from single instances of a behavior. In language, at least three instances are needed. Yet, much language assessment in the clinical fields relies on single instances. Such an assessment is vulnerable to distortion and misrepresentation.

*Conditionality* means that behavior is the product of the contexts in which it occurs (Deese, 1969). The implication is that it is necessary to account for the contexts of a behavior as well as for the behavior itself. This is especially true for language (cognitive-linguistic-communicative systems and processes), wherein various contextual influences and determinates are so evident (Bates, 1979; Bloom, 1970, 1973; Muma and Zwycewicz-Emory, 1979). A linguistic assessment should take into account co-occurring systems because new aspects of language are selectively inserted into old ones. Yet, the various sentence imitation and comprehension tests impose their own co-occurring systems. Slobin and Welsh (1971) suggested utilizing a child's own best spontaneous utterances in sentence imitation as a means of appraising his/her linguistic knowledge for his/her co-occurring systems. This suggestion is applicable for comprehension as well.

The rather considerable research in phonology shows that sounds are influenced by other sounds in context. These are coarticulatory functions (Daniloff and Hammarberg, 1973). Again, the articulatory assessment tests on the market essentially have ignored the phonological contexts within a child's system while imposing contexts on the child which may or may not be relevant. Indeed, Locke (1980a) showed that the various widely used speech discrimination tests lacked validity on this basis (Goldman, et al. 1970; Wepman, 1973; etc.).

*Complexity* needs to be appropriately preserved in clinical assessment; otherwise, the assessment outcome will result in distorted or irrelevant information, *data* rather than *evidence*. Language is complex. It entails complex underlying cognitive - linguistic - communicative systems and processes. The extent to which the clinical fields vest assessment in various short profiles is the extent to which misrepresentation and distortion contribute to the enterprise. Unfortunately, the clinical fields are notorious for the use of simple, quick, and easy tests (Geffner, 1981; Hammill and Bartel, 1978; Reid and Hresko, 1981; Wallace and Larsen, 1978). One rather vacuous argument is that the clinical fields must deal with large numbers of clients and therefore they need simple, quick, and easy tests. This turns out to be a contradiction of purposes, because the simple, quick, and easy tests distort and misreport what is claimed to be measured. This defines an irony. Specialists in learning disabilities and some traditionally oriented speech-language pathologists claim to have competencies in language, yet they unwittingly violate a fundamental aspect of language by reducing it to simple irrelevant dimensions in clinical assessment.

*Dynamism* refers to the fact that behavior changes with use or the lack of use. The more one uses his/her cognitive skills or language, the more adept he/she becomes. The implication for assessment is that assessment is always ongoing and open-ended rather than finite and exact. Indeed, contrary to the simplistic linear concept of development espoused in the clinical fields, there is evidence of various curvilinear functions in the acquisition of language, e.g. inflectional systems— (Cazden, 1968; Palermo and Eberhart, 1968), phonological system — phonetic inventories (Ingram, 1976), syntactic systems — dampened oscillatory functions (Menyuk, 1964), markedness (Donaldson and McGarrigle, 1974; Eilers, Oller, and Ellington, 1974), and various revision and hesitation phenomena such as false starts, buildups, and buttressing (Gallagher, 1977; Muma and Muma, 1979; Weir, 1962). The age referenced approach upon which the clinical fields are oriented is too simplistic, gross, and taxonomic and it is based on unwarranted notions of linear acquisition. Paraphrasing Brown (1973), the rate of language learning is notoriously varied, whereas the sequence is highly stable. This means that the clinical assessment process should be predicated on developmental sequences rather than on age.

*Ecology* refers to one's natural environment. It is imperative that the assessment of language be vested in natural circumstances rather than on test performance alone so that the outcome can be regarded legitimately as representative and relevant. Unfortunately, the clinical fields have dismissed a considerable amount of literature, whereby they ignore (or only give passing consideration to) a child's natural behavior but use test scores and developmental profiles which merely claim to provide age references. The result is that the assessment process becomes 'ecologically invalid' (Bronfenbrenner, 1974, 1977). Again, reviews (Locke, 1980 a,b,; Muma, 1981; Rees, 1981) have shown that some so-called clinical experts in language reveal a calloused ineptitude because they miss what they claim to measure.

The clinical fields are shifting away from psychometric tests and developmental profiles because they are rather weak in validity. The shift is toward descriptive procedures, because they are more valid in dealing with relativity, conditionality, complexity, dynamism, and ecology.

*Sampling* is another major issue in language assessment. There are three main issues in language sampling which need to be reconsidered by the clinical fields: spontaneity, variability of settings, and stability of structure and function. These issues could be subsumed under representativeness. That is to say, a primary objective in language sampling is to obtain a representative sample from which inferences can legitimately be made about an individual's competencies. Spontaneity is essential because the language sample can be credited to an individual's linguistic skills. Unfortunately, some clinicians use non-spontaneous samples, responses to forced questions, imitations, and highly rehearsed utterances. As a reference, if a language sample does not include false starts, revisions, buildups, and other hesitation phenomena, it is probably an unrepresentative sample.

Variability of setting refers to the fact that language samples must be taken from several (minimum of three) different contexts. The more contexts sampled, the greater the likelihood of representing the individual's repertoire. Stability of structure and function refers to the language sample size. Most language samples in the clinical fields are 100 utterances. This has become traditional. However, there is no theoretical or empirical reason to justify a language sample of 100 utterances. A casual consideration alone will show that a 100-utterance sample will easily misrepresent an individual's linguistic skill. It should be patently obvious that 100 utterances of a clinician's speech, for example, would misrepresent his/her language skills; yet, clinicians use 100 utterances to guage a client's language knowledge. A more appropriate reference for a language sample size is stability of information, structurally and/or functionally. After sampling in three contexts, if a particular structure or function continues to be manifest in new ways, it is necessary to sample further; however, if the last sample replicates previous manifestations, the sample is sufficient.

## Seven Basic Issues

Clinical assessment should be considered from the perspective of seven basic issues (Muma and Muma, 1979). Such a consideration defines rather serious limitations for the psychometric normative tests and developmental profiles, and it shows that a descriptive approach is more powerful and appropriate. The issues are: clinical complaint, problem/no problem, nature of a problem, individual differences, intervention implications, prognosis, and accountability as shown in Table 9-2.

**TABLE 9-2**
**Seven basic clinical assessment issues compared between psychometric and descriptive procedures.**

| *Clinical Assessment Issues* | *Psychometric* | *Descriptive* |
| --- | --- | --- |
| Clinical complaint | Yes | Yes |
| Problem/no problem | (Yes) | Yes |
| Nature of a problem | No | Yes |
| Individual differences | No | Yes |
| Intervention implications | No | Yes |
| Prognosis | ? | ? |
| Accountability | No | Yes |
| | Data | Evidence |

The *clinical complaint* is a concern that someone had a problem. Both the psychometric and descriptive approaches deal with the clinical complaint by reporting the concern, identifying the referring source, and obtaining various identifying information about the individual who presumably has a problem i.e., age, sex, birthdate, address, etc.

The *problem/no problem* issue is an attempt to identify if there is a problem or not. This is the purpose of the psychometric normative test approach. If a score is found to be aberrant, it is concluded that a problem exists; otherwise no problem is thought to exist. The main faults with this approach are the categorical nature of the norms and the relevance of the norms. Natural problems are rarely categorical. They are complex conditions varying in nature and complexity. The categorical nature of norms is deceptive, often resulting in labeling a clinical disorder without understanding the nature of the problem (Hobbs, 1974,a,b). The problem of relevance is that a norm must be relevant to an individual's presumed disorder in order for the assessment process to be valid. In recent years, a large number of widely used assessment tests and procedures have been found to be irrelevant to what is claimed to be measured, i.e., digit memory span, attention, vocabulary, mean length of utterance, auditory processing, sentence and linguistic knowledge, speech discrimination, cognition, communication, etc. Thus, while the psychometric normative tests and developmental profiles strive to deal with the problem/no problem issues, they fall considerably short because they utilize a priori classifications (norms) which may not be relevant, they are categorical in nature, and furthermore, they lack power (Muma, 1981; Muma and Muma, 1979). Descriptive procedures, on the other hand, overcome these limitations by virtue of relativity, conditionality, complexity, dynamism, and ecology.

The *nature of the problem* is not addressed in the psychometric normative approach per se. It is typically dealt with on a 'logical' basis after the data are in. The result of this process is that a problem merely becomes labeled, i.e., auditory sequencing, visual decoding, short attention span, speech discrimination, language age, etc.

Descriptive procedures can deal directly with the nature of a problem by specifying relevant patterns and the conditions in which a behavior occurs. For example, a developmental profile may index a language age for an individual because he/she uses pronouns; this merely constitutes a labeling process. However, a descriptive approach would detail various patterns of pronoun use in terms of types, co-occuring systems, and referential use. Such descriptions would specify the nature of a problem by indicating that the individual does well with pronouns in some contexts for certain uses but that he/she may not do well with other pronouns in other contexts and other uses.

*Individual differences* constitute a central issue in clinical assessment. It is virtually impossible to find two individuals with the same clinical disorder whose problems are identical. Indeed, a characteristic of clinical populations is heterogeniety. This means that individual differences should be a focal issue in clinical assessment. This proposition is typically given verbal recognition but its implementation falls considerably short of what is needed. The typical implementation is to assess children individually using normative tests and developmental profiles which obviate individual differences. Furthermore, the typical intervention efforts are to label a child (expressive language, auditory sequencing, short attention span, distractible, etc.) and then to subject the child to prepackaged programs which again obviate individual differences. Thus, a paradox exists in the clinical fields. On the one hand, the learning disability teacher, resource teacher, and others claim to be experts in dealing with exceptional children, but they miss an essential issue, individual differences. The descriptive approach is addressed directly to individual differences by virtue of its reliance on patterns of behavior *within* a system or process, contextual determinants, and natural instances.

*Intervention implications* are important in assessment. Thus, assessment should provide specific information about intervention. Because psychometric norms and developmental profiles merely label a child, intervention implications are reduced to categorical issues, such as the child is retarded or has a learning disability. Operationally, this categorization process results in simplistic notions about whether the child should have one-to-one or group therapy, whether therapy should be highly structured or not, whether the room should be cleared of "distractions," etc. Issues about content, sequencing, pacing, context, mediation, and reinforcement are only given passing consideration because they are usually prepackaged.

On the other hand, the descriptive approach is much more explicit about the nature of the problem, especially in regard to the relativity and conditionality for natural behavior. Accordingly, intervention implications are more discernible, under the premise that it is necessary to exploit a child's own systems and processes in contexts. Thus, language intervention becomes an enterprise not only of deducing the nature of a problem through relativity but also of identifying contextual influences and determinants. For example, the coarticulation research has shown that it is insufficient to assess speech difficulties according to initial, medial, or final word positions and omissions, substitutions, and distortions. Rather, it is necessary to identify the phonological contexts in which various difficulties occur so intervention can focus on these contexts (Daniloff, Schuckers, and Hoffman, in press). Similarly, in syntax, it is necessary to identify co-occurring systems (Muma, 1973, 1981) and processes, such as revisions (Gallagher, 1977), to ascertain the loci of learning in certain contexts.

*Prognosis* is an attempt to forecast progress. Unfortunately, there is very little prognostic information about language learning. The reason it is so difficult to provide prognostic statements is that language learning is the product of many underlying complicated systems and processes. Paraphrasing Brown (1973), language learning occurs in spurts of unknown duration and the rate of learning is notoriously varied.

The prognostic aspect of assessment is complicated further because the clinical fields have unwittingly used developmental profiles for prognostic purposes. These profiles simply do not have a prognostic capability. They were not generated on such information, the developmental increments cut across systems and processes rather than trace them, and the age references are unreliable because of large variances. Yet, diagnosticians and special educators strive to give prognostic statements based upon developmental profiles.

Descriptive approaches also lack prognostic power. We simply cannot say how long it will take an individual to learn a given dimension of language. We say with some certainty where a child is in developmental sequence and what co-occurring systems may evidence change as a function of intervention. These are issues of accountability.

*Accountability* is an effort to show the effect or impact of intervention on a child. When a child's behavior changes while he/she is participating in intervention, these changes are usually attributed to the intervention. This may or may not be the case. It is simply very difficult to say with certainty what effect intervention has had. This is complicated by the fact that language intervention entails very complex cognitive-linguistic communicative systems and processes and that the acquisition processes are not confined to the particular intervention activities employed with a child. And of course a child may improve without intervention and even in spite of some intervention.

Accountability is justified in some instances. When a child has had significant problems which were alleviated after intervention, there is reason to attribute some progress to intervention. When a clinician can show that there is a direct relationship between the nature of a problem, what was done in intervention, and present performance, there is sufficient evidence for accountability. When a clinician can truly predict an outcome as a function of intervention, he/she can claim accountability. When a clinician can substantiate that an acquired behavior is sustained, generalized, or fits into a hierarchy of subsequent behaviors, that too would constitute evidence for accountability. Descriptive approaches have the capabilities to provide these kinds of evidence, whereas normative tests and developmental profiles do not.

In summary, descriptive procedures are more valid than psychometric tests and developmental profiles because they provide *evidence,* whereas the latter merely categorize and label. It is for this reason that the major authorities in language and language acquisition use descriptive procedures but rarely, if ever, use psychometric tests and developmental profiles, i.e., Brown, Bates, Bloom, Bowerman, Nelson, Slobin, Greenfield, Halliday, Dore, etc. And it is for this reason that the clinical fields are shifting toward descriptive procedures.

# Substantive Advancements: Some Illustrations

Some major substantive advancements have occurred which have resulted in some major substantive improvements in language assessment.

## Cognitive systems

In the past two decades the perspectives on cognition have shifted away from such simplistic notions as intelligence per se and intelligence testing to an emphasis on a large variety of cognitive skills. Some of these skills have only a general relationship to language and language learning, whereas others are more specifically related. It is more useful to understand how an individual functions than to try to determine some level of overall performance. Unfortunately, school diagnosticians and other special education personnel perpetuate intelligence testing or estimation via the Peabody Picture Vocabulary Test (Dunn, 1965). It is unfortunate because there is a substantial literature that has defined serious problems with this and similar tests (Wechsler, 1975). Piagetian psychology, Guilford's model, and Bruner's cognitive stages are notable alternatives.

The clinical fields are also notoriously naive in their understanding of concept development. Four major developments have occurred in which it is possible to appreciate the nature of an individual's concepts. One development pertains to markedness in concept formation, the idea that it is possible to ascertain what Flavell (1977) called the status, validity, and accessibility of one's concepts by appraising static and dynamic attributes for ostensive and relational terms (Bowerman, 1976; Nelson, 1974). A second development deals with learned equivalence and learned distinctiveness (Dollard and Miller, 1950), and a related perspective is vertical and horizontal concept formation (Vygotsky, 1962). The third major development is the view that the focal and peripheral exemplars are evidence of prototypic and extended knowledge of one's concepts (Anglin, 1977; Burger and Muma, 1980; Rosch, 1973). The fourth major development deals with the roles of various mediators (function, labels, class names, exemplars) and mediating agents (peers, siblings, parents, etc.) in concept formation.

A review of how special education deals with concept formation shows virtually no appreciation of these developments, yet special education teachers claim to deal with concept development (Hammill and Bartel, 1978; Reid and Hresko, 1981; Wallace and Larsen, 1978).

## Linguistic systems

Both the speech-language pathologist and the learning disability teacher, as well as the other special education teachers, claim expertise in language but frequently render services of questionable value. For example, the Peabody Picture Vocabulary Test (Dunn, 1965) is supposed to measure vocabulary, yet it violates a fundamental principle of word knowledge: one word/many referents and one referent/many words. Moreover, it fails to deal with intentional meaning and combinatorial meaning. Last but not least, it employs an a priori set of words instead of assessing a child's own words. Given these rather serious problems with validity, it would be expected that the PPVT would not be used, yet it is probably the most widely used test in the clinical fields.

The Illinois Test of Psycholinguistic Abilities (Kirk, McCarthy, and Kirk, 1968) is another example of a test which is widely used in the clinical fields but has dubious validity. It is predicated on Osgood's psycholinguistic model. This model conceptualizes language in terms of modality performance, that is, expressive language, integration, and receptive language. Unfortunately, a modality model neglects the essential issues of language: underlying cognitive-linguistic-communicative systems (Muma, 1978; 1981), or alternatively, content, form, and use (Bloom, 1974; Bloom and Lahey, 1978).

The applied fields seemingly have a penchant for quantifying behavior. Lee's (1974) efforts to quantify language, the various developmental profiles which presumably assess linguistic age, and the mean length of utterance as a robust index of language age are wrought with serious deficiencies. Rather than quantifying linguistic skill as Lee did, it is more appropriate to describe the particular systems in particular contexts for particular functions. Quantification omits essential information and is therefore rather capricious. More elaborate and sophisticated attempts to quantify linguistic structure have not proved to be very useful (Johnson, 1966).

There are several problems with the developmental profiles which claim to measure language age. (A) They are predicated on the faulty assumption that the normal language learning processes are the same for everyone. However, the psycholinguistic literature shows that there are several different strategies of language acquisition (Muma, 1978; 1981; Bloom and Lahey, 1978). (B) They are predicated on the assumption that the rate of learning is stable, thereby warranting the use of an age reference. However, Brown (1973) and others have documented the fact that the rate of learning is notoriously varied but the sequence is highly stable. Thus, sequence (Prutting, 1979) should be used as a reference for language learning rather than age. (C) Developmental profiles have false precision in their claims to assess language development in increments of less than six months, because the natural variances are at least this large. These variances are evidenced by the fact that language acquisition occurs in spurts of unknown duration.

Mean length of utterance (MLU) was regarded as one of the best indices of language acquisition. Perhaps this view extends back to a study by Darley and Moll (1960), where they held that mean length response (MLR) was the single best indicator of language development. However, MLU is based on a morpheme count for spontaneous utterances. The detailed delineation of changes in MLU as a function of movement through Brown's (1973) five stages gave further credence to MLU as a developmental index. Nevertheless, Brown (1977) no longer wants his stages perpetuated because they are undergoing revision. And, research on MLU has shown that it has only a narrow range of value as an acquisition index (Shriner, 1969). The range is roughly 1.0 to 3.5, then it changes to a performance index. This range indicates that MLU has little value, because even the low values occur at a time when it is more useful to specify which particular structures and functions (Slobin, 1973) are manifest with their attendant co-occurring systems (Harris, 1965; Muma, 1973). Yet, the clinical fields continue to rely on MLU.

The clinical fields perpetuate the notion that speech is separate from language. Yet, the literature has shown that speech is a part of language. Indeed, speech difficulties are traceable to other aspects of the linguistic system. They are not phoneme specific (Ferguson and Garnica, 1975), as special education continues to believe. In recent years assessment and intervention for phonological disorders have made major improvements. Speech-Language Pathologists shifted away from considering phonemes in the initial, medial, and final positions of words and considering articulation disorders in terms of omissions, substitutions, and distortions. The current orientation is to appraise various simplifications, phonotactic processes, and co-articulatory processes (Daniloff, Schuckers, and Hoffman, in press; Ingram, 1976). The previous approach was not as powerful in accounting for a child's speech. Similarly, Locke (1980 a,b) has shown that the widely used speech discrimination tests, such as the Goldman, et al. 1980, and Wepman, 1973, are essentially invalid.

### Communicative Systems

Curiously, the applied fields have claimed expertise in language but have neglected to deal with language as an ongoing active dynamic process in communicative context. The psycholinguistic literature over the past decade has shown that the cognitive and communicative (pragmatic) aspects of language are primary, as contrasted to the structural aspects. Brown's definition of language in 1957 foretold this orientation: language is a cognitive socialization process. Yet, the clinical fields have perpetuated a rather non-productive taxonomic modality perspective in terms of expressive language, integration, and receptive language as evidenced by the ITPA.

Communicative systems are very complex; they include various intents, perception of available references, perception of encoder or decoder perspectives, code matrix, code complexity, turntaking, paragraphing, adjusted messages, revision and other hesitation phenomena, and anaphoric reference. Elsewhere, I have posited how these various aspects may interplay in a communication game (Muma, 1975) which becomes fully acquired by around 10 years of age. The clinical fields are beginning to incorporate various pragmatic dimensions in assessment and intervention. Consequently, the clinical fields are beginning to realize that many of the previously held notions were naive and even detrimental, i.e., digit memory span, mean length of utterance, exclusive modality orientations, taxonomic approaches with baseline frequency counts removed from context, a priori tests and intervention programs, and so on.

## Clinical Intervention

With the clinical fields incorporating communicative or pragmatic perspectives, major changes have begun to occur not only in assessment but also in intervention. Heretofore the clinical fields based their intervention on a behavioristic philosophy, but there is a shift toward mentalism as shown in Table 9-3.

*Behaviorism* held that a child is a passive learner waiting to be taught and that stimulation is necessary and sufficient. The role of the clinician was to determine content, sequencing, pacing, mediation, and reinforcement for the learning processes. Thus, the learning processes were presumed to be under the control of the learning expert, the teacher or clinician. Moreover, it was necessary to predicate the assessment process on normative tests and to provide group instruction. This logic led to the development of many a priori assessment practices and procedures which merely categorized and labeled children while saying virtually nothing about the nature of a problem. Muma (1978) held that this logic also begot a priori intervention of dubious value. Such intervention programs were addressed

**TABLE 9-3**
**A comparison between behaviorism and mentalism in intervention.**

| *Behaviorism* | *Mentalism* |
| --- | --- |
| Passive learner | Active learner |
| Stimulation necessary and sufficient | Stimulation necessary but insufficient |
| Teacher readiness | Child readiness |
| Teacher criteria:   ⋮ content, sequence, pacing, mediation, reinforcement | Child criteria: content, sequence, pacing, mediation, reinforcement |
| Group performance | Individual performance |
| Assessment: immediate, direct, parcelled | Assessment: delayed indirect, integrated |

to learning vocabulary words and building sentences outside of a meaningful communicative context. The clinical fields had invented and perpetuated the notion that language training should be highly structured to overcome the so-called short attention span or distractibility of learning disabled children. Such notions reflect a lack of professional insight about attention, memory, and language rather than insights into the actual learning problems of children. Chomsky (reported in Cazden, 1972) warned that highly structural a priori programs are potentially detrimental to natural learning processes. Both Piaget (1954) and Bruner (1964, 1975 a,b, 1978) had defined cognitive and language learning as active dynamic processes, yet the clinical fields' utilization of a behavioristic orientation ignored fundamental issues of active dynamic processesing. Indeed, behaviorism has become so institutionalized in the clinical fields that assessment and intervention policies are now cast in behavioristic terms, notably Public Law 94-142. The irony is that this law contains mentalistic issues such as individualized assessment and readiness, but these issues can become corrupted.

*Mentalism* contrasts significantly with behaviorism in intervention. Mentalism holds that the learning processes are active and dynamic and that stimulation is necessary but insufficient. This means that it is inappropriate to subject a child to a normative assessment or an a priori 'canned' intervention program. Mentalism holds that cognitive and language learning take several different forms, therefore it is necessary to ascertain which strategies a given child is employing. Indeed, the literature shows that there are several strategies of cognitive and language learning (Muma, 1978, 1981). With several strategies, intervention issues about content, sequence, pace, mediation, and reinforcement are, by definition, the primary province of the child rather than of the teacher or clinician. For this reason a mentalistic model for intervention contrasts with the instruction model of behaviorism. Mentalistically, the goal is to facilitate learning by exploiting a child's natural predisposition for learning. This means that it is necessary to ascertain an individual's strategies of learning, his/her readiness to learn within a developmental sequence for various systems or processes, and contextual influences and determinants. Issues such as these rest on relativity, conditionality, complexity, dynamism, and ecology.

It is noteworthy that while the learning disability teacher claims to have expertise in language learning, this expertise is defined in terms of an instruction model (Hammill and Bartel, 1978; Reid and Hresko, 1981; Wallace and Larsen, 1978). Clearly, the behavioristic philosophy has prevailed at the cost of a more appropriate mentalistic and interactionistic model (McLean and McLean, 1978; Muma, 1975).

## Three Basic Intervention Components

A serious incorporation of the contemporary psycholinguistic literature in intervention would logically include peer modeling, parallel talk, and parent participation as shown in Table 9-4.

**TABLE 9-4**
**Three basic intervention components.**

*Peer Modeling*
  Target child - peer match
  Natural ongoing behavior: utility
  Selective

*Parallel Talk*
  Tuned
  Action patterns
  Available reference
  Salience to an event
  Presumed attention
  Intent
  - - - - - - -
  Ten techniques

*Parent Participation*
  Observational
  Active participant:
    produce activities
    clinician role
  Counseling and informative

*Peer modeling* entails the use of the behavior of a peer as a model to induce positive change in the behavior of a target child. Thus, a target child who is having difficulties with the pronominal system could engage in activities with another child who does not have difficulties with the pronominal system. This child will then provide spontaneous examples of the pronominal system from which information can be extracted either indirectly or with selective inducement by a clinician's parallel talk. It is easier for a child to learn from a peer model than from an instructional model because language is used in a spontaneous natural way, with intent and available reference supporting it. This defines language as purposeful and contextually related (referential and linguistic). In this arena, the behavioristic notions of carryover or generalization became moot issues, because they are inherent with peer modeling.

*Parallel talk* is a procedure whereby a clinician strives to be tuned (Bruner, 1975a, 1978) to the cognitive-linguistic-communicative needs of a child as the child uses language in social commerce. A clinician codes ongoing events in ways that correspond to a child's readiness to code (Bruner, 1975a, 1978), his action patterns (Bates, 1979; Greenfield and Smith, 1976), available reference (Olson, 1970), salience to an event Macnamara, 1972), presumed attention (McCall and Kagan, 1969), and intent (Bruner, 1975b; Dore, 1975; Halliday, 1975). Parallel talk is predicated on an appropriate descriptive assessment which delineates the nature of one's language in communicative contexts so a clinician can be on target most of the time.

The application of the five children initiated and clinician response models previously reported: correction, expansion, expatiation, expatiation complex, and alternatives (Muma, 1971) comprise part of the parallel talk procedure. The other five models: completion, revision, combination, alternative replacement, and replacement, need to be predicated on a child's own target structures and co-occurring systems to realize their full potency.

Unfortunately, the clinical fields are not well versed in parallel talking. The prevailing attitude is behavioristic and instructional. Most clinicians talk too much or say the wrong thing. They are insufficiently tuned to the language learning needs of a child. They are seemingly ignorant of a fundamental principle of language learning — *payoff*. If an utterance works as intended, it gets paid off. When pay off occurs, a child talks more and with more variety. Unfortunately, the instructional model, in which children are told to wait their turn and then perform in ways directed by a teacher, undermines the use of language for one's intent as it relates to an event and opportunities for appropriate pay off. In short, much of what has been going on in special education (learning disabilities, resource room, etc.) in instructional models has been contradictory to some language learning principles.

*Parent participation* is essential to language intervention. Parents want to play an effective role and they can. It is helpful to have parents begin in observing target behaviors, co-occurring systems, available reference, communicative intent, hesitation phenomena, and so on, then they can begin to take an active role in intervention. Initially, parents can bring in relevant activities. This relieves the clinician of the mundane busy work so he/she can utilize professional skills observing, reporting, and evaluating performance. After several weeks, parents can play a more active role by selectively carrying out certain activities. The clinician can provide feedback so parents can legitimately extend intervention to the home. We have a very high percentage of the parents participate in this way. We are convinced that such participation constitutes a significant portion of a successful program.

Parent participation is important for another reason — counseling. As parents become involved, they learn more about their child's problems and their role in improvement. In this way, they come to more fully appreciate the various efforts of clinicians.

## Summary

This is truly a new era in Speech-Language Pathology in which *technicians* are becoming *clinicians*. In clinical assessment, there is increased concern about *validity*. Face validity and construct validity are viewed from the perspectives of relativity, conditionality, complexity, dynamism, and ecology. Accordingly, there is a shift away from the psychometric normative test model, which merely categorizes and labels, to a descriptive model which can deal more appropriately with the seven basic assessment issues: clinical complaint, problem/no problem, nature of a problem, individual differences, intervention implications, prognosis, and accountability.

In clinical intervention, the behavioristic instructional model was shown to be inappropriate, whereas a mentalistic model is appropriate. Accordingly, language intervention is shifting toward practices and procedures that deal with a child as he/she strives to use language naturally. Three basic intervention components in this regard are peer modeling, parallel talk, and parent participation.

## References

Anglin, J. *Word, object and concept development.* New York: W.W. Norton 1977.

Bates, E. *The emergence of symbols.* New York: Academic Press 1979.

Bloom, L. *Language development: Form and function in emerging grammar.* Cambrige, Mass.: MIT Press 1970.

Bloom, L. *One word at a time: The use of single-word utterances before syntax.* The Hague: Mouton 1973.

Bloom, L. Talking, understanding, and thinking. In R. Schiefelbusch and L. Lloyd (Eds.), *Language perspectives: Acquisition, retardation, and intervention.* Baltimore: University Park Press 1974.

Bloom, L., & Lahey, M. *Language development and language disorders.* New York: Wiley 1978.

Bowerman, M. Semantic factors in the acquisition of rules for word use and sentence construction. In A. Morehead and D. Morehead (Eds.), *Normal and deficient child language.* Baltimore: University Park Press 1976.

Bronfenbrenner, U. Developmental research, public policy, and the ecology of childhood. *Child Development,* 1974 *45,* 1-5

Bronfenbrenner, U. Toward an experimental ecology of human development. *American Psychologist,* 1977, *32,* 13-31.

Brown, R. Development of the first language in the human species. *American Psychologist,* 1973, *28,* 97-106.

Brown, R. Personal correspondence 1977.

Bruner, J. The course of cognitive growth. *American Psychologist,* 1964, *19,* 1-15.

Bruner, J. From communication to language - a psychological perspective. *Cognition,* 1975a, *3,* 255-288.

Bruner, J. The ontogensis of speech acts. *Journal of Child Language,* 1975b, *2,* 1-19.

Bruner, J. Learning the mother tongue. *Human Nature,* 1978, 42-49.

Burger, R., & Muma, J. Cognitive distancing in mediated categorization in aphasia. *Journal of Psycholinguistic Research,* 1980, *9,* 37-47.

Cazden, C. The acquisition of noun and verb inflection. *Child Development,* 1968, *39,* 433-448.

Cazden, C. *Child language and education.* New York: Holt, Rinehart, and Winston 1972.

Daniloff, R., Schuckers, G., & Hoffman, P. *Articulation: Theory and treatment.* Boston: Addison-Wesley (in press).

Daniloff, R., & Hammarberg, R. On defining coarticulation. *Journal of Phonetics,* 1973, *1,* 239-248.

Darley, F., & Moll, K. Reliability of language measures and size of language samples. *Journal of Speech Hearing Research,* 1960, *3,* 166-173.

Deese, J. Behavior and fact. *American Psychologist,* 1969, *24,* 515-522.

Dollard, J., & Miller, N. *Personality and psychotherapy.* New York: McGraw-Hill 1950.

Donaldson, M., & McGarrigle, J. Some clues to the nature of semantic development, *Journal of Child Language,* 1974, *1,* 185-194.

Dore, J. Holophrases, speech acts, and language universals. *Journal of Child Language,* 1975, 2, 21-40.

Dunn, L. *Peabody picture vocabulary test.* Circle Pines, MN: American Guidance Service, 1965.

Eilers, R., Oller, D., & Ellington, J. The acquisition of word-meaning for dimensional adjectives: the long and short of it. *Journal of Child Language,* 1974, *1,* 195-204.

Ferguson, C., & Garnica, O. Theories of phonological development. In E. Lenneberg and E. Lenneberg (Eds.), *Foundations of language development.* New York: Academic Press, 1975.

Flavell, J. *Cognitive development.* Englewood Cliffs, NJ: Prentice-Hall, 1977.

Gallagher, T. Revision behaviors in the speech of normal children developing language, *Journal of Speech Hearing Research,* 1977, *20,* 303-318.

Geffner, D. Assessment of language disorders: Linguistic and cognitive functions. In K. Butler (Ed.), *Topics in language disorders,* 1981, *1,* 3, 1-10.

Goldman, R., Fristoe, M., & Woodcock, R. *Goldman-Fristoe-Woodcock test of auditory discrimination.* Circle Pines, MN: American Guidance Service, 1970.

Greenfield, R., & Smith, J. *Communication and the beginnings of language: The development of semantic structure in one-word speech and beyond.* New York: Academic Press, 1976.

Halliday, M. Learning how to mean. In E. Lenneberg and E. Lenneberg (Eds.), *Foundations of language development.* New York: Academic Press, 1975.

Hammill, D., & Bartel, N. *Teaching children with learning and behavior problems.* Boston: Allyn and Bacon, 1978.

Harris, Z. Co-occurrence and transformation in linguistic structure. In J. Fodor, and J. Katz (Eds.), *The structure of language.* Englewood Cliffs, NJ: Prentice-Hall, 1965.

Hobbs, N. (Ed.). *The Future of children: Categories, labels, and their consequences.* San Francisco: Jossey-Bass, 1974a.

Hobbs, N. (Ed.). *Issues in the classification of children: A sourcebook on categories, labels, and their consequences.* San Francisco: Jossey-Bass, 1974b.

Ingram, D. *Phonological disability in children.* New York: Elsevier, 1976.

Johnson, N. The influence of associations between elements of structured verbal responses. *Journal of Verbal Learning and Verbal Behavior,* 1966, *5,* 369-374.

Kagan, J. On the need for relativism. *American Psychologist,* 1967, *22,* 131-142.

Kirk, S., McCarthy, J., & Kirk, W. *The Illinois test of psycholinguistic abilities.* Urbana, IL: University of Illinois Press 1968.

Lee, L. *Developmental sentence analysis.* Evanston, IL: Northwestern University Press, 1974.

Locke, J. The inference of speech perception in the phonologically disordered child. Part I: A rationale, some criteria, the conventional tests. *Journal of Speech Hearing Disorders,* 1980a, *45,* 431-444.

Locke, J. The inference of speech perception in the phonologically disordered child. Part II: Some clinically novel procedures, their use, some findings. *Journal of Speech and Hearing Disorders,* 1980b, *45,* 455-468.

Macnamara, J. Cognitive basis of language learning in infants. *Psychological Review,* 1972, *79,* 1-13.

McCall, R., & Kagan, J. Individual differences in the infant's distribution of attention to stimulus discrepancy. *Developmental Psychology,* 1969, *2,* 90-98.

McLean, J., & McLean, L. *A transactional approach to early language training.* Columbus, Ohio: 1978.

Menyuk, P. Alteration of rules of children's grammar. *Journal of Verbal Learning and Verbal Behavior,* 1964, *3,* 480-488.

Messick, S. Test validity and the ethics of assessment. *American Psychologist,* 1980, *35,* 1012-1027.

Muma, J. Language intervention: Ten Techniques. *Language, Speech, and Hearing Services in the Schools,* 1971, *5,* 7-17.

Muma, J. Language assessment: The co-occuring and restricted structures procedure. *Acta Symbolica,* 1973, *4,* 12-29.

Muma, J. The communication game: Dump and play. *Journal of Speech and Hearing Disorders,* 1975, *40,* 296-309.

Muma, J. *Language handbook: Concepts, assessments, intervention.* Englewood Cliffs, NJ: Prentice-Hall, 1978.

Muma, J. *Language primer.* Lubbock, TX: Natural Child Publisher, 1979.

Muma, J., Lubinski, R., & Pierce, S. Language assessment: Data or evidence? In Lass, N. (Ed.), *Speech and language,* 1982.

Muma, J., & Muma, D. *Muma assessment program.* Lubbock, TX: Natural Child Publisher, 1979.

Muma, J., & Pierce S. Language intervention: Data or evidence? In J. Panagos (Ed.), *Language intervention with the learning disabled: Topics in learning and learning disabilities,* 1981, Vol. 1, No. 2, 1-12.

Muma, J., & Zwycewicz-Emory C. Contextual priority: Verbal shift at seven? *Journal of Child Language,* 1979, *6,* 301-311.

Myers, P., & Hammill, D. *Methods for learning disorders* (2nd. Ed.). New York: Wiley, 1976.

Nelson, K. Concept, word and sentence: Interrelations in acquisition and development. *Psychological Review,* 1974, *81,* 267-285.

Olson, D. Language and thought: Aspects of a cognitive theory of semantics. *Psychological Review,* 1970, *77,* 257-273.

Piaget, J. *The construction of reality in the child.* New York: Basic Books, 1954.

Palermo, D., & Eberhart, W. On the learning of morphological rules: An experimental analogy. *Journal of Verbal Learning and Verbal Behavior,* 1968, *7,* 337-344.

Prutting, C. A. Process/pra/ses/n: The action of moving forward progressively from one point to another on the way to completion. *Journal of Speech and Hearing Disorders,* 1979, *44,* 3-30.

Rees, N. Saying more than we know: Is auditory processing disorder a meaningful concept? In R. Keith (Ed.), *Central auditory and language disorders in children.* San Diego: College-Hill Press, 1981.

Reid, D., & Hresko, W. *A cognitive approach to learning disabilities.* New York: McGraw-Hill, 1981.

Rosch, E. On the interval structure of perceptual and semantic categories. In T. Moore (Ed.), *Cognitive development and the acquisition of language.* New York: Academic Press, 1973.

Shriner, T. A review of mean length of responses as a measure of expressive language development in children. *Journal of Speech Hearing Disorders,* 1969, *34,* 61-67.

Slobin, D. Cognitive prerequisites for the development of grammar. In C. Ferguson and D. Slobin (Eds.), *Studies of child language development.* New York: Holt, Rinehart, Winston, 1973.

Slobin, D., & Welsh, C. Elicited imitation as a research tool in developmental psycholinguistics. In C. Lavatelli (Ed.), *Language training in early childhood education.* Urbana: University of Illinois Press, 1971.

Vygotsky, L. *Thought and language.* Cambridge, Mass.: MIT Press, 1962.

Wallace, G., & Larsen, S. *Educational assessment of learning problems.* Boston: Allyn and Bacon, 1978.

Wechsler, D. Intelligence defined and undefined: A relationistic appraisal. *American Psychologist,* 1975, *30,* 135-139.

Weir, R. *Language in the crib.* The Hague: Mouton, 1962.

Wepman, J. *Auditory discrimination test.* Chicago: Language Research Associates, 1973.

# 10

# DEVELOPMENTAL LANGUAGE DISORDERS: A THEORETICAL PERSPECTIVE

*Diane M. Kirchner*
and
*Elizabeth Skarakis-Doyle*
University of California at Santa Barbara

> *Suppose that what is important about kangaroos is that they hop. Ordinarily they do this by application of both legs and the tail. One could argue, however, that the basis for hopping in the kangaroo is "really" its hind legs . . . On the other hand, one might support the theory that it is the tail that is essential . . . Finally, I could maintain a third position which is: It's both. To prove this, all we do is cut off a little bit of both the tail and the legs. And we find that indeed the animal still can hop; it doesn't like to and doesn't do as good a job as a normal kangaroo but it does in fact manage to hop, because these different organs have been maintained in balance. The conclusion from all these experiments would be that neither the legs nor the tail is the essential basis for hopping; rather it is balance between them.*
>
> *(Bever, 1975)*

## Introduction

*D*evelopmental language disorders have been a primary focus of speech/language pathologists' clinical and research interests in the past ten years. Basic research into the nature of the disorders, as well as applied investigations of assessment and remediation techniques have flourished. However, this has not always been the case in this field. Indeed, developmental language disorders as a specialty area, has its roots not in speech and language pathology, but in several allied disciplines including: neurology (adult aphasiology), psychiatry, pediatrics and deaf education. It was not until the early 1950's that speech and language pathologists, such as Mildred McGinnis and Helmer Myklebust, began to synthesize information from those disciplines to create the specialized field of developmental language disorders. However, in these early years terminology reflected the influence of the medical fields. Developmental

language disorders were known as "delayed speech" or "childhood aphasia."
In 1960 the Institute on Childhood Aphasia convened at Stanford University to
develop guidelines for the diagnosis and treatment of childhood aphasia. Conferees were charged with the responsibility of answering basic questions such as:
Is there a problem such as "childhood aphasia?" If so, what is its etiology? How
should such a term be defined? What is the nature of the problem?

Participants in the conference unanimously agreed on the existence of the entity termed childhood aphasia. They generally agreed that a "brain deficit" (West,
1962) was the etiology, but could specify it no further. Most agreed on the following definition:

> Impairment of language function (expressive or receptive) resulting from
> maldevelopment or injury to the central nervous system, prenatally,
> paranatally, or postnatally, (... not later than the normal time for develop-
> ment of speech ...). The language deficiency may or may not be associated
> with other cerebral or neurological pathology or dysfunction. Excluded are
> language problems associated primarily with: 1) mental deficiency, 2) hear-
> ing impairment, 3) CNS damage affecting the    peripheral speech
> mechanism, 4) emotional disturbance and 5) delayed maturation in
> language development resulting from social or emotional factors or
> physical factors not primarily due to CNS involvement. (p. 1)

However, conferees could not agree on the exact nature of the disorder. While
this conference generated interest in the problem, at best we are left knowing
what a developmental language disorder is not, rather than what it is. Presently, a
definition of the problem and its characteristics still remain elusive.

Contemporary investigations have provided preliminary descriptions of these
children's linguistic behavior, but have not succeeded in answering the basic questions raised at the Stanford conference. Fifteen years after the Stanford Institute,
Menyuk (1975) once again posed the fundamental question regarding children
with language disorders, What is the problem? Two reasons may be suggested as
to why the basic questions remain unanswered. First, current research has produced a class of data which cannot be accounted for by popularly accepted
theoretical premises. Over the past 15 years, this residue class of data has grown
too large to ignore any longer. Clearly the size of this pool of data signals the need
for a new, more comprehensive theoretical framework. Second, the
methodological complexities in studying language disorders have become apparent in the past fifteen years and also indicate the need for a new framework.
Naremore (1979) has stated: "The complexity of language behavior is such that
we destroy what we are most interested in by virtue of attempting to measure it"
(p. 173). Although she maintains that it is methodological failure that impedes
progress in developing new theoretical constructs, it is the position of this paper
that inadequate theoretical constructs, are responsible for methodological short-
comings. A theoretical framework that is sensitive to the unique aspects of the
language disordered system is needed. In the discussion to follow such a

framework will be presented. As necessary background to this theoretical position, the paper will begin with a review of research conducted in the area of developmental language disorders, followed by a critique of assumptions and models this research was based on. The proposed theoretical framework will then be presented and supported by several case studies.

# Review of Research in Developmental Language Disorders

Speech and language pathologists began serious investigations into the cause and nature of developmental language disorders over two decades ago. Early attempts to understand these phenomena were based on a "specific disabilities" model (Kirk and McCarthy, 1961; Mykelbust, 1954; Osgood, 1957). The basic assumption of this model was that particular specific abilities including perceptual, symbolic, and planned motor acts were required for language. Thus, disordered language is explained as a result of a deficit in receiving, processing, or expressing language via the central nervous system. Research based on this model was largely inconclusive. The exact relationship between specific deficits and the manifested linguistic behavior remains unclear.

Dissatisfaction with the specific disabilities model along with a growing amount of research in language acquisition prompted researchers to turn to a different model for understanding language disorders. The "normal developmental model" (Bloom and Lahey, 1978; Prutting, 1979; Rees, 1972) assumes that it is possible to describe a language disordered child's communication skill by comparing their proficiency to children acquiring language normally. Specifically, this model assumes that communicative behavior develops in a sequentially invariant manner over a period of time and that normal and language disordered children both progress through the same sequence. The sequence of development is dependent on complexity. Earlier behaviors are presumed less complex and learned earlier while more advanced behaviors are more complex and, therefore, learned later. The rate at which a child progresses through this developmental sequence is variable across children.

Studies based on the normal developmental model have generally been descriptive, relying on a corpus of spontaneous utterances as the data base. Based on Chomsky's 1957 theory of transformational grammar, the original research was syntactic in nature. Utterances are transcribed and coded for type and frequency according to syntactic taxonomic categories. Then, comparisons are made between the structures produced by language disordered and normal children of the same age or younger.

Menyuk (1964) was the first to specifically compare the syntactic knowledge of language disordered children and normal children of the same age followed two years later by Lee (1966). Both of these investigators, while using slightly different analysis procedures, obtained basically the same results. Differences in both the range of structures and frequency with which these structures were used appeared in the disordered children. Qualitative analyses of the utterances produced by language disordered subjects in both studies suggested that language disordered children used nongrammatical sentences (i.e., approximations to well-formed sentences) more often than normal children.Further, both researchers discovered that those approximations were constituent omissions rather than substitutions as were typical of the normal children. These findings support the notion that language disordered children are not merely slower in following a normal pattern of development, but also fail to produce certain types of structures.

In the years to follow, investigators have looked systematically at the structural knowledge of the language disordered child (Bax and Stevenson, 1977; Leonard, 1972; Morehead and Ingram, 1973). Some have studied the acquisition of specific linguistic structures in language disordered populations such as production of the copula and verbal auxiliary (BE) (Ingram, 1972a), question forms (Ingram, 1972b), and grammatical morphemes (Cousins, 1979; Johnston and Schery, 1976) (see Appendix 10-1).

The majority of these studies conclude that there are few differences between the syntactic structures used by normal and language disordered children when matched for language level. Most researchers suggest that the disordered child follows a similar, invariant but delayed order of acquisition of specific linguistic structures compared to children developing language normally. However, Bax and Stevenson (1977) and Cousins (1979) results are contradictory to this position. Both of these investigators conclude that the acquistion and use of certain syntactic structures are qualitatively different in language disordered children. Thus, investigators disagree on whether the language disordered child has deviant or delayed structural knowledge. However, all agree that knowledge is characterized by a high frequency of fragmentary or partial syntactic forms not typical of the normal child at the same age or linguistic stage.

As interest in the area of psycholinguistics grew, the research emphasis shifted away from the syntactic to the semantic bases of language, particularly as a result of the contributions of Bloom (1970) and Brown (1973). Studies were subsequently designed to investigate the type and frequency of basic semantic relations present in disordered language users (Freedman and Carpenter, 1976; Leonard, Bolders, and Miller, 1976) (see Appendix 10-2).

Freedman and Carpenter (1976) concluded that the language disordered children in their study demonstrated at least as flexible use as the normal group with regard to semantic relations, Leonard et al. (1976) suggested that what differences exist in the language disordered child's use of semantic relations were consistent with an earlier level of development. Neither group of investigators reported evidence for qualitatively different rule systems, where basic semantic relations are concerned, in language disordered children.

In the mid-1970's, Bates (1976) was the first to attempt to delineate a theory of language in context. As a result, a number of investigators sought to study the pragmantic abilities of language disordered children (Gallagher and Darnton, 1978; Shatz, Bernstein, and Schulman, 1980; Skarakis and Greenfield, 1982; Snyder, 1978) (see Appendix 10-3).

Snyder (1978) and Skarakis and Greenfield (1982) were interested in the language disordered child's ability to mark new and old information. Snyder found that her young language disordered subjects were unable to verbally encode new information at a level greater than chance and concluded that these children demonstrated deficits in forming verbal presuppositions. Skarakis and Greenfield (1982), using language disordered children beyond the one-word stage, found that the disordered group manifested the same developmental sequence of strategies for deemphasizing old information but a subgroup of children differed in the proportional use of those strategies.

Other investigators have studied the language disordered child's response to specific speech acts. Gallagher and Darnton (1978) looked at the language disordered child's responses to contingent queries and were particularly interested in revision strategies. These investigators concluded that the disordered children revise linguistic forms just as do normal children. But, again, the language disordered subjects demonstrated a proportionately different distribution of revision strategies. Shatz et al. (1980) examined language disordered children's responses to directives under varying contextual conditions. In this study, language disordered children were found to be qualitatively much like normal children with regard to early response behavior and followed a qualitatively similar course of development when compared to normal children. Still, the language disordered children did appear to have more difficulty in generating informing responses and in using information from prior linguistic context than did normal children.

While our understanding of language disorders has broadened considerably over the past two decades, the results of research in this area are fragmented and contradictory. The only consistent conclusion from research in this area is that "language disordered children may learn to speak slowly and late, but little else about their language has proven remarkable" (Johnston, 1982).

As Naremore (1979) suggested, a number of methodological obstacles contribute to the difficulty in fully understanding the nature of language disorders in children. First, many of the processes contributing to language acquisition and disorders are unavailable for direct observation. We can only infer what these processes might be from observing the manifested linguistic and cognitive behavior in a child or group of children. Second, language disordered children represent a heterogeneous population. As such, it is unlikely that we will be able to identify a single finding or set of findings that characterize the population as a whole. Even matching for mean length of utterance (MLU) does not fully equate subject groups. MLU is a superficial measure which is restricted to grammatical assessment and tells us nothing about cognitive or comprehension skills in the same group of children. Miller, Chapman, and Bedrosian (1977) state that research which has failed to establish its subject's status on all variables, cognition, comprehension, and production, may have inadvertently used groups so heterogeneous so as to be useless for drawing conclusions about language and communication delays. Geschwind (1979), referring to the population of language disordered children states:

"...we do not have a classification scheme that we know is correct. This means that studying children in groups may be based on the fallacious assumption that they have similar language behavior." (p. 180)

Third, literature to date is composed of mostly cross-sectional studies and only a few longitudinal investigations of disordered children.

Clearly, depending on the particular methodology employed, results are variable (Cousins, 1979; Johnston and Schery, 1976). Cross-sectional studies do provide useful results, however, the longitudinal study of single subjects during early development is necessary if we wish to understand the processes underlying the developmental phenomena we observe and measure (Dennenberg, 1979). Finally and most importantly, there are problems at the conceptual level.

Part of the reason why differences between disordered and normal language users are difficult to interpret in the experimental literature is the use of the normal developmental model for comparison purposes. Prutting (1973) states that the model provides terminology and methodology for clinical assessment and remediation purposes. We are able to categorize linguistic structures and sequence treatment goals accordingly. While it is tempting to use the developmental stage model as an explanatory concept, Hutt (1973) warns against the danger in confusing a taxonomy with an explanatory system. A model which provides descriptive labels and guidelines for programming tells us very little about how the component parts underlying linguistic behavior are organized or about potential mechanisms responsible for change. In other words, the predictive power of such a model is weak at best.

In the sections to follow we propose a framework which extends the normal model. Expansion of the currently accepted version of this model includes the addition of concepts which account for the unique patterns of communicative behavior in the language disordered child. As a result, the explanatory power of the normal model is enhanced.

# A Theoretical Framework for Developmental Language Disorders

## Basic Assumptions

In order to develop a theoretical framework sensitive to the unique aspects of the disordered language system, four basic assumptions must be stated. These assumptions are derived from several theoretical constructs integral to research in the social and biological sciences. The first of these assumptions is taken from General Systems Theory (Boulding, 1956; Von Bertalanffy, 1950) which developed in reaction to the increasing specialization of science. Systems Theory is that which attempts to understand properties and principles of "wholes" or organization. Watzlawick, Beavin, and Jackson (1967) were prominent among those who applied this theoretical position to human communication. The second and third assumptions are derived from the genetic-biological school of thought in the field of psychology (Bates, Bretherton, Camaioni, and Volterra, 1979; Piaget, 1952; Tinbergen, 1951). The fourth, and final assumption, is taken from the work of Bates and MacWhinney (1979) who propose a functionalist approach to the acquisition of language. In the discussion to follow, each assumption will be discussed in greater detail.

The first assumption maintains that communicative behavior should be regarded as an "open system." An open system is one that interacts with its environment. Von Bertalanffy, "father" of this theoretical position states:

"Every living organism is essentially an open system. It maintains itself in a continuous inflow and outflow, building up and breaking down of components...being so long as it is alive...maintained in a so-called steady-state." (p. 9)

There are several properties which are characteristic of open systems.
1. **Wholeness**-This property refers to the notion that each part of the system is related to every other part. An alteration in one element will result in a change in all parts as well in the total system. Thus, an open system is not simply the composite of independent parts, but rather a cohesive inseparable whole.
2. **Nonsummativity**-The second property of an open system maintains that such a system cannot be considered the sum of its parts. In fact, analysis which artifically segments the system destroys that which is under investigation. The system cannot be analyzed by varying the parts one at a time because each part is dynamic and intricately intercorrelated with each other part (Watzlawick, et al. 1967).
3. **Equifinality**-The third property refers to the suggestion that an open system may reach a particular final state independent of its initial condition. That is to say, the end state is not causally related to the initial state of the system. Thus, different initial conditions may yield the same final results and vice-versa. The same initial conditions may result in different final outcomes.

In summary, communicative behavior should be considered a dynamic system comprised of inseparable parts which directly influence each other and the system as a whole. Changes in the system are more likely due to the interaction of parts with the environment rather than to the initial state of the system.

The second assumption is based on the genetic-biologic inheritance of the language user. First, the language user has the ability to change behavior in order to meet environmental demands, that is, adapt. While adaptation is a basic tendency of the organism, the ways in which adaptation occurs differ from individual to individual. Second, the genetic make-up of every individual (language disordered or not) has a unique range of possible expressions in response to environmental stimuli or a "range of reaction."

Two related factors are essential to the organism's expression of this range of behavior — timing and proportion. Timing relationships which are genetically regulated, determine onset times and sequencing of individual components of the system. Even a slight alteration in the growth or the development curve of any single component may significantly affect the characteristics of the system as a whole. In addition, timing differences may result in qualitatively different interaction among parts. Proportion is a quantitative notion and refers to the extent to which one element of a system is developed compared to the others. In the case of normal development, one might suggest that components of the system exist in sufficient proportion and advance at similar rates. As such, normal communication patterns are allowed to emerge. Conversely the range of behavior manifested by the disordered communicator may be the result of asynchronous rates of advancement among component parts, insufficient proportion in some or all elements, or both.

The third assumption, equilibration, unifies the two components of the previous assumption. In an effort to adapt, any living system strives for a state of balance or equilibrium. Due to the individual's genetic make-up, this state may be achieved in a unique way or be expressed in a unique manner. The concept of equilibrium is applied widely throughout the physical and social sciences. Piaget (1952) believed that three types of equilibrium are possible:

1. A state in which the parts predominate and consequently the whole is distorted.
2. A state in which the whole predominates with consequent deformation of the parts.
3. A state in which the system as a whole and its parts are preserved in a reciprocal relationship.

Depending on the type of equilibrium, the behavioral manifestations of adaptation may be variable.

The final assumption of the proposed framework is based on the general notion of formal causality discussed by Bates and colleagues (1979). Formal causality refers to the "principles or laws that govern the range of possible outcomes in a given situation" (p. 16). Applied to language, Bates and MacWhinney (1979) propose a "functionalist approach" to understanding the development of grammar. They maintain that surface forms of language are determined by multiple sources (e.g., genetic predisposition and environment) but are largely the result of the problem of communicating non-linear meaning through the linear speech channel. In other words, the acoustic-articulatory modality through which language is usually realized imposes powerful constraints on the surface forms which can emerge. Four other possible constraints on linguistic outcomes were delineated by Slobin (1977):

1. *Clarity*-Preserve as much as possible, a transparent, one to one relationship between underlying meaning and surface form.
2. *Processibility*-Alternative surface forms differ in their relative demands on memory and perceptual clarity. Thus, the most critical information to be communicated is presented in the most mnemonically and perceptually salient position of the message.
3. *Efficient and Rapid Processing*-Operate to ease the memory load in the production and comprehension of speech.

4. *Expressivity*-Information pressures on language to convey both semantic and pragmatic content. The user must encode ideational, social, and rhetorical information.

This final assumption maintains that constraints specific to the task of communicating interact with requisite component behaviors to produce surface forms. Thus, an intersystem relationship is responsible for the final outcome — language.

The previously stated assumptions can be synthesized to form the following framework. First, communicative behavior is characterized as a dynamic system comprised of inseparable parts. Interaction occurs both "intersystem" or between the system and its environment and "intra system," between the parts and the whole. Second, the genetic-biologic inheritance of the language user provides for regulation of onset, sequencing, and proportion of intrasystem components, as well as assures adaption to intersystem communicative demands through the process of equilibration. Third, the model specifies that the task of linguistic communication entails certain constraints due to its particular nature. These constraints interact with biologically regulated intrasystem components during any equilibration process. The result is a range of expression which is not causally related to the initial state of the system.

The previously described systemic components and interactions occur in the "normal" language user, but take on special importance when intersystem relationships are disrupted. As such, this framework is particularly sensitive to the language disordered system. Application of these concepts is more clearly seen in the following discussion.

## Application to Developmental Language Disorders

How does this framework account for the unique aspects of the disordered language system? In the case of the language disordered child we might assume there is either a genetic or lesion based disruption in the growth of component skills requisite to the development of normal communication. There may be asynchronous rates of advancement of the component parts, insufficient proportion in some or all elements of the system, or both. The task constraints involved in learning and using language delineated by Bates and MacWhinney (1979) and Slobin (1977) occur both intra- and inter-system. As such, they may interact at either level with the disordered child's communicative requisites to result in an imbalance of systems. In other words, the child with a developmental language disorder must meet the same communicative demands imposed by such task constraints as the normal language learner. Yet, due to onset and rate differences in developing communicative requisites interacting with task constraints, the language disordered child is left in a state of disequilibrium. When such an imbalance occurs, the natural tendency of the child is to adapt through an equilibration process. As Bever (1975) states:

"Organisms remain whole organisms even when they sustain specific deficits; this reduces and distorts the apparent effects of a deficit especially if the deficit occurs early in development when the organism is relatively malleable " (p. 82).

Due to the individual child's genetic make-up and combination of deficits, the process through which a state of equilibrium is achieved and the final outcome may vary across children. In general, however, that group of processes ultimately responsible for a state of equilibrium fall under the heading of "compensatory strategy."

Menyuk (1975) introduced the basic notion of "compensatory mechanism" related to developmental language disorders from a neurological framework. She proposed that compensatory mechanisms, a variety of neurological substrates, and experience may form the bases for the heterogeneity of this population. In the proposed framework, the concept of compensatory strategy is viewed more specifically as a behavioral rather than neurological process. Nelson (1973) defined a strategy as "...a method of controlling and manipulating information. It may reflect a genetically based predisposition or it may be learned in the course of organism-environment interaction" (p. 85).

The natural tendency of the language disordered child, as with any living organism, is to compensate when damaged in order to maintain a balance of systems. The end result is adaptation to communicative demands. To meet the desired goal of adaptation the language disordered child employs a compensatory strategy or alternative means of controlling information. A compensatory strategy may be characterized by behaviors common to a normal communicative repertoire. However, reliance on the use of these types of behaviors is excessive compared to a child without a language disorder and it may persist beyond a linguistic stage that can be considered appropriate. Behaviors not seen in normal children, such as jargon terms may also be employed as compensatory strategies. Compensatory strategies such as gesture, simplification and revision will be illustrated in the case studies to be presented. The language disordered child, then, organizes him/herself around the relative strengths and weaknesses of his/her communicative system. Those behaviors which are strengths are available to be employed as compensatory strategies. A variety of compensatory strategies may be available to a single child and that variety may be extensive among the population of developmentally language disordered children.

As Curtiss (1981) has stated, single case methodology reveals "the qualitative character of a phenomenon, its inner nature" (p. i). Based on this premise the following case studies are presented to "illuminate" the notion of compensatory strategy in the language disordered child.

## Case Studies

*Case 1:*
D was a 3 year 3 month old boy. At this age, MLU was 3.15 morphemes and 2.82 words based on a language sample of 374 utterances. The primary

characteristic of this child's language deficit is a severely restricted spontaneous linguistic repertoire. The compensatory strategy employed by this child is that of repetition (present in 50% of the total sample). It takes the form of partial or complete repetitions of self (33% of all repetitions) or another person (67% of all repetitions). The following examples are taken from his language sample: Adult = (A) and Child = (D).

Example #1
(A) Do you have a favorite toy?
(D) Favorite. (Picks up car and hands it to clinician)
(A) That one?
(D) That one.

Example #2
(A) The boy is walking over there?
(D) Yeah
(A) He's walking fast.
(D) I find you gone.
　 Kids gone.
　 I find kids gone.
　 Kids gone.

In the first example, D's heavy reliance on the adult communicative partner to lead the conversation is demonstrated. A large proportion of his repetition appeared to serve a variety of communicative functions other than to copy or segment (Keenan, 1977). In this case it is to answer a question. The second example demonstrates D's reliance on partial self-repetition used to reduce the effort involved in sentence production. D retains the whole or part of a previous utterance as a framework for subsequent utterances. In this way, a partial repetition strategy served to compensate for the linguisitc deficit by extending the range of possible sentences available in the context of an otherwise restricted repertoire. For this child, the repetition strategy clearly serves as a means of sustaining discourse while simplifying the task of speech production. This child is able to compensate for a linguistic deficit by incorporating all or part of a prior utterance into subsequent utterances as if to avoid structuring his entire utterance from scratch (Clark, 1974).

*Case 2:*
B was a 3 year 7 month old male whose language disorder was characterized by highly unintelligible speech and fragmentary, or simple syntactic structure. At this age his mean length of utterance (MLU) was between 2.5 and 3.0 morphemes. The following utterances are taken from a 100 utterance spontaneous language sample.

Example #1
　 aʊ  dɛ  dæ  kaʊ  wɪ  dɪs
　 I'll get that cow with this.

Example #2

æn    æn    aʊ    pu    hɪ    hoʊ    ɔf

And and I'll pull his horn off

Example #3

dæ    ʌ    noz

that a nose

B exemplifies the use of simplification or the systematic reduction of syllable complexity as a compensatory strategy. The child relies heavily on this strategy; 68% of his final consonants and 38% of unstressed syllables are deleted in the 100 utterance sample. Based on the previously presented model it is possible that simplification, a behavior common in all young children's language, was employed to meet task constraints such as acoustic-articulatory channel limitations, and rapid and efficient processing. Obviously both the child's phonology and syntax are affected by the simplification strategy. However, he has adapted to communicative demands, which is the function of a compensatory strategy.

*Case 3:*

Q was a young boy age 4 years and 7 months. At the time of this analysis, he had been enrolled in language therapy for 1 year. Q's language deficit was characterized by a problem of word retrieval and production. The variety of compensatory strategies employed to reduce the effects of the word retrieval problem include: (1) Stallers and interjections to allow more processing time and maintain a place in the conversation:

Example #1

These are all my friends and this, this -

um, this - um, um.....my dinosaur

(2) Overuse of pronouns without establishing a referent:

Example #2

Uh, huh, and, and then he - and he tried to get one and he eats them all up and he gets his legs, see?

(3) Substitution of a function for a name:

Example #3

Hey I have...I have one of these. It, it, it, it, blows out the fire.

(4) Revision:

Example #4

Not this - um - cause he broke his...somebody broke it.

(5) Introduction of a subtopic:
Example #5
    And this is a horse. Watch. He's, he's...Look at all - at all those other horses.

It is important to note than in an attempt to circumvent the primary problem of word retrieval the entire linguistic system of this child appears impaired. Q shows deficits at the phonological ("maks" for "masks," "fireflea" for "firefly"), semantic (substitution of a jargon word for the desired production "renchter" and "loosh"), syntactic (reduced utterance length), and pragmatic (introduction of subtopics, inappropriately long pauses) levels. Thus, when some areas of the linguistic system "compensate" for the word-finding deficit, the effects of the retrieval problem are apparent across language components.

*Case 4:*
J, an 8 year 5 month year old male, was diagnosed as having a developmental language disorder. At this age his MLU was 6.0 morphemes. The following utterances are taken from a 150 utterance spontaneous language sample.
Example #1
    Context: Adult and child discussing the child's vacation in the mountains:
    "This, this was how much snow"
        Child puts hand to forehead to indicate snow level

Example #2
    Discussing driving home very fast (Adult = A, Child = J).
    (A) So you really gunned it?
    (J) And go like this
        Child pushes foot to floor as if on an accelerator pedal

Example #3
    Discussing skiing:
    (A) Just sort of sink into the snow?
    (J) Yeah, and then you go (sound effect of falling) when you start skiing
J exemplifies the use of gesture and vocal sound effects as a compensatory strategy, employing it in 10% of his 150 utterance language sample. J uses gestures, pantomime or vocal sound effects to fill-in a missing lexical item or to clarify a vague referent. However, the child is using these behaviors to compensate for difficulties in lexical retrieval. He succeeds in remaining a participant in the communicative interaction by drawing on the strength of his nonlinguistic pragmatic skills despite deficits in lexical retrieval.

The preceding case studies have demonstrated how several language disordered children have met performance constraints inherent in the acoustic-articulatory channel, as well as demands for rapid and efficient processing. Despite the disruption in their linguistic communicative systems, all of the children adapted to these constraints and thus, were able to participate in communicative interactions. While the disruption may be similar, as in the cases of J and Q (i.e., word retrieval), each child demonstrated a different means for adapting. J's primary strategy was to employ gesture and pantomime to fill-in for missing lexical items and clarify vague referents. On the other hand, Q employed a range of compensatory strategies from the over use of pronominalization, to the less effective substitution of jargon words. Thus, it is clear that a variety of compensatory strategies are available to any single child, as well as across children. These cases also demonstrate that compensatory strategies are generally behaviors found in a normal child's repertoire. The distinguishing characteristic is the child's heavy reliance upon the behavior. This occurs either in frequency of use as demonstrated by B, or by remaining in the repertoire beyond an appropriate linguistic stage as in D's case. Occasionally, an atypical behavior such as creation of jargon words may also be employed. Regardless of the specific nature of the compensatory strategy, the purpose is the same. The language disordered child draws on systemic strength — whether it be cognitive, linguistic, or social to minimize the effects of the primary linguistic deficit.

## Discussion

The proposed framework characterizes the language disordered child as having a disrupted linguistic communication system. This results in an imbalance between the child and the communicative demands of learning and using language. As a living organism the child strives to adapt to these demands and hence, achieve a state of equilibrium. Compensatory strategies or alternative means for achieving equilibrium are employed in the service of adaptation and allow the child to participate in communicative interaction.

The addition of concepts such as compensatory strategies to the normal model helps to explain a number of important unanswered issues regarding developmental language disorders. The first contribution of the proposed framework is that the broader theoretical framework offers resolution to an issue raised by Johnston (1982). That is, why don't the results of research coincide with clinical observation? Even though the majority of research results indicate that language disordered children are merely delayed versions of normal children, clinical experience suggests otherwise. This discrepancy may be due to limitations in the theoretical constructs that research is based upon.

Peters (1977) suggests that data is heavily influenced by what we expect to find on the basis of our theoretical preconceptions and techniques we have already developed for handling linguistic data in general. This appears to be the case in the language disorder research reviewed previously. Still, there is always a class of phenomena that do not fit our expectations, our descriptive techniques, or our theoretical constructs, the residue class.

"If the residue class remains a small proportion of the total data we may ignore it while we deal with the more tractable data ... But if the residue class grows so large that we can neither ignore it nor describe it within the current paradigm, then we are faced with the choice of either setting aside the data as unanalyzable or drastically modifying our outlook" (Peters, 1977, p. 560).

In the past, the residue data resulting from research in language disorders has been ignored and only quantitative differences have been reported as significant. However, reviewing Appendices 10-1 and 10-3, this residue class has cumulatively grown too large to ignore. To summarize these data, several studies revealed that constituent omission rather than substitution, thus generally less well-formed utterances, were more frequent in the language of the disordered child (Lee, 1966; Leonard, 1972; Menyuk, 1964; Morehead and Ingram, 1973). In addition, fewer question forms and transformations and fewer major lexical categories were noted in the language of disordered children. Further, a different sequence of acquisition for grammatical morphemes from that observed in normal children has been described (Cousins, 1979). Other studies have revealed that certain linguistic structures and pragmatic strategies were found to be used more frequently by disordered children than by normals at an equivalent linguistic level; particularly the contractible verbal auxiliary (Ingram, 1972b), progressive tense and plural markers (Morehead and Ingram, 1973), phonological and reduced revision strategies (Gallagher and Darnton, 1978), and pronominalization strategies for marking old information (Skarakis and Greenfield, 1982). Each investigation's results considered separately are unremarkable. Johnston's conclusion that language disordered children are different only in that they learn to speak slowly and late is then understandable. However, when residue results are considered collectively with the quantitative differences reported, a qualitatively distinct pattern of communication emerges. The accumulation of enough quantitative differences can yield a qualitative distinction between disordered and normal language users.

A second important contribution of this framework is that it makes it possible to understand the heterogeneity and range of variation within the population of language disordered children. In general, a language disorder must not be conceptualized as a single deficit. Instead, it should be characterized as the result of an interaction between a number of related components each contributing to the configuration of the disorder as a whole. The contributions made by various components of the system act independently and in combination with one another. However, the way in which the components combine to produce the manifested linguistic behavior may be different across children depending on stage of development, degree of deficit, and age (e.g., some components may be more severely depressed than others and contribute more to the overall outcome).

However,the variety of manifested behaviors is not infinite due to task constraints limiting possible outcomes to the problems of learning and using language. Instead, the concept of compensatory strategy suggests the idea of subgroups of language disorders; a notion that is not unfamiliar to the study of developmental language disorders (Affolter, Brubaker, and Bischofbergen, 1974; Aram and Nation, 1975; de Ajuriaguerra, Jaeggi, Guignard, Kocher, Maquard, Roth, and Schmid, 1976; Rosenthal, Eisenson, and Luckau, 1972; Wolfus, Moscovitch, and Kinsbourne, 1980).

Because there may be a variety of compensatory strategies available to individual children and because the final state of equilibrium may vary, so might the resultant language disorder. As Menyuk (1975) suggests, the language behavior of children with developmental disorders may be characterized by at least three possibilities: (1) some aspects of language being acquired at a later age than that of normally developing children, (2) some aspects being acquired differently, and (3) some aspects not being acquired at all. It is also possible that some aspects of language may be acquired the same as normally developing children. The process and product of adaptation may be variable across children yielding a finite number of potentially different outcomes which can be subgrouped. The proposed framework can account for different outcomes or subgroups of developmental language disorder, the normal model alone cannot.

A third contribution of the proposed framework is its implication for the competence/performance distinction in defining developmental language disorders. In 1965 Chomsky defined these notions as follows. Competence is the intuitive knowledge which an idealized speaker-hearer may be presumed to have of his own language. It enables him to recognize as grammatical, non-anomalous utterances he has never heard before and to produce such utterances. Performance is the use of this competence by an individual speaker-hearer. Performance is therefore clouded by such grammatically irrelevant conditions as memory limitations, distraction, shifts of attention and interest, and errors in the speaker's application.

Researchers in speech-language pathology applied the competence notion in defining developmental language disorders. Linguistic behavior was considered disordered or deviant if intuitive knowledge of grammatical structure was significantly different from a normal child at the same linguistic stage. Investigations based on the competence notion have been reviewed previously. Their results suggest that language disordered children have the same linguisitc knowledge or "competence" as normal younger children. However, this conclusion fails to bring us closer to a definition of developmental language disorders than we were in 1960. Recall, Chomsky employed the competence/performance distinction strictly for purposes of formal structural description. This theory, as Bates and MacWhinney (1979) state "...is one of sentences not people (p. 168)." Thus, it is not well suited for direct application to language disordered children.

The present framework permits the introduction of constructs such as compensatory strategies and task constraints for defining developmental language disorders. These are performance rather than competence issues, but constitute an elaboration of Chomsky's description of performance beyond memory and attention factors. The theoretical framework for understanding developmental language disorders presented in this paper suggests that they are more profitably viewed as a disorder of performance rather than competence.

Schwartz (1981) provides a useful analogy for understanding these performance deficits. The language disordered child is like the inept dancer who knows the necessary movements comprising the dance, but can only carry them out partially. In other words, the necessary knowledge or "competence" is intact, but interference in the system permits only its partial realization. However, the language disordered child's use of compensatory strategies, such as simplification or repetition, may also be responsible for partial realization. Under task constraints a partial form may be all that the child can produce to remain a communicative interactant. To reiterate, if the research to date indicates competence is intact in the language disordered child, then performance parameters must receive empirical attention. Chomsky has said that studying the "observed use of language ... cannot constitute the actual subject matter of linguistics if it is to be a serious discipline." However, it is a necessary investigation if the understanding of developmental language disorders is to be a serious endeavor.

The preceding discussion has shown that the normal developmental model cannot predict language disorder. It is necessary to, but not sufficient for the understanding of this problem. The proposed framework expands the currently accepted version of the normal model with concepts such as task constraints and compensatory strategies in the service of adaptation which can account for the unique aspects of the disordered system. As such, this framework has important implications for future research in developmental language disorders and in clinical application. First, a shift in focus from competence to performance aspects of the language disordered child's system is warranted. Future research should attempt to identify performance factors such as task constraints and compensatory strategies. This would lead to identification of population subgroups, which in turn would allow more precise subject descriptions. Such a shift in focus might also bring a merger of two separate areas of investigation; those directed toward processing factors and those directed toward linguistic description.

The framework also has implications for clinical application. It suggests that assessment of the language disordered child should focus on relative strengths and weaknesses which would lead to identification of potential or manifested compensatory strategies. Thus, clinical intervention may take the form of teaching the child to use his/her strengths to minimize limitations, as well as to increase effectiveness of the child's demonstrated compensatory strategies. For both research and clinical areas, the framework also implies that the normal developmental model should be retained for taxonomic and methodological purposes. However, the unique aspects of the language disordered system must be recognized beyond those aspects shared with a normal system. The language disordered child should no longer be considered merely a delayed version of a normal child.

# References

Affolter, F., Brubaker, R., and Bischofbergen, W. Comparative studies between normal and language disturbed children based on performance profile. *Acta-Otolaryngologica*, 1974, Supp. 323.

Aram, D., & Nation, J. Patterns of language behavior in children with developmental language disorders. *Journal of Speech and Hearing Research*, 1975, *18, 229-241.*

Bates, E., Pragmatics and sociolinguistics in child language. In D. Morehead and A. Morehead (Eds.), *Normal and deviant child language*. Baltimore, MD.; University Park Press, 1976.

Bates, E., Benigni, L., Bretherton, I., Camaioni, L., & Volterra, V. *The emergence of symbols: Communication and cognition in infancy*. New York: Academic Press, 1979.

Bates, E., & MacWhinney, B. A functionalist approach to the acquisition of grammar. In E. Ochs and B. Schieffelin (Eds.), *Developmental pragmatics*. New York: Academic Press, 1979.

Bax, M.C.O., & Stevenson, P. Analysis of a developmental language delay. *Proceedings of the Royal Society of Medicine*. 1977, *70,* 727-728.

Bever, T. Some theoretical and empirical issues that arise if we insist on distinguishing language and thought. *Annals of New York Academy of Sciences*, 1975, No. 263, 76-83.

Bloom, L. *Language development: Form and function in emerging grammar.* Cambridge, MA: MIT Press, 1970.

Bloom, L., & Lahey, M. *Language development and language disorders*. New York: John Wiley and Sons, Inc., 1978.

Boulding, K.E. General systems theory - skeleton of science. *Management Science*, 1956, Vol. 2.

Brown, R. *A first language: The early stages*. Cambridge, MA: Harvard University Press, 1973.

Chomsky, N. *Syntactic structures*. The Hague: Mouton, 1957, *Aspects of the theory of syntax*. Cambridge, MA: The MIT Press, 1965.

Clark, R. Performing without competence. *Journal of Child Language*, 1974, 1, 1-10.

Cousins, A. Grammatical morpheme development in an aphasic child: some problems with the normative model. Paper presented at the 4th Annual Boston University Conference on Language Development, 1979.

Curtiss, S. (Ed.) NCLA Working papers in Cognitive Linguistics, Winter 1981, Vol. 3.

Dennenberg, V.H. Dilemmas and designs for developmental research. In C. Ludlow and M.E. Doran-Quine (Eds.), *The neurological bases of language disorders in children: Methods and directions for research.* Bethesda, MD: NIH Publications, 1979, No. 79-440.

de Ajuriaguerra, J., Jaeggi, A., Guignard, F., Kocher, F., Maquard, M., Roth, S., & Schmid, E. The development and prognosis of dysphasia in children. In D. Morehead and A. Morehead (Eds.), *Normal and deficient child language.* Baltimore, MD: University Park Press, 1976.

Freedman, P.P., & Carpenter, R.L. Semantic relations used by normal and language impaired children in Stage I. *Journal of Speech and Hearing Research,* 1976, *19,* 784-795.

Gallagher, T., & Darnton, B. Conversational aspects of the speech of language disordered children: Revision behaviors. *Journal of Speech and Hearing Research,* 1978, *21,* 118-135.

Geschwind, N. Discussion of R. Naremore's "Studying children's language behavior: Proposing a new focus." In C. Ludlow and M.E. Doran-Quine (Eds.), *The neurological bases of language disorders in children: Methods and directions for research.* Bethesda, MD.: NIH Publication, 1979, No.79-440.

Hutt, S.J. Constraints on learning: Some developmental considerations. In R.A. Hinde and J. Stevenson-Hinde (Eds.), *Constraints on learning: Limitations and predispositions.* New York: Academic Press, 1973.

Ingram, D. The acquisition of questions and its relation to cognitive development in normal and linguistically deviant children: A pilot study. *Papers and Reports on Child Language Development.* Committee on Linguistics Stanford University, 1972a, *4.*

Ingram, D. Acquisition of the English verbal auxilliary and copula in normal and linguistically deviant children. *Papers and Reports in Child Language Development.* Committee on Linguistics Stanford University, 1972b, *4.*

Johnston, J. The language disordered child. In N. Lass, J. Northern, D. Yoder, and L. McReynolds (Eds.), *Speech, language and hearing.* Philadelphia, PA.: W.B. Saunders Co., 1982.

Johnston, J., & Schery, T. The use of grammatical morphemes by children with communication disorders. In D. Morehead and A. Morehead (Eds.) *Normal and deficient child language.* Baltimore, Md.: University Park Press, 1976.

Keenan, E.O. Making it last: The role of repetition in discourse. In C. Mitchell-Kernan and S. Ervin-Tripp (Eds.), *Child discourse.* New York: Academic Press, 1977.

Kirk, S., & McCarthy, J. *The Illinois test of psycholinguistic abilities:* An approach to differential diagnosis. *American Journal of Mental Deficiency,* 1961, *66,* 399-412.

Lee, L. Developmental sentence types: A method for comparing normal and deviant syntactic development. *Journal of Speech and Hearing Disorders,* 1966, *31,* 311-330.

Leonard, L. What is deviant language? *Journal of Speech and Hearing Disorders,* 1972, *37,* 427-446.

Leonard, L. Bolders, J., & Miller, J. An examination of the semantic relations reflected in the language usage of normal and language disordered children. *Journal of Speech and Hearing Research,* 1976, *19,* 371-392.

Menyuk, P. Comparison of grammar of children with functionally deviant and normal speech. *Journal of Speech and Hearing Research,* 1964, *7,* 109-121.

Menyuk, P. Children with language problems: What's the problem? In D. Dato (Ed.), Georgetown University Roundtable on Language and Linguistics. Washington, D.C.: Georgetown University Press, 1975, 129-144.

Miller, J., Chapman, R., & Bedrosian, J. Defining developmentally disabled subjects for research: The relationship between etiology, cognitive development, language and communicative performance. Paper presented at the 2nd Annual Boston University Conference on Language Development, 1977.

Morehead, D., & Ingram, D. The development of base syntax in normal and linguistically deviant children. *Journal of Speech and Hearing Research,* 1973, *16,* 330-352.

Myklebust, H.R. *Auditory disorders in children: A manual for differential diagnosis.* New York: Grune and Stratton, Inc. 1954.

Naremore, R. Studying children's language behavior: Proposing a new focus. In C. Ludlow and M.E. Doran-Quine (Eds.), *The neurological bases of language disorders in children: Methods and directions for research.* Bethesda, Md.: NIH Publication, 1979, No. 79-440.

Nelson, K. Structure and strategy in learning to talk. *Monographs of the Society for Research in Child Development,* 1973, *38,* No. 1-2.

Osgood, C. Motivational dynamics of language behavior. *Nebraska Symposium on Motivation.* Lincoln, NB: University of Nebraska Press, 1957.

Peters, A. Language learning strategies: Does the whole equal the sum of the parts? *Language,* 1977, *53,* 560-573.

Piaget, J. *The origin of intelligence in children.* M. Cook (tr.). New York: Basic Books, 1952.

Prutting, C.A. Process /pra/ses/ n: The action of moving forward progressively from one point to another on the way to completion. *Journal of Speech and Hearing Disorders,* 1979, *37,* 283-304.

Rees, N., Bases of decisions in language training. *Journal of Speech and Hearing Disorders,* 1972, *37,* 283-304.

Rosenthal, W., Eisenson, J., & Luckau, J. A statistical test of the validity of diagnostic categories used in childhood language disorders: Implication for assessment procedures. *Papers and Reports on Child Language Development.* Committee on Linguistics Stanford University, 1972, *4.*

Shatz, M., Bernstein, D.K., and Schulman, M.A. The responses of language disordered children to indirect directives in varying contexts. *Applied Psycholinguistics,* 1980, *1,* 295-306.

Skarakis, E.A., & Greenfield, P.M. The role of new and old information in the verbal expression of language disordered children. *Journal of Speech and Hearing Research.* (1982).

Slobin, D. Language change in childhood and in history. In J. Macnamara (Ed.), *Language learning and thought.* New York: Academic Press, 1977.

Snyder, L. Communicative and cognitive abilities and disabilities in the sensorimotor period. *Merrill-Palmer Quarterly,* 1978, *24,* 161-180.

Schwartz, A. Personal communication. Santa Barbara, California, 1981.

Tinbergen, N. *The study of instinct.* Oxford: Clarendon Press, 1951.

von Bertalanffy, L. An outline of general system theory. *British Journal of Philosophical Science,* 1950, Vol. 1

Watzlawick, P., Beavin, J.H., & Jackson, D. *Pragmatics of human communication.* New York: W.W. Norton and Co. Inc., 1967.

West, R. (Ed.), Childhood aphasia. Proceedings of the Institute on Childhood Aphasia. San Francisco: California Society for Crippled Children and Adults, 1962.

Wolfus, B., Moscovitch, M., & Kinsbourne, M. Subgroups of developmental language impairment. *Brain and Language,* 1980, *10,* 152-171.

## Appendix 10-1
### Syntactic Studies

• Reported as a significant finding
▼ Reported as a residual finding

| Author | Study | Results: |
|--------|-------|----------|
| Menyuk (1964) | Analysis of spontaneous speech samples according to Chomsky's tripartite view of syntactic structure. | • Language disordered children did not use the same range of structures as normal children. |
| | Compared language disordered children to normal children of the same age. | • Significant differences existed in the use of structures involving sentence permutations or elaborations. <br><br> • Used non-grammatical sentences more frequently than normal children. Majority of errors were omissions as opposed to substitutions. |
| Lee (1966) | Compared sentence types used by normal child 3.4 years and a language disordered child 4.7 years old. | • Differences in both structure and frequencies with which utterances were produced. |
| Leonard (1972) | Compared frequency of structures used in nine normal and nine language disordered children matched for age. | • Significant differences in frequency with which 14 structures were used. |

# Appendix 10-1 (continued)
## Syntactic Studies

| Author | Study | Results: |
|--------|-------|----------|
| | | • Structures and morphemes character-istic of the adult linguistic system were more frequently used by normal children. |
| | | • Structures representing underdeveloped forms particularly constituent omissions were more frequent in the language of the disordered children. |
| Ingram (1972a) | Examined the development of production of the copula and verbal auxiliary (BE) in a group of language disordered children. | • Differences between normal and dis-ordered children is one of quantity rather than quality. |
| | | • Disordered group progressed through the same stages but more slowly and used the forms less frequently. |
| | | ◂ Disordered children used the contract-ible verbal auxiliary more frequently than the normal chldren. |

# Appendix 10-1 (continued)
## Syntactic Studies

| Author | Study | Results: |
|--------|-------|----------|
| | | ◀Concludes that linguistic deviance in this group results from a disorder of performance rather than linguistic competence. |
| Ingram (1972b) | Analyzed spontaneous questions asked by normal children and 10 language disordered children. | • Language disordered children asked questions less frequently than normal children of the same linguistic level. |
| | | ◀Language disordered children performed much the same as normal children with regard to question type except for a more frequent use of "what" questions in the disordered group. |
| Morehead and Ingram (1973) | Investigated syntactic structure in the spontaneous speech of 15 normal and 15 language disordered children matched for MLU. | • Found few differences in the syntactic structures used by both groups. Phrase structure or basic sentence types did not differ between the groups. |

# Appendix 10-1 (continued)

## Syntactic Studies

| Author | Study | Results: |
|--------|-------|----------|
|        |       | • Onset time for base syntax was found to be delayed as much as 3.5 years and acquisition times was nearly 2.5 years longer in the disordered children. |
|        |       | ▼Transformation analysis indicates that 4 of them occurred more frequently in the normal samples and two more frequently in the disordered samples. |
|        |       | ▼Language disordered children used significantly fewer major lexical categories per syntactic structure type. |
|        |       | ▼Language disordered children acquire minor lexical categories, before, after, and at the same linguistic stage as normals. |
|        |       | ▼Generally, the language disordered children had less well-informed utterances than normal children at the same stage of linguistic development. |

## Appendix 10-1 (continued)
### Syntactic Studies

| Author | Study | Results: |
|---|---|---|
| Johnston and Schery (1976) | Studied the acquisition of grammatical morphemes by linguistically deviant children compared to normals. | • Invariant order of acquisition of grammatical morphemes in the disordered group but at later linguistic stages. |
| Bax and Stevenson (1977) | Case study of a 3.5 year old child with general language delay and behavioral problems. Analyzed syntax (Crystal, et al., 1978). | • Predominantly simple clause structures and numerous instances of breakdown of syntactic structure.<br><br>• Many utterances were deviant and cannot be analyzed using a normal model of syntactic development. |
| Cousins (1979) | Studied the acquisition of grammatical morphemes by linguistically deviant children compared to normal children. | • The majority of morphemes were not acquired in the same order nor at the same MLU levels reported for normal children. |

## Appendix 10-2
### Semantic Studies

| Author | Study | Results: |
|---|---|---|
| Leonard, Boulders, and Miller (1976) | Analayzed spontaneous language samples from 3 and 5 year normal and disordered children to compare semantic relations. | • Under matched age conditions disordered children use *essive* + *designated* more frequently than 3 and 5 year old normals, and *verb* + *agentive* more frequently than the 3 year old normals. <br><br> • When matched for language level these frequency differences disappeared. <br><br> Concluded that the language disordered child's use of semantic relations is consistent with an earlier level of development and what differences exist are related to language level and are not evidence for qualitatively different rule systems. |

## Appendix 10-2 (continued)
### Semantic Studies

| Author | Study | Results: |
|---|---|---|
| Freedman and Carpenter (1976) | Compared the semantic relations used in the utterances of 4 language disordered children at the two-word stage with those used by normal children matched for linguisitic level. | • At stage I level of linguistic development the language impaired children demonstrate a linguistic system no different than normal children at the same stage. |
| | | ◂ Language disordered children did use *introducer* + *entity* more frequently than the normal group. |
| | | Concluded that while language disordered children possess the neccessary cognitive prerequisites for coding semantic relations - deficit lies in the higher more complex aspects of the linguistic system. |

# Appendix 10-3
## Pragmatic Studies

| Author | Study | Results: |
|---|---|---|
| Snyder (1978) | Subjects were 15 language disabled children between 20 and 30 months matched to a group of normal children for MLU. MLU range was 1.0 to 1.12.<br><br>Studied verbal encoding of new and old information. | • When verbal and non-verbal (e.g., pointing) were considered together - both normal and disabled children selectively verbalized the changing objects. When examining verbal encoding only, a statistically significant difference was discovered between the groups. The language disabled group did not verbally encode new information at a level greater than chance.<br><br>Concluded that language disabled children have deficits in forming verbal presuppositions. |

## Appendix 10-3 (continued)
### Pragmatic Studies

| Author | Study | Results: |
|--------|-------|----------|
| Gallagher and Darnton (1978) | Investigated language disordered child's responses to contingent queries. | • Language disordered children revise linguistic forms just as normal children do. But, the language disordered children demonstrated a proportionally different distribution of revision strategies. Though both groups employed the same range of strategies, language disordered children used more phonetically changed and reduced response revisions and less substitution of elements than the normal children. |
| Shatz, Bernstein, and Shulman (1980) | Examined language disordered children's responses to directives under varying contextual conditions. | • Language disordered children were found to be qualitatively much like normal children with regard to early response behavior.<br>They showed evidence of an early action response strategy and followed a qualitatively similar course of development to normal children. Did appear to have more difficulty both in generating informing responses and in utilizing information from prior linguistic context than the normal characteristic. |

## Appendix 10-3 (continued)
### Pragmatic Studies

| Author | Study | Results: |
|---|---|---|
| Skarakis and Greenfield (in press) | Examined language disordered children's ability to verbally encode new and old information.<br><br>Subjects were children beyond the one-word stage as in Snyder's study. | • Language disordered children selectively mark new information in verbal communication just as normal children do. Language disordered children exhibit the same developmental sequence of strategies for de-emphasizing the old information.<br><br>• Children at an MLU of 3 tended to omit old information and children at an MLU of 5 tended to pronominalize it. Although both groups demonstrated the same strategies, a subgroup of disordered children demonstrated a proportionally different combination of those strategies than would be expected at their MLU level. |

# 11

# SCIENTIFIC INQUIRY AND COMMUNICATIVE DISORDERS: AN EMERGING PARADIGM ACROSS SIX DECADES

*Carol A. Prutting*
University of California at Santa Barbara

## Introduction

*H*istory has a great deal to teach us since themes reappear time and again. This chapter was written from the perspective of the philosophy of science. Within the field of science there are two distinct philosophies. At one end there is the hermeneutic doctrine with adherence to a priori knowledge, the assumed, and the interpretive aspects of phenomena. At the other end we have the positivistic philosophy concerned with natural phenomena and their spatiotemporal properties derived by the methods of empirical science. This broad context, from both hermeneutic and positivistic philosophies of science, provides us with a basic understanding from which to operate in our field. Thomas H. Shriner, as my doctoral advisor at the University of Illinois, gave me an appreciation and respect for science. It is with Tom's spirit in mind that this paper was developed.

An article entitled "Pathological Conditions, Speech Deficits" was published in the *Quarterly Journal of Speech Education* in 1920. In this article Woobert described speech correction as one of the most important of all possible disciplines for the acquisition of knowledge valuable to the prosperity and happiness of the human race. So began our promise for a field devoted to the betterment of our society.

Five years later, in the Spring of 1925, Robert West, Smiley Blanton, John Muyskens, and G. Oscar Russell met at the home of Lee Travis in Iowa City to discuss the possibility of forming an organization interested in the individual with a communicative disorder. That same year the American Academy of Speech

Correction was founded and its purpose was defined as "the promotion of *scientific,* organized work in the field of speech correction." (Paden, 1970, p. 9). The thought at the time was to include only the "scholars" in the field. Robert West was quoted as saying, "we were a group of brash young people who wanted to start something " (Paden, 1970, p. 9). Membership was given to the present members of the National Association of Teachers of Speech who were engaged in clinical work, academics in the area of speech correction and those individuals conducting research leading to the understanding of communicative disorders.

One of the first scientific experiments reported in the newly founded organization was conducted by Travis in 1925. The experiment consisted of firing a blank pistol (without warning) close to the subject who was a stutterer. The subject's speech was immediately analyzed for differences in pitch and compared to normal levels. Travis was criticized by the rhetoricians because of his inhumane treatment of the subject. Consequently, the Academy of Speech Correction decided to exclude rhetoricians since they were not able to appreciate the "scientific method!" Hence, this was our beginning of scientific inquiry toward the understanding and treatment of the individual with a communicative disorder.

The purpose of this paper is to review certain basic principles from the history and philosophy of science. It is believed that the basic perspective and insights which have been developed over time are relevant to the field of Speech/Language Pathology formerly referred to as Speech Correction. Since we are nearing the end of our sixth decade it should be insightful to review and take note of our progress leading to our current state of affairs in light of a philosophy of science framework. The four parameters most often dealt with in science are as follows: science/real world, objectivity/subjectivity, system/entities, and theoretical/applied. These parameters will serve as a framework for the paper. The parameters are presented in pairs and are to be viewed on a continuum. That is, both are seen as a continuous succession or whole, no part of which can be distinguished from each other except by arbitrary division.

## Science/Real World:
## Philosophy of Science Perspective

Science has often been thought of as a lofty endeavor performed by individuals who do not necessarily walk on the same ground as the common man. The picture is of a man who is not concerned with everyday matters and removed from the dailiness of it all. As time progressed, Asimov (1979) says, "Science developed a low habit of becoming applicable to the work of the world and, as a result, those whose field of mental endeavor lies in the liberal arts (minus Science) tend to look down on scientists today as being in altogether too great a danger of dirtying their hands" (p. 23). There is no doubt that science, or the art of knowing about the universe in which we live, has upgraded the quality of everyday life. Bronowski (1977) in a personal statement said, that he would be concerned with the relation of science to the ordinary world. Kuhn (1962) in his classic book,

*The Structure of Scientific Revolutions* stated that science is predicated on the assumption that scientists know what the real world is like. There seems to be a consensus that science has everything to do with the world in which we live.

Questions have been asked about how scientists work and the fruits of their creativity. Koestler (1967) attempted to outline the patterns of scientific discovery. He hit on a pattern of playfulness or l'art pour l'art technique. Koestler illustrated how numerous scientific discoveries began with a spirit of playfulness or fooling around. He pointed out that the telescope, for instance, was invented first as a toy after which Galileo put it to use for astronomic investigation. In the second century B.C. Hero of Alexandria built a steam engine for purposes of play. Two thousand years later the steam engine was put to practical use. Apollonius of Perga in the fourth century studied the geometry of conic sections as a pastime. Thousands of years later Kepler employed this as a framework for understanding the elliptical orbits of the planets. Some time ago, Chevalier de Mere asked Pascal's advice for a system of gambling so he could win at the games. From this evidence for playing dice came the theory of probability. So often, we see great discoveries grow out of and are a product of a spirit of play.

Einstein in 1945 was asked, along with other eminent mathematicians in America, to discuss his methods for discovery. He wrote, "Taken from a psychological viewpoint, this combinatory play seems to be the essential feature in productive thought—before there is any connection with logical construction in words or other kinds of signs which can be communicated to others " (Hadamard, 1949, p. 171).

Major advances in knowledge seem to have developed from an attitude of lightness and play, something which scientists engage in through concentration and focus over time. It seems to be a very private endeavor whose origin begins with wonderment and playfulness. It is not something one decides to do apart from his/her life. Edison once remarked that you can labor for a long time over the solution to something then, one day  while eating an apple, the solution comes. Kepler quoting Virgil's Eclogus stated that "Truth appears as a teasing hussy: you chase after her until you almost collapse; then when you have gotten up she smilingly surrenders" (Koestler, 1967, p. 146). "The history of discovery is full of such arrivals of unexpected destinations and arrivals at the right destination by the wrong boat" wrote Koestler (1967, p. 145). Science is concerned with the understanding of everyday events. Creative acts of discovery in science are rarely bred in a sterile laboratory but rather from a consideration of real world phenomena.

## Science/Real World:
## Speech/Language Pathology

Early on in our history Van Riper (1939) stated, "a severe speech defect, because it provokes rejection and other penalties due to its communicative unpleasantness, causes a low in self-esteem, in ego strength. Thus, in all its various aspects and functions, speech is defective when it calls attention to itself, interferes with communication, or causes its possessor to be maladjusted" (p. 18). This view of communication problems centered on everyday consequences in daily life. Van Riper used the acronym "PFAGH." The letters represented the following: P = penalty, F = frustration, A = anxiety, G = guilt, and H = hostility. The acronym was used by Van Riper to remind people in the field of the hidden part of a speech disorder. He believed that it was extremely penalizing to have a speech disorder in a society which prides itself on the ability to communicate effectively. Van Riper hypothesized that the extent of the diminished social identity was related to various factors such as, the severity of the disorder, the type, the individual's age, the presence of compensatory strategies, as well as the attitudes of his associates.

During the early decades there was a series of studies which investigated the disordered client's social standing and personality. (Blackman and Battin, 1957; Brissney and Trotter, 1955; Freestone, 1948; Hawk, 1948; Henrikson, 1945). From outside of the field as well, communicative abilities were tied to the socialization process. Miller (1951) stated, "communication, if it is anything at all, it is a social event" (p. v). It is of interest to take note that in the language preface, Miller states his reason for writing *Language and Communcation*. He was asked to teach a course in the area and could find no textbook so he wrote one.

The point of view of considering the person with a communicative disorder in the context of one's daily life and one's relationships with others is demonstrated in the writing of Wood (1953). In reference to a basic philosophy of speech correction he wrote, "Its philosophy is that every individual is worthwhile and that his speech is the most important tool he has for getting along in life. Whatever we do for his speech, that we do also for his whole being " (p. 263). In the first edition of *Handbook of Speech Pathology* (Travis, 1957) this same message was clear in the preface, "a speech disorder is a disorder of the person as well as a disorder in the reception and transmission of spoken language" (v.).

This broad understanding of communication and socialization was also translated into the goals of remedial work as well. Hawk (1948) wrote, "It is part of our function as speech pathologists to aid not only in speech rehabilitation but also in helping the individual to better understand himself in the world in which we must live and function" (p. 312). The remedial goal according to Hawk was to find a place in society in which the communicatively disordered individual could best function. Backus (1957) concurred with Hawk and wrote, "Therapy should be conceived of as including the use of speech in social situations " (p. 1026). She advocated a plan for remediation which dealt with the psychological as well as physiological aspects of communication.

A person's communicative abilities were directly linked to personality and Johnson (1946) states this most colorfully.

Leaving any consideration of language behavior out of a discussion of personality would be somewhat like leaving the cheese out of a cheese souffle. As a matter of fact, most of the key terms that we customarily use in talking about personality are seen, on close scrutiny, to refer somehow to reactions that are made to and with words and other symbols. To speak of attitudes, fears, hatreds, anxieties, conflicts, likes and dislikes, self-evaluations, delusions, etc. is to indicate, even though obscurely as a rule, those kinds of behavior in which language plays a heavy, often a very dominant role (p. 243).

What was important to these early contributors was for remediation to have a positive effect on personal development and changes in communicative abilities were seen as social changes as well.

What followed during the next three decades was a change in our definition of a speech disorder. In the first as well as the second edition of the *Handbook of Speech Pathology* a speech disorder was defined as, "any deviation of speech outside of the range of acceptable variation in a given environment" (Travis, 1957, 1971). Someone must have asked the question: How much of a deviation in speech must one have in order to be considered outside of the acceptable range? The response which remains with us today is: one or two standard deviations below the norm on a standardized test in one of the following areas: phonology, syntax, and or semantics.

In the name of accountability, however, some of us feel that we displaced the person and society from the definition of a communicative disorder. There is some indication that there is a move back clinically to viewing communication disorders from a social perspective (Prutting, 1982). This trend started in the child language literature and has greatly influenced the perspective from which we view communication (Bates, 1976; Halliday, 1975). We may want to merge the earlier views with our later views and consider a societal/clinical appraisal of the individual with a communicative disorder.

We have come full circle in our understanding. This is a common phenomenon in all of science. Koestler (1967) stated, "The creative act is not an act of creation in the sense of the Old Testament. It does not create something out of nothing; it uncovers, selects, re-shuffles, combines, synthesizes already existing facts, ideas, faculties, skills" (p. 120). This is a decade in which we shall once again connect up individuals and their place in society with our appraisal of the disordered. Hence, the paradox in science as mentioned by Koestler (1967), "The more original a discovery the more obvious afterwards (p. 119).

# Objectivity/Subjectivity: Philosophy of Science Perspective

Gould (1981) in a recent book, *The Mismeasure of Man* stated that there is a myth that science is an objective enterprise. Presumably, scientists are able to shuck the constraints of their culture and view the world as it really is. Instead Gould argues that science is a social act and at its core is subjectivity. Kuhn (1962) saw subjectivity not as a factor tainting scientific choice to be tolerated until it could be dismissed but as an essential and discussable constituent of scientific practice. Of course it never bothered Piaget (1926) to go beyond the observable. Scheffler (1967) summarizes the view that science consists of various degrees of subjectivity by saying, "In place of a community of rational men following objective procedures in the pursuit of truth, we have a set of isolated nomads, each of which forms belief without systematic constraints" (p. 19).

Scheffler has described three main areas where subjectivity enters into the pursuit of knowledge. These three are: observation, categorization, and terminology. The first premise that exists is that observation supplies the scientist with data independent of our conceptions and assertions. Medawar (1979), with this same idea in mind, wrote that observation is not a passive experience yielding sensory information. He stated, "observation is a critical and purposive process; there is a scientific reason for making one observation rather than another. What a scientist observes is always a small part only of the whole domain of possible objects to observation. Experimentation is also a critical process, one that discriminates between possibilities and gives direction to further thought" (p. 82). Scheffler (1967) raises an insightful point with which any scientist is familiar, "Observational support for an assignment contrary to an accepted hypothesis needs to persist longer and fight harder for a hearing than observational data which accord with expectation " (p. 44). The point of course may be summarized by saying that the astronomers Kepler and Tycho did not see the same thing when they looked. It is apparent that observation of natural phenomena in its physical state, is mediated by a person's concepts. It is not merely a sensory visual experience.

The second paradox as mentioned by Scheffler concerns the notion that taxonomies and categorical systems are objective instruments of science. Categories are developed from what an individual believes, which we have already seen determines what an individual perceives. Categorical systems cannot be tested for truth value. Taxonomies and categorizing of data are not able to make predictions and are products of observations.

The last consideraton involving the premise that science is objective is concerned with the language used by particular communities of scientists. The scientist can be isolated within his own meanings. Bronowski (1978a) wrote "I am saying that science is exactly an expression of human language capacity in a special, formal way " (p. 46). Koestler (1967) says that "language can become a screen which stands between the thinker and reality. This is the reason why true creativity often starts where language ends" (p. 177). He goes on to say that words may serve as decoys or straight-jackets, crystalizing thoughts and giving precision to vague images.

Some scientists have argued that there is subjectivity within observational research but not experimentation. Whether one categorizes behavior as one sees it or selects one's favorite variable to manipulate, all of science has a subjective component to it. Scientific evidence or verification is always a relative affair. Huxley has said the real tragedies of science are the slayings of beautiful hypotheses by ugly facts (reported in Koestler, 1967). Verification is a matter of degree. Einstein once said, "the facts are wrong" (Einstein, 1949). Experimental verification never yields absolute certainty. Data can usually be interpreted in a number of ways. A scientific statement remains tentative by its very nature. In a book entitled *The History of Science,* Sir Lawrence Bragg (1951) concluded that "the essence of science lies not in discovering facts, but in discovering new ways of thinking about them."

There are many ways in which to do research as described by Medawar (1979). The Baconian approach suggests that truth is all around and one needs to observe things as they really are—this is the essence of science. Others select the Aristotelian approach which requires a preconceived notion and then to act out in some calculated manner the preconceived idea. Conversely the Galilean method discriminates between different ways of doing something which either gives confidence in one's view or permits one to correct the view. Finally, the Kantian philosophy views the world as a product of our a priori knowledge. The belief here is that knowledge exists independent of experience. While all of these approaches appear diverse, they are nevertheless all concerned with asking questions, in different ways, about cause, order, or chance. Bronowski (1978b) claims that all scientific inquiry revolves around these questions. One needs to realize that what one believes determines what questions to ask and how to ask them.

Scientists are individuals asking similar questions but inquiring in different ways. Medawar (1979) has described the different types of scientists, "Among scientists are collectors, classifiers and compulsive tidiers-up; many are detectives by temperament and many are explorers; some are artists and others artisans. There are poet-scientists and philosopher-scientists and even a few mystics "(p.3). Regardless of the philosophy or personality of the scientist, one's intuitions are central to the business of scientific inquiry. Truth is supposed to be an outgrowth of objective methods used by objective scientists. Most scientists agree that things can be disproved but not proved in the truest sense. All of which is to say that science is a highly subjective enterprise. Objectivity is a myth Ph.D. candidates are often lectured about and truth the carrot for their hopes and aspirations. "Science searches the common experience of people; and it is made by people, and it has their style"—Bronowski (1978b, p. 14).

## Objectivity/Subjectivity: Speech/Language Pathology

If one reviews our history it appears that intuitions were important and were thought to be extremely valuable in our clinical work. You can find in some of the earlier writing reference to a subjective definition of a speech disorder. For instance, Berry and Eisenson wrote (1942), "Subjectively, an individual's speech is defective if more attention is paid to how he speaks than to what he says (p. 1). In our current literature there is mention of the value of a clinician's subjective impressions for assessment purposes (Muma, 1978). Today, there appears to be an effort to employ objective means clinically. As Gould (1981) mentions, we live in an age which assumes numbers to be king. However, at some point, a number must be interpreted. In our current manner of assessing communicative disorders, even with the use of standardized tests, subjectivity is present. Someone determines what to test, how to test, and how to interpret the results. In this sixth decade standardized tests are the most widely used procedure for determining if a disorder exists and its degree of severity.

Our methodology has changed considerably over time. Our early studies were done without the use of easily obtained tangible evidence using accessible high technology, unlike today. Many of our earlier assessment procedures depended upon astute observations and a rich background of clinical experience. These were the tools most often utilized.

Other aspects of our methodology have held up throughout the six decades. For instance, the mean length of utterance was first discussed in 1925 by Nice. This measure was utilized in our earlier studies on normal language development (McCarthy, 1930; Templin, 1957) as well as more recently (Brown, 1973). Specific rules for calculating the MLU and how to interpret it in relationship to language development were provided by Brown (1973). This measure served as the basis for his classical study with Adam, Eve, and Sarah in the early sixties. Currently this procedure has been the most widely used index on which to match both normal and disordered children for research purposes. The MLU is thought to be a highly objective tool. Years ago, Shriner (1969) wrote that the MLU had a narrow range of value as an acquisition index. He cited the range to be roughly 1.0 to 3.5. The use of one parameter or data base (MLU), although appropriate for a certain acquisition period, is not appropriate in order to make assumptions about the entire communicative system (see Kirchner and Skarakis-Doyle this volume). While the procedure is highly regarded, it alone cannot do justice to the description of children's language. So we can see, over six decades, the development of a procedure and new insights as to its use. How much subjectivity went into the making of the tool referred to as MLU? As with all advances even subjectivity is a part of something which is sustained over time.

Earlier we reviewed the idea that our language choices permit certain insights at the expense of others. In 1965 Hardy, in a classic paper asked those interested in language to agree on the use of specific terminology. He suggested that those individuals concerned with language disorders, "agree to use the term aphasia in broad reference to an individual's incapacities in language comprehension and use, and then go on to describe and demonstrate as thoroughly as possible what these incapacities are and what residual, or possibly substitute capacities are available" (p. 5). Using the term aphasia made sense at the time given that the field was utilizing Fairbank's theory of the speech mechanism as a servo system (Fairbank, 1954). With the use of the term aphasia one viewed the individual with a language disorder as having a breakdown somewhere in the channel, transmitter and/or receiver. It is likely that the term "aphasia" colored our observation and categorization of the individual with a disorder. Today we believe aphasia may be only one type of language disorder. We now use terms like disorder, delay, or deviance to imply that no known etiology can be found for the problem.

Early in the fourth decade of our field came a new theory and with it came a different terminology and a different set of goals (Chomsky, 1957). How we viewed language determined what we did and along with the theory came a detailing of linguistic knowledge by means of writing grammars. Menyuk (1969) wrote: "This knowledge or competence is reformulated by writing the grammars of language which consist of structural descriptions of the possible sentences of the language" (p. 1). Different terminology such as transformations and phrase structures were used. An important question asked by some was — Is there a psychological reality to transformations? There was a word but many wanted to know what the behavioral correlate would be. Others accepted and used the term and assumed a behavioral correlate.

There is a balancing act to be played between the notions of subjectivity and objectivity. We have seen a change in clinical procedures, changes in terminology employed and something which both of these are related to — changes in theory construction. It is tempting to think of this sixth decade as one in which we are more objective about the assessment and treatment of communicative disorders. However, in the name of objectivity many events occur according to Jakobovits (1970). He addressed a group of Speech and Hearing majors at the University of Illinois in 1970. The author did not know at the time but, in retrospect he was discussing objectivity and subjectivity. He said,

I have seen dozens of worthwhile Ph.D. dissertation proposals watered down to worthlessness by a committee of experimentalists who insisted on the straightjacket of the ANOVA design. I have witnessed the rejection of bold imaginative articles by the editors of experimental journals due to the fact that the investigators refused to operationalize into meaninglessness the measurement of some real but subjective phenomenon. At the same time, I have seen in print an unlimited number of reports with absolutely impeccable designs with significance levels of one in five thousand dealing with mean differences of a few percentage points on variables whose relation to the world outside the laboratory was not even mentioned. (Jakobovits, 1970, p. 5)

In the name of objectivity Jakobovits points out some limitations when carried too far. Speaking about the other side — subjectivity — Jakobovits goes on to discuss the common sense aspect of science or "Buba psychology." Buba is the Yiddish word for grandmother. What this means is whenever one implements an experiment you could tell your grandmother about it and she invariably would say, "I knew that, why didn't you ask me?" In other words there is the common sense side to science.

It may be healthy in our sixth decade to realize we invent reality, we do not discover it. Interpretation is always a part of science no matter how objective we desire it to be. Clinicians need to feel as secure with their clinical impressions as they do with reporting a test score. In this matter we stand to learn something from the examples of our earlier contributors to the field.

# System/Entities:
# Philosophy of Science Perspective

The "either/or" elementalisitic way of thinking began with Aristotle. This entity way of thinking still dominates Western thought. Renaissance scientists such as Copernicus, Galileo, and Kepler broke away from the Aristotelian way of thinking. They utilized arithmetic and geometry in order to understand the relationship and regularities in nature. By viewing the universe in this way they were able to see the vital role the sun played in relationship to other planets.

Fuller (1975) proposed a systems approach to understanding as well. He defined synergy as, "the behavior of whole systems unpredicted by the behavior of their parts taken separately" (p. 3). Restated, the behavior of any components of subsystems is not equal to, that is, does not predict, the behavior of whole systems. Watts, discussing this subject, stated, "It becomes suddenly clear that things are joined together by the boundaries we ordinarily take to separate them" (1963, p. 212). Whenever one perceives figure and ground it is likely that one focuses on one dimension of the relationship and ignores the other. In Eastern philosophy plurality or duality is inherent in their way of conceptualizing as demonstrated by the dualism of Yang and Yin, the principles of Taoist philosophy.

It appears that the most detrimental aspect of a separate entity approach or way of thinking is reflected in the American educational system of today. Fuller (1975) has written, "We are in an age that assumes the narrowing trends of specialization to be logical, natural, and desirable" (p. xxv). According to Fuller specialization leads to extinction. What happens is that general adaptability is no longer possible for the organism to cope with change and this is where the destruction comes into play.

The concern over highly specialized and narrow curricula is not new and has been with us for some time. Fisch and Cope (1882, reprinted 1952) suggested that a liberal education required an individual to think logically. They go on to say, "But the higher places in science in the coming years are for those who succeed in adapting the methods of one science to the investigation of another..."(p. 337).

It is well known that many of the great scholars of our age have been broadly educated. Fuller, Piaget, and Chomsky — all have had an interdisciplinary education and have excelled as scholars in more than one field. Many of the earlier contributors to mankind also have had a broad understanding of multidisciplines such as Newton, Maxwell and Descartes. Fisch and Cope (1882, reprinted 1952) concluded by stating, "but so far as he wants an intellectual education, it is precisely logic that he wants" (p. 337).

With the lack of a broad education utilizing a systems framework and with today's goals of a competency based education with contractural agreements and minimal requirements we are headed in a tenuous direction. As Fuller has suggested certain highly specialized disciplines may cease to exist.

# System/Entities:
# Speech/Language Pathology Perspective

With regard to our own field and the treatment of communicative disorders one can look at our unit of measurement over time to reveal our understanding of the system. We moved from exploration of a small unit of information for research purposes, the phoneme, to a larger unit, the utterance or sentence. Currently, with the interest in pragmatics our unit of behavior includes the dyad. It seems like we have moved closer to understanding the communicative system by moving from an entity approach to a systems approach. The phoneme could certainly be considered a part or component of the communicative system and therefore we could not necessarily predict, from this analysis, the behavior of the whole system. The dyad provides more information and an opportuntiy to study the phenomena in a more holistic manner.

In our own planning for the education of a Speech/Language Pathology student we started out with a broad curriculum. Wood in 1953 remarked, "one of the salient features of speech correction is the natural systematic eclecticism which has resulted from the necessity for drawing together elements from so many fields: psychology, neurology, medical science, genetics, physics, physiology, education, and many others " (p. 259). Today curriculum development is often determined by governing accreditation professional boards and not necessarily academics. Many of the Speech/Language Pathology programs have few if any required courses in literature, philosophy, or art. The impression given is that in order to know how to function professionally one needs to have numerous facts across numerous speech and language areas. Thomas (1982) discussed the education students are receiving in the sciences. He says that students are misled into "thinking that bafflement is simply the result of not having learned all the facts. They should be told that everyone else is baffled as well — from the professor in his endowed chair down to the platoons of post-doctoral students in the laboratories all night" (Thomas, 1982, p. 45). He calls for an intellectual attitude which consists of "informed bewilderment." Thomas (1981) also discussed the need for college students to be let in on the contemporary arguments in order to stimulate their interest. He suggests that lecturers believe that before students can appreciate the arguments they need to master the "fundamentals." Thomas writes, "I would be willing to see some experiments along this line, and I have in mind several examples of contemporary doctrinal dispute in which the drift of the argument can be readily perceived without deep or elaborate knowledge of the subject" (p. 49).

Data about the success of a highly specialized academic program would aid one in determining the worth of such an approach. While we do not have data on how Speech/Language students perform in relationship to students of other disciplines, we have data on our companion area — Audiology. Herbenick (1981) found that Audiology was ranked 88th out of a possible 98 areas of study based on the combined scores on the verbal, quantitative, and analytic portion of the Graduate Record Exams. We ranked higher than areas such as education, general speech, and physical education. Ringel (1982) has discussed these results. He says, "It is perhaps this combination of relatively weak exposure to literature, philosophy, language, the arts, logic and the basic sciences that contribute to the GRE performance as reported. It remains for our profession to decide on the importance of these areas of study for success in our discipline. Presently, there is every indication that our students are bright and highly motivated but as a group they are also poorly prepared to compete on national tests of general knowledge " (p. 10).

With regard to performance in our own specific discipline we have data on the percentage of individuals who failed the National Examinations in Speech, Language  Pathology and Audiology. This information is from both individuals trained in programs accredited by the Education Training Board (ETB) and those from non-accredited programs for 1971-73 and for 1980-81. The results are as follows:

### Comparisons of Percentage of Individuals Failing the National Examinations

|  | ETB Accredited | Non-ETB Accredited |
|---|---|---|
| 1971-73 | Speech, Language Pathology   7.3 Audiology   10.7 | Speech, Language Pathology  14.5 Audiology  26.0 |
| 1980-81 | Speech, Language Pathology  25.0 Audiology  32.0 | Speech, Language Pathology  40.0 Audiology  40.0 |

*Note: The 1971-73 and 1980-81 data represent two different examinations for both Speech, Language Pathology and Audiology.

In addition to performing poorly on the Graduate Record Examinations, a test of general knowledge, we see an increase in the number of individuals who failed the National Examinations within our own discipline over the past decade. The trend in both cases is not in a positive direction.

We are reminded of the description by Wood almost thirty years ago when he wrote "A Philosophy of  Speech Correction." He declared, "I call attention here to the broader implications of speech correction which are sometimes overlooked in the university training program" (p. 257). We may want to spend some time looking back at our beginning and the broad perspective we had on education in contrast to today. We may want to rethink when specialization should begin academically. We may want to determine how students can best be educated to think and problem solve in the area of communicative disorders as well as in other areas. How can we educate students to view the importance of research in their clinical practice? There may be alternatives to our present way in which standards are met. Many of these questions will be dealt with by the Self Study Committee of the American Speech, Language and Hearing Association. This is a special committee set up for three years to study our profession. The ability of this group to synthesize the state-of-the-art and to propose changes within the profession are of the utmost importance for our future. When we moved to a highly specialized curriculum and imposed standards which primarily favored applied work we all became painfully aware of the trend which occurred. In the last two decades there has been a mass exodus of scientists from Speech, Language and Hearing Programs. It is time to rethink our focus and direction. As a discipline our future could be most promising. Recently, the Bureau of Labor Statistics surveyed 250 occupations in terms of which fields were most likely to have substantial gains in employment opportunities in the 1980's. Speech, Language Pathology and Audiology were at the top of the list along with computer programmers and aerospace engineers (*Forbes,* July 5, 1982).

# Theoretical/Applied:
# Philosophy of Science Perspective

Medawar (1979) has written, "one of the most damaging forms of snobbism in science is that which draws class distinction between pure and applied science. The word "pure" was originally used to distinguish a science of which the axioms or first principles were known not through observation or experiment " (p. 45). In an article entitled "Pure or Impure: The Interplay of Sciences and Technology" Asimov (1979) has stated that the division between theory and applied or pure science and technology began with the Greeks. "They divided science into two parts; one deals only with the difficult, the obtruse, the elegant, the fundamental—in other words, "pure science," a truly liberal art. The other type of science is any branch that goes slumming and becomes associated with such mechanical arts as medical, agriculture and industry — clearly a form of impure science " (p. 23).

There are many examples in history to suggest that the separation is indeed man-made. Asimov (1979) says, "The advances of knowledge of the physical universe rest on science and technology; neither can flourish without the other" (p. 23). He goes on to say that technology is the older of the two because long before man speculated about the universe —the hominids were hitting rocks in order to make a sharp edge. Examples of the interrelationship between theory and applied work are numerous. Einstein's theory of relativity is perhaps one of the best examples of pure science. His theory describes moving objects at sizable fractions of the speed of light. This idea of relativistic motions was put to use in the form of radio-isotopes for use in the medical and industrial fields. Asimov concludes by suggesting, "there is only one scientific endeavor on earth — the pursuit of knowledge and understanding — and all divisions into disciplines and levels of purity are but man-made ways of obscuring that fundamental truth" (p. 28).

Recently Volpe (1981) has addressed the same issue under the name of theory and practice. He mentions how these two notions are often treated as separate in education. He speaks of the fact that in many applied fields theory and application are placed in opposition to each other. Often in application fields, relevance of curriculum is perceived narrowly in terms of what is concrete, answers and is instantly applicable. Volpe says, "only the purposive interplay of conceptual schemes and practical experience can bring about the transformations necessary to enhance the adaptive potential of both the professional and his or her profession" (p. 42). Theory can influence practice via a Kantian approach and experience can color or develop theories ala a Galilean approach. For education to flourish both theory and practice are essential. Theory explication permits one to conceptualize the problem. As Volpe points out, the separation of theory and practice ignores the necessary and essential role of representation and reflective abstraction in the advancement of knowledge. According to Volpe, "overlooking this dimension will make professional programs technical training courses. The practitioners they produce will not be equipped to participate in the growth of professional knowledge" (p. 50).

As stated earlier, important themes recur over time. Tyndall in 1895 wrote:

Keep your sympathetic eye upon the originator of knowledge. Give him the freedom necessary for his research, not overlooking him, either with duties or tuition or of administration, nor demanding from him so-called practical results — above all things, avoiding that question which ignorance so often addresses to genuis: what is the use of your work? Let him make truth his object, however unpractical for the time being it may appear. If you cast your bread thus upon the waters, be assured it will return to you, though it may be after many days (p. 225).

Through his message we hear that science will always lead, at some point, to application. This demonstrates its existence on a continuum. It is clear that whether one refers to theory and practice, science and technology, or theory and application they co-exist. Both, in different ways, lead to advances in science for the mutual benefit of society.

# Theoretical/Applied:
# Speech/Language Pathology Perspective

The fallacy of separating science from application has been discussed. A year ago Feldman (1981) in delivering the presidential speech at the American Speech, Language and Hearing Association discussed the need for science but separated it from application. Feldman remarked, "In addition, the development of new knowledge and improvement in clinical application cannot occur without a strong scientific effort. But that effort must not be confused with the essence of the profession itself. That essence is the delivery of service to persons with speech-language and hearing disorders " (1981, p. 945). As a leader in our sixth decade of growth Feldman disappointingly demonstrated short sightedness, in my opinion, by his lack of understanding the relationship between science and application. He communicated this message to the entire American Speech, Language and Hearing Association membership, some 35,312 individuals (Feldman, 1981).

In that same speech, Feldman went on to recommend the establishment of a professional doctorate. His argument was that the amount of research activities our students experience in the course of doctoral study takes up time and weakens clinical training. Feldman suggested that a "smattering of research training" is irrelevant to the development of clinical abilities. A "smattering" may indeed be inadequate but a substantial background is invaluable. Feldman's argument was not in that direction. Ringel (1982) has eloquently spoken out in opposition to Feldman's ideas on the subject. It should be remembered that our earliest leaders prided themselves on being scientists as well as practitioners. It is no wonder we had such a solid foundation upon which to build.

A preliminary analysis of the data from a national survey conducted by the American Speech, Language and Hearing Association suggests that Ph.D. respondents and M.A. respondents considered theory and research as low priorities within their academic programs (Self Study Committee meeting, 1982). Feldman's argument for a professional doctorate may be irrelevant since the data from the self study nationwide survey can be interpreted in such a way as to suggest we may already be offering a professional doctorate under a different name. We need to continue to offer a Doctor of Philosophy Degree and elevate science in our educational programs because it offers a context from which to understand and critique our clinical pursuits.

Thenen and Ewing (1979) performed a study in the related discipline of psychology. Academic clinical psychologists were asked about their views of graduate curricula. In this study only 7% supported a strictly professional degree. In another study Bornstein and Wollersheim (1978) questioned clinical psychologists and found them to be active in research activities. This study demonstrates that practitioners in psychology do engage in research activities even though their prime responsibilities are with clients. The implication, of course, of the study is that a background of research is important and necessary in the education of clinical professionals although one's prime efforts may be directed toward application.

Seventy-two years ago this theory/application issue was discussed by Flexner (1910) as cited by Ringel (1982). His report had a substantial influence on the decisions made regarding medical curricula. He wrote:

> The conservative in medical education makes much of what he conceives to be a fundamental opposition between medical practice and medical science; occasionally a despairing progressive accepts it. The family doctor represents the former type. One can ask of him - so the conservative thinks - only that he be more or less well grounded in things as they are when he gets his degree. The momentum with which he is propelled from the medical school must carry him to the end of his days - on a gradually declining curve; but that cannot be helped. The other type - the scientific doctor - either himself "investigates," or has a turn for picking up increases due to others. How profound is the opposition here depicted? Opposition of course there is between all things in respect to time and energy. The doctor who puts on his hat and goes out to see a sick baby cannot just

then be making an autopsy on a guinea-pig dead of experimental dysentery. But does the opposition go any deeper? Is there any logical incompatibility between the science and the practice of medicine?

The main intellectual tool of the investigator is the working hypothesis, or theory, as it is more commonly called. The scientist is confronted by a definite situation; he observes it for the purpose of taking in all the facts. These suggest to him a line of action. He constructs a hypothesis, as we say. Upon this he acts, and the practical outcome of his procedure refutes, confirms, or modifies his theory. Between theory and fact his mind flies like a shuttle; and theory is helpful and important just to the degree in which it enables him to understand, relate, and control phenomena.

This is essentially the technique of research: wherein is it irrelevant to bedside practice? The physician, too, is confronted by a definite situation. He must seize its details, and only powers of observation trained in actual experimentation will enable him to do so. The patient's history, conditions, symptoms, form his data. Thereupon he, too, frames his working hypothesis, now called a diagnosis. It suggests a line of action. Is he right or wrong? Has he actually amassed all the significant facts? Does his working hypothesis properly put them together? The competency of the physician is in proportion to his ability to heed the response which nature thus makes to his ministrations. The progress of science and the scientific or intelligent practice of medicine employ, therefore, exactly the same technique    (pp. 54-55).

The analogy to our field should be obvious. The emerging paradigm suggests that Speech, Language Pathology, as with any discipline, can be viewed as a microcosm characterized and governed by the same principles in which science is grounded. As noted earlier the field was founded for the purpose of promoting the scientific study of speech correction. Today, our purpose still reads, "to encourage basic scientific study of the processes of individual human communication" (Spahr, p. vii, 1981). Science comes from the Latin word "Scientia" which means "to know." There are many levels of knowing. The promise in our sixth decade is for a renewed intellectual spirit in which it is realized that our understanding of an individual with a communicative disorder can only be as strong as our understanding of the basic tenets of science.

# References

Asimov, I. Pure and impure: The interplay of science and technology. *Saturday Review,* June 9, 1979, 22-28.

Backus, O. Group structure in speech therapy. In L. Travis (Ed.), *Handbook of speech pathology.* New York: Appleton-Century Crofts, Inc. 1957, 1025-1064.

Bates, E. *Language in context.* New York: Academic Press, 1976.

Berry M., & Eisenson, J. *Speech disorders: Principles and practices of therapy.* New York, Appleton-Century-Crofts, 1942.

Blackman, R., & Battin, R. Case study of delayed speech. *Journal of Speech and Hearing Disorders,* 1957, *22,* 381-384.

Bornstein, P., & Wollersheim, J. Scientists-practitioner activities among psychologists of behavioral and non-behavioral orientations. *Professional Psychology,* 1978.

Bragg, Sir L. *The history of science.* London: Cohen West, 1951.

Brissey, F., & Trotter, W. Social relationships among speech defective children. *Journal of Speech and Hearing Disorders,* 1955, 20, 277-283.

Bronowksi, J. *A sense of the future.* Cambridge: The MIT Press, 1977.

Bronowski, J. *Magic, science, and civilization.* New York: Columbia University Press, 1978a.

Bronowski, J. *The common sense of science.* Cambridge: Harvard University Press, 1978b.

Brown, R. *A first language.* Cambridge: Harvard University Press, 1973.

Chomsky, N. *Syntactic structures.* The Hague: Mouton, 1957.

Einstein, A. *Autobiographical notes.* In P. Schilpp (Ed.), *Albert Einstein: Philosopher-scientist.* New York: Tudor Publishing Co., 1949.

Fairbanks, G. Systematic research in experimental phonetics. I. A theory of the speech mechanism as a servosystem. *Journal of Speech and Hearing Disorders,* 1954, *19,* 133-139.

Feldman, A. The challenge of autonomy. *Asha,* 1982, *23,* 941-946.

Fisch, M., & Cope, T. Logic and a Liberal Education - Editor's note. In P. Wiener and F. Yound (Eds.), *Studies in the philosophy of C.S. Peirce.* Cambridge: Harvard University Press, 1952, 289-290.

Flexner, A. *Medical education in the United States and Canada.* Boston: Merrymount Press, 1910.

*Forbes,* July 5, page 10, 1982.

Freestone, N. The wish for defective speech. *Journal of Speech and Hearing Disorders,* 1948, *13,* 119-130.

Fuller, R. *Synergetics.* New York: Macmillian, 1975.

Gould, S. *The mismeasure of man.* New York: W.W. Norton and Co., 1981.

Hadamard, J. *The psychology of invention in the mathematical field.* Princeton: Princeton University Press, 1949.

Halliday, M. *Learning how to mean.* London: Edward Arnold, 1975.

Hardy, W. On language disorders in young children: A reorganization of thinking. *Journal of Speech and Hearing Disorders,* 1965, *30,* 5-8.

Hawk, W. Personality measurement in speech correction. *Journal of Speech and Hearing Disorders,* 1948, *13,* 307-312.

Henrickson, E. A semantic study of identification of speech defects. *Journal of Speech Disorders,* 1945, *10,* 169-1972.

Herbenick, R. How philosophy students compete on basic skills. *Proceedings of the American Philosophical Association,* 1981, *54,* 469-476.

Jakobovits, L. Needed: Radical reconstruction of scientific psychology. Paper presented to Sigma Alpha Eta, University of Illinois, Champaign-Urbana, IL. May 24, 1970.

Johnson, W. *People in quandaries.* New York: Harper and Brothers, 1946.

Kirchner, D., & Skarakis-Doyle, E. Developmental language disorders: A theoretical perspective. In T. Gallagher & C. Prutting (Eds.), *Pragmatic assessment and intervention issues in language.* San Diego: College-Hill Press, 1983.

Koestler, A. *The act of creation.* New York: The Macmillan Co., 1967.

Kuhn, T. *The structure of scientific revolution.* Chicago: University of Chicago Press, 1962.

Medawar, P. *Advice to a young scientist.* New York: Harper and Row, 1979.

Menyuk, P. *Sentences children use.* Cambridge: MIT Press, 1969.

Miller, G. *Language and communication.* New York: McGraw Hill, 1951.

Muma, J. *Language handbook.* Englewood Cliffs, NJ: Prentice-Hall, Inc., 1978.

McCarthy, D. The language development of the preschool child. *Institute of Child Welfare Monograph, No. 4,* Minneapolis: University of Minnesota Press, 1930.

Nice, M. Length of sentences as a criterion of a child's progress in speech. *Journal of Educational Psychology,* 1925, *16,* 370-379.

Paden, E. A history of the American Speech and Hearing Association 1925-1958. Washington, D.C: *American Speech and Hearing Association,* 1970.

Piaget, J. *The language and thought of the child.* London: Routledge and Kegan Paul Ltd., 1926.

Prutting, C. Pragmatics of social competence. *Journal of Speech and Hearing Disorders.* May 1982, *47,* 123-134.

Ringel, R. The science in speech science. In *Human Communication Disorders: What has happened since West went east.* Symposium presented at Department of Speech of Brooklyn College of The City University of New York, Brooklyn, May 6, 1982.

Scheffler, I. *Science and subjectivity.* New York: Howard W. Sams and Co. Inc., 1967.

Self-study Committee Meeting, American Speech, Language and Hearing Association, Tucson, AZ, April 22, 23, 1982.

Shriner, T. A review of mean length of responses as a measure of expressive language development in children. *Journal of Speech and Hearing Disorders,* 1969, *34,* 61-67.

Spahr, F. (Ed.). *American Speech Language Hearing Association 1981 directory supplement.* South Bend, IN: 1981.

Templin, M. Certain language skills in children, their development and interrelationships. *Institute of Child Welfare Monograph, No. 26,* Minneapolis: University of Minnesota Press, 1957.

Thomas, L. Debating the unknowable. *The Atlantic Monthly,* July 1981, 49-52.

Thomas, L. The art of teaching science. *The New York Times Magazine,* March 14, 1982, 40-45.

Thenen, M., & Ewing, D. Roles, functions, and training in clinical psychology: A survey of academic clinicians. *American Psychologist,* 1979, *25,* 550-554.

Travis, L. *Handbook of speech pathology.* New York: Appleton-Century Crofts, Inc., 1957, (second edition, 1971).

Travis, L. Muscular fixation of the stutterer's voice under emotion. *Science,* 1925, *62,* 207-208.

Tyndall, J. *Six lectures on light.* London: Longmans, Green, and Co., 1895.

Van Riper, C. *Speech correction: Principles and methods.* Englewood Cliffs, New Jersey, 1939.

Volpe, R. Knowledge from theory and practice. *Oxford Review of Education,* 1981, *7,* 41-51.

Watts, A. *The two hands of God: Myths of polarity.* New York: Harper 1963.

Woobert, C. Pathological conditions, speech defects. *Quarterly Journal of Speech Education,* 1920, *6,* 62-75.

Wood, K. A Philosophy of speech correction. In C. Van Riper (Ed.), *Speech therapy: A book of readings.* New York: Prentice Hall, 1953, 258-263.

# INDEX